THE STATE OF INTERDEPENDENCE

Globalization, Internet and Constitutional Governance

For other titles in the Series see p. 261

INFORMATION TECHNOLOGY & LAW SERIES 19

THE STATE OF INTERDEPENDENCE

Globalization, Internet and Constitutional Governance

Rudolf W. Rijgersberg

T·M·C·ASSER PRESS

The Hague

The *Information Technology & Law Series* is published
by T·M·C·Asser press
P.O. Box 16163, 2500 BD The Hague, The Netherlands
<www.asserpress.nl>

The *Information Technology & Law Series* is an initiative of IT*e*R, the National Programme for Information Technology and Law, which is a research programme set up by the Dutch government and the Netherlands Organisation for Scientific Research (NWO) in The Hague. Since 1995 IT*e*R has published all of its research results in its own book series. In 2002 IT*e*R launched the present internationally orientated and English language *Information Technology & Law Series*. This series deals with the implications of information technology for legal systems and institutions. It is not restricted to publishing IT*e*R's research results. Hence, authors are invited and encouraged to submit their manuscripts for inclusion. Manuscripts and related correspondence can be sent to the Series' Editorial Office, which will also gladly provide more information concerning editorial standards and procedures.

Editorial Office
eLaw@Leiden, Centre for Law in the Information Society
Leiden University
P.O. Box 9520
2300 RA Leiden, The Netherlands
Tel. +31(0)715277846
E-mail: <ital@law.leidenuniv.nl>
Web site: <www.nwo.nl/iter>

Single copies or Standing Order
The books in the *Information Technology & Law Series* can either be purchased as single copies or through a standing order. For ordering information see the publisher's web site.

ISBN 13: 978-90-6704-331-1
ISSN 1570-2782

Cover and lay-out: Oasis Productions, Nieuwerkerk a/d IJssel, The Netherlands
Printing and binding: Koninklijke Wöhrmann BV, Zutphen, The Netherlands

To Cleo, with love and gratitude

PROLOGUE

This book is about interdependence. More specifically, it is about the implications of interdependence for constitutional governance. It is the result of an intellectual journey that started in the nineties when a conference in Bilbao on 'Sovereignty and National Identity' first triggered my interest in constitutional democracy as the archetypical form of a modern political organization. Coincidentally, these years also gave rise to the Internet revolution and saw the birth of a new field of academic research in globalization studies.

Since then, much work has been done on globalization, the Internet and constitutional governance. This book, however, is not a repetition of arguments. What I have wanted to show in this book is how globalization, as a process which increases transnational interdependence between actors, is shaping modern governance in the public interest and what this means for the role of the State as vehicle for decision-making in the public interest. The Internet forms an interesting testing ground for examining these potential transformations since it is the most inclusive and important manifestation of this phenomenon.

Whereas the odyssey leading to this book has led me to touch upon a variety of disciplines, including philosophical logic, the foundations of law and constitutional theory over a considerable length of time, the vast amount of research was conducted in the last four years at the Department of Legal Theory at the University of Groningen and at the Netherlands Institute for International Relations 'Clingendael'. I particularly wish to thank Henry Prakken, Frans Nelissen and Aernout Schmidt for their valuable comments on earlier drafts of this book. A special debt of gratitude is due to Kees de Vey Mestdagh for his encouragement and thought-provoking comments throughout the research and writing process.

Groningen, summer 2010 *Rudolf Rijgersberg*

TABLE OF CONTENTS

LIST OF ABBREVIATIONS

ADR	alternative dispute resolution
ALAC	At Large Committee (ICANN)
ARPA	Advanced Research Projects Agency
ASCII	American Standard Code for Information Interchange
ASO	Address Supporting Organization
AT&T	American Telephone and Telegraph
BBC	British Broadcasting Corporation
CALEA	Communications Assistance for Law Enforcement Act
CCNSO	Country Code Names Supporting Organization
ccTLD	country code Top Level Domain
CIA	Central Intelligence Association
CNNIC	China Internet Network Information Center
CORE	Council of Registrars
CPC	Communist Party China
CS	case study
DNS	Domain Name System
DNSSEC	Domain Name System Security
DSL	Digital Subscriber Line
e2e	end-to-end
EC	European Commission
EES	Escrowed Encryption Standard
ESMTP	Enhanced Simple Mail Transfer Protocol
EU	European Union
FAA	Foreign Assistance Act
FBI	Federal Bureau of Investigation
FCC	Federal Communications Commission
Fermilab	Fermi National Accelerator Laboratory
FISA	Foreign Intelligence Surveillance Act
FTAIA	Foreign Trade Antitrust Improvements Act
FTC	Federal Trade Commission
FTP	File Transfer Protocol
GAC	Governmental Advice Committee (ICANN)
GCI	UN Global Compact Initiative's
GigaNet	Global Internet Governance Academic Network
GOFA	Global Online Freedom Act
GSNO	Generic Names Supporting Organization
gTLD	generic Top Level Domain
HTTP	Hypertext Transfer Protocol
IAB	Internet Architecture Board
IAHC	International Ad Hoc Committee
IANA	Internet Assigned Number Association

ICANN	Internet Corporation for Assigned Names and Numbers
ICCB	Internet Control and Configuration Board
ICCPR	International Covenant for Civil and Political Rights
ICPs	Internet Content Providers
IDN	International Domain Name
IDNA	Internationalized Domain Names in Applications
IEC	International Electrotechnical Commission
IEEE	Institute for Electronics and Electrical Engineering
IESG	Internet Engineering Steering Group
IETF	Internet Engineering Task Force
IGF	Internet Governance Forum
INTA	International Trademark Association
IP	Internet Protocol
IPv4	Internet Protocol version 4
IPv6	Internet Protocol version 6
IRA	Intergovernmental Regional Association
IRTF	Internet Research Task Force
ISO	International Standards Organization
ISOC	Internet Society
ISP	Internet Service Provider
ITA	Information Technology Agreement
ITU	International Telecommunication Union
ITU-T	International Telecommunication Union
JTC	joint technical committee
LEAF	Law-Enforcement Access Field
MAC	Media Access Control
MILNET	military part of the Internet
MoU	Memorandum of Understanding
MRC	Madison River Communications
NC	Nominating Committee
NGO	Non Governmental Organization
NIST	National Institute of Standards and Technology
NRC	National Research Council
NSF	US National Science Foundation
NSI	Network Solutions Incorporated
NTIA	National Telecommunications and Information Administration
OCCSSA	Omnibus Crime Control and Safe Streets Act
OECD	Organization for Economic Cooperation and Development
ORSN	Open Root Server Network
PDO	People's Daily Online
PKE	Public Key Encryption
PM	Prime Minister
POP	Point of Presence
POP3	Post Office Protocol version 3
PSTN	Public Switched Telephone Network
QoS	quality of service
RFC	Request For Comments
SLD	Sub Level Domain

SMTP	Simple Mail Transfer Protocol
SSO	Standard Setting Organization
TACD	TransAtlantic Consumer Dialogue
TCP/IP	Transmission Control Protocol over Internet Protocol
TLD	Top Level Domain
TNC	Trans National Corporation
UDHR	Universal Declaration of Human Rights
UDRP	Universal Dispute Resolution Policy (ICANN)
UK	United Kingdom
UN	United Nations
UNDHR	United Nations Declaration of Human Rights
US	United State of America
USDoC	United States Department of Commerce
USDoJ	US Department of Justice
USDoS	United States Department of State
VoIP	Voice over IP
WGIG	Working Group on Internet Governance
WGs	working groups
WIPO	World Intellectual Property Organization
WSIS	World Summit on the Information Society
WTO	World Trade Organization
WWII	World War II

LIST OF FIGURES

Chapter 1
INTRODUCTION

1.1   RESEARCH OBJECTIVE

The modern State[1] is unlikely to be the end configuration of organized political life. Throughout history, both the nature and manifestation of political organization have continuously adapted to the specific needs of the age. Despite the natural tendency of organizations to retain a certain status quo, there is no reason to suggest that the dominant form of political organization, the State, has lost the ability to adapt to changing circumstances. Today's needs are shaped by a process of globalization increasing the level of transnational interdependence between actors in terms of social, economic and political activity. As such, this process is likely to inform the next transformation of organized political life. This inquiry sets out to shed some light on the consequences of this transformation for the modern State in the view of its constitutional commitments and responsibilities using the Internet's interdependency-imposing nature as foundation for the inquiry. In investigating the way in which traditional public commitments and responsibilities take shape on the Internet, this inquiry aims to further our understanding of how globalization influences decision making in the public interest.

The vast amount of literature on the effects of globalization on the State roughly divides into three categories. The first strand of literature stresses the economic dimension of globalization. The emphasis in this class of literature is on the integration of markets with an emphasis on the internationalization and intensification of trade and capital flows. As a corollary, it stresses the rise in economic power of Transnational Corporations (TNCs) and the advanced role of multi-national economic institutions determining the development of the global economic order.[2] The second strand of globalization literature emphasizes the political dimension of globalization. This class of literature tends to focus on international legal institutions and the need for democratic representation and accountability mechanisms in decision-making procedures affecting the public. In addition, it stresses the rise of alternative political actors like Non-Governmental Organizations (NGOs) and Intergovernmental Regional Associations (IRAs) within the context of the Interna-

---

[1] In order to avoid confusion between the state as a 'nation state' and the state as 'element in a federal structure', I use a capital 'S' for the former category.

[2] See for example, Gilpin, R. and Gilpin, J.M., 2001; Hutton, W. and Giddens, A., 2000.

R.W. Rijgersberg, The State of Interdependence
© 2010, T·M·C· ASSER PRESS, *The Hague, and the author*

tional political order.[3] A third strand of literature stresses the cultural dimension of globalization. This class of literature emphasizes a unification of language and values throughout the world, sometimes referred to as the 'McDonaldization of society'.[4]

As the three categories outlined above indicate, there is a wide variety in the globalization literature. One of the reasons for this is that the globalization process manifests itself differently depending on one's field of interest. Because the impact of the process touches upon almost every aspect of our daily lives, there are as many ways to approach the phenomenon academically. The normative component in many of the debates has generated a vast amount of literature in and of itself. Despite these differences in approach and opinion however, the core of the phenomenon is relatively undisputed. Globalization is essentially a process increasing the level of transnational interdependence between actors.

In addition to agreeing on the essence of globalization, nearly all scholars share a uniform conclusion regarding the role of the State in a world characterized by increased transnational interdependence. The power of the individual State is declining. The State as a sovereign entity is no longer able to determine its own course of action independently from other actors. In itself, this is not a very interesting conclusion. It merely seems tautological to conclude that due to an increased transnational interdependence States lose part of their traditionally independent sovereign power to determine their own affairs. Consequently, a great deal of globalization literature then is devoted to identifying the structures of power emerging from novel political alliances, the increased influence of NGOs and TNCs in the global world order and the effects of cultural assimilation. Characteristically these debates tend to take place at the abstraction level of the international stage, taking States to be politically self-interested units in the international world order. Whereas in itself, these lines of inquiry are very interesting to pursue, there seems to be an area that is largely ignored in the literature: the effects of globalization on constitutional governance as such.

The concept of the modern State is often associated with the Peace of Westphalia (1648). This Peace divided Europe into sovereign States religiously divided into Protestant and Catholic units. The treaties signed at the Peace marked the birth of a system of sovereign (nation-)States. Whereas before the Westphalian 'world order', the world consisted of a mesh of competing interests and powers both in territorial and religious terms, the Peace of Westphalia neatly divided the world along territorial lines into sovereign States, enjoying absolute and exclusive control and power, each promoting their own interests on the international stage.[5] Consequently, many writers associate the modern State with the Peace of Westphalia and view

---

[3] See for example, Baylis J. and Smith, S., 2005, and Koenig-Archibugi, M. and Zorn, M., 2006.

[4] See for example, Ritzer, G., 1998. For a more general exposition of cultural globalization see, Tomlinson, J., 1999, and Jameson, F. and Miyoshi, M., 1998.

[5] Shaw, M.N., 2003, pp. 25, 1015 and 1161. For an exposition on the concept of sovereignty see, Hinsley, F.H., 1986.

States as self-interested political units that form the building blocks of the international world order.

Today's State however, is more than a mere building block in the international world order. Over the years it has evolved into a territorially organized political arrangement for promoting the interests of its subjects. This latter conception of State is relatively new and was not yet established with the Peace of Westphalia. The leaders in the recently established Westphalian world order were absolute rulers lacking both the philosophical conviction and the institutional tools to promote the interests of their subjects. The radical change since the Peace of Westphalia suggests a turning point in the way we have come to understand our main form of political organization. Within this inquiry, the conception of the State as a promoter of its subject's interests distinguishes the modern era of Statehood from its premodern era.

In order to identify the interest of the citizens adequately one needs a mechanism to determine these interests combined with securities against possible abuse of government power. Whereas the seeds of democracy and other limits on government powers were planted well before the emergence of the modern State, these limits were only unequivocally secured through the codification of the State-subject relation in constitutional documents. Consequently, constitutions mark the beginning of a new era in political organization, that of the modern State.

For a long time, the State seemed to be autonomous in promoting the interests of its citizens both within the confinements of its borders as beyond. In the course of the 20th century, States gradually lost their sovereign power to determine their own affairs and became increasingly dependent on organizations operating outside their territorial boundaries. Consequently, the State has gradually become just a player among many (albeit perhaps still the most important one) rather than the sole constituent of today's world order. Whereas this particular development is well documented in the globalization literature, it is less clear what effect the globalization process has on the constitutional commitments and responsibilities that govern the relation between the individual subject and the State. This latter question is the one this inquiry sets out answer.

If the first distinguishing feature of this book is its conception of the modern State as a constitutional democracy as opposed to a Westphalian unit in an international world order, a second distinguishing feature is the way in which it uses the Internet to investigate the effects of globalization on democratic constitutional governance. The role of the Internet as *catalyst* to the globalization process is well established. Due to its border-transcending nature, the Internet increases the cross-border flow of information and communication and serves as platform for location-independent, real-time business transactions. The Internet, however, can also serve as an instrument, as *lens* for investigating the effects of globalization. The reason is that the Internet's very network architecture imposes a type of transnational interdependence between actors that is on the one hand (a) similar in key respects to the type of interdependency emerging within the globalization process. On the other hand, the Internet is also (b) immediate and comprehensive in nature. This latter characteristic of the interdependency generated by the Internet's network architecture is central to this inquiry because it allows for an investigation into the effects of globalization on the relation between the State and its subjects under extreme conditions. In addition, the Internet as a global medium naturally delineates the focus of the research, making the endeavor better manageable.

The set up for the book can be summarized as follows. Constitutional commitments and responsibilities of States towards their citizens do not significantly differ on line and off line. The transnational interdependence created by the Internet architecture is similar in kind to the increased interdependence that characterizes the globalization process. Because the Internet, due to its very nature, takes the notion of interdependence to its logical extreme, it magnifies the effects that are only emerging due to the globalization process. Consequently, the political transformations that are discerned on the Internet, can serve as precursor to emerging political transformations in the context of the general globalization process.

Areas of concern

In order to focus the inquiry, it is useful to divide the main focus of the research into four areas that are (1) relevant to the traditional constitutional commitments and responsibilities of States, and (2) are also relevant in terms of increased transnational interdependence ('interdependence' for short). The four areas that this book deals with concern (a) global (infrastructure) governance (b) global standard setting, (c) the promotion of fundamental values abroad, and (d) the development of national policies.

(a) *Global infrastructure governance.* Transnational interdependence increases the need for global governance mechanisms. Central to the modern State are its constitutional accountability mechanisms, viz. democracy and other limitations on power abuse. Whereas the constitutional format seems to work on various territorially defined areas, the absence of an effective, global State-based umbrella organization suggests that global governance is likely to diverge from the traditional State-based format. This in turn, is likely to have consequences for the way in which constitutional responsibilities take shape in an interdependent context.

(b) *Global standard setting.* Standards facilitate trade in a variety of ways. This is one important reason why States traditionally play an important role in standard setting processes. In addition to facilitating trade, standards also form an important tool for State control. For example, accountancy standards establishing a uniform valuation of assets, directly affect the State's ability to levy taxes. Within the realm of technological standardization, standards can influence the State's ability to monitor the communications of its subjects. The existing variety in standards suggests that different States have different interests in standards. The globalization process, in contrast, implies a need for globally uniform Standards. In absence of a global State-based umbrella organization that is able to perform an oversight role, global standard setting is likely to take on a novel format.

(c) *The promotion of fundamental values abroad.* Constitutions are essentially consolidated values. Globalization seems to offer new opportunities for exporting fundamental values and interests beyond State borders. The operations of private actors increasingly transcend national borders. In addition to extending their protective role beyond their territorial borders, States are increasingly tempted to use these corporations to actively promote their values abroad. One way of doing this, is to legally impose requirements upon private actors operating abroad, a phenomenon which is in this inquiry referred to as 'extraterritorial regulation'. This type of regulation has effects on the State's constitutional commitments and responsibilities because it blurs the traditional distinction between national and international legal frameworks.

(d) *The development of national policies.* The early constitutional State granted a considerable government free zone in order for civil society and the market economy to flourish. In the course of the last century, the States have gradually claimed an increased control over the private lives of their subjects, particularly in the economic realm. A transnational context has constitutional implications because national policies have extraterritorial effects. Since one of the most prominent areas in which governments employ regulation is in stimulating the economy, the fourth question designed to investigate the effects of transnational interdependency concerns its effect on the development national innovation policies.

In order to establish an empirical foundation, the inquiry takes one particular State, the United States of America (US) as a case in point The challenges and consequences the US faces in trying to address key issues and players in four case studies form indicators to the changing role of the State in the light of its constitutional commitments and responsibilities.

1.2 METHODOLOGY

The methodology used in the overall inquiry is primarily fundamental in nature. As opposed to applied research, fundamental research is not primarily designed to discover a solution to a practical problem. It is rather aimed at gaining knowledge and understanding for its own sake, in this case in order to formulate hypothesis as a basis for theory formation about the consequences of the globalization process for the modern State in the light of its constitutional commitments and responsibilities. In order to do this, a combination of techniques is used. Whereas the overall inquiry uses the grounded theory approach, it also uses explanatory and empirical techniques in order to answer the main question of this inquiry.

1.2.1   The grounded theory approach

The nature of this inquiry is primarily theory-oriented. It aims to contribute to the formulation of a theory concerning the effects of globalization on democratic constitutional governance and uses elements of the grounded theory approach in order to achieve this. The grounded theory approach differs considerably from the traditional empirical research. The empirical research cycle consists of (a) a definite research question, followed by (b) a hypothesis derived from a theoretical framework, (c) a definition of the research object or scope and (d) a method of verifying the hypothesis.[6] The grounded theory approach is less predictable. Its hermeneutical approach,[7] primarily aimed at *understanding and interpreting* as opposed to *explaining* a phenomenon, allows theoretical concepts to 'emerge' from the data (research objects) under investigation, an approach that stands in sharp contrast to the hypothetical-deductive approach used in the empirical sciences.

Whereas the grounded theory approach improves the creative process iteratively and allows for a more 'open' and neutral starting point in approaching the research objects, it also runs the risk of developing tunnel vision and spending too much time on dead-ends in the formation of theoretical concepts. In order to avoid these traps, a disciplined and continuous 'moving back and forth' between empirical data and theoretical concepts during the course of the research is required, hereby allowing the context and scope to vary as one goes along. One of the major insights this iterative approach has generated during the course of this investigation is the use of the Internet as lens through which to examine the effects of globalization and insight that has changed the set-up of the inquiry and has broadened its scope.

1.2.2   The explanatory components

Whereas the overall inquiry adapts the grounded theory approach aimed at interpreting a particular phenomenon, a part of the research is explanatory in nature. The first explanatory component of the inquiry sets out to clarify why the constitutionalization of the relation between the State and its subjects formed a crucial step in the formation of modern political organization. It also explains that even within this constitutional setting, the relation between the State and its subjects is susceptible to change. To this aim, a conceptual model is developed to depict the interaction between three constitutive elements of the constitutional democracy: government, civil society and the market. This conceptual triangle, which is labeled *Triangle of Liberty*, clarifies the changing nature of the relation between these elements over time. As such, it forms an important heuristic device for clarifying the peculiarities of constitutional governance and the concept of transnational interdependence in the light of the globalization process.

---

[6] Chalmers, A.F., 1999.
[7] Glaser, B.G. and Strauss, A.L., 1967.

The second explanatory component sets out to clarify the relation between globalization and the Internet by applying a model developed by David Held[8] in order to determine the level of globalization at various stages of technological development to the Internet. It shows that the very architecture of the Internet establishes a kind of interdependency similar in key respects to the type of interdependence emerging within the globalization process. In addition it shows that the Internet takes level of transnational interdependence between actors to its logical extreme in terms of both its spatio-temporal dimension and its organizational dimension. This observation renders the Internet an ideal environment to examine in detail the way in which constitutional commitments and responsibilities take shape in an interdependent context. Improving our understanding of the transformations of political organization in the Internet context will help to formulate adequate policies that are tailored to the interdependent context generated by the globalization process in general.

1.2.3 The empirical components

A thorough understanding of the effects of globalization on the modern State in the light of its constitutional commitments and responsibilities cannot do without an empirical component. The case studies are designed to do just this. Strictly speaking, the notion 'case study' applies to practice-oriented as opposed to theory-oriented research.[9] Theory-oriented or fundamental research, aims to develop, test or illustrate particular scientific theories. In the case of this inquiry, it is used to explore the parameters along which lines a possible new theory of State or political organization can be developed. Within the context of theory-oriented research, the goal is always to generalize particular cases. In practice-oriented research, this is not necessarily the case. In practice-oriented research, case studies are generally conducted 'on location', for example by questioning groups that are involved in transformation processes, or observing people's behavior when using the Internet.

This inquiry takes a more liberal interpretation of the term 'case'. The approach is empirical in that it assesses the actual State practices in terms of regulation and decisions. It is not practice-oriented in the sense that the empirical investigation is conducted 'on location'. In order to distinguish the more empirical part of this inquiry from the more theoretical part, the in-depth examination of the specific ways in which one prominent constitutional democracy (the US) attempts to achieve its particular objectives, is subsumed under the label 'case studies' within this inquiry.

1.3 RESEARCH METHODS

With the methodological approaches clarified, it is time to specify the ways in which this inquiry sets out to answer the central research question more specifically. The

[8] Held, D., 1999, p. 21ff.
[9] Verschuren, P. and Doorewaard, H., 1999, p. 146.

first research object, the essence of globalization (transnational interdependence) and its relation to the Internet has already been touched upon in outlining the explanatory components of the research. This part of the research uses social sciences literature on globalization and technical literature on the Internet. Its second research object is still in need of some specification. The following section provides more insight into the way in which this inquiry sets out to investigate the modern State. The last method of inquiry in need of clarification is the case study component. The criteria and contents of the case studies are taken up in the Sections 1.3.2 and 1.3.3.

1.3.1 The modern State

The previous sections have already touched upon the historical approach to the State. Since 'modern' suggests something 'pre-modern' this inquiry necessarily has a historical component. This serves two purposes. First, it shows why, within this inquiry, the emergence of constitutions mark the beginning of the modern era in Statehood. Secondly, it aims to show that democratic constitutional governance is dynamic in nature, which makes the modern State inclined to respond to challenges.

Constitutionalization marks the beginning of the modern State and constitutions form the basis for the relation between States and their subjects. Constitutions are both prescriptive and descriptive in nature. Similar to many other laws, constitutions are normative in that they lay down the rules of the game. For example, constitutions dictate the way in which governments should act on behalf of their citizens and determine how to fulfill positions within parliament and government. They are also descriptive in nature in that they describe the values, responsibilities and commitments of a given community. In this latter capacity, they are particularly interesting within the context of this inquiry. Since constitutions differ from other laws in that they are more difficult to amend than generic laws, they capture the most fundamental values, commitments and responsibilities of a modern State. For the same reason constitutions are also easily identified allowing a clear delineation of the investigation.

States come in many guises. In order to obtain a uniform generalization of the concept 'State', the focus in this inquiry is on constitutional democracies. More specifically, the modern State within the context of this inquiry is an abstraction of Western industrialized States. This limitation in scope has two reasons. First, it minimizes the critical argument aimed at pointing out the discrepancy between the constitution interpreted as a description of a particular state of affairs (democratic representation, constitutional liberties etc.) and its materialization (the actual democratic representation and constitutional liberties). In focusing on the constitutions of Western industrialized states, the discrepancy between is and ought that could be raised against this approach is minimized. Secondly, and more importantly, since Western industrialized States constitute the majority of the world's advanced States in terms of political stability and economic openness and power, their stake in the globalization process is larger than that of other States. As such, the implications of globalization on constitutional governance are likely to be more intense and significant than in other States.

1.3.2   Case study framework

The aim of this inquiry is to obtain a better understanding of the consequences of the globalization process for the organization of political life. The previous section explained that the general concept of 'the State' used in this inquiry is an abstraction from based on the common features of Western industrialized States. The case study component in this inquiry however, only allows for an investigation of the relation of one particular State. The investigation of this particular State is conducted in the light of the key elements derived from a careful examination of the Western industrialized States mentioned above. The case study component forms the empirical basis for the inquiry using a desk-research approach based on legal documents, policy statements and academic literature.

The case studies are selected based on their relevance to the Internet as a distinct realm characterized by complete, immediate and location-independent interdependency between actors. Two criteria for picking the case studies are particularly relevant in this respect. First, the case studies need to relate directly to the interdependency-imposing nature of the Internet. In addition, the case studies need to concern the State in its capacity as promoter of its citizen's interests, pertaining to traditional constitutional commitments and responsibilities. The following analytical model (Figure 1) is designed in order to select a variety of relevant case studies and analytically distinguishes the influence of States into two categories, the *field* of influence and the *mode* of influence.

FIELD OF STATE INFLUENCE

		INTERACTION	INTERCONNECTION
MODE OF STATE INFLUENCE	INSTITUTIONAL	**CASE STUDY I**	**CASE STUDY II**
	REGULATORY	**CASE STUDY III**	**CASE STUDY IV**

Figure 1. Case study framework

The *fields* of State influence on the Internet coincide with the Internet's main functionalities. The Internet's prime role is to establish *communication*, enabling hosts to exchange information and ideas. Its secondary but more fundamental role is establishing the *interconnection* between hosts. This latter role forms a precondition for establishing the exchange of information on the Internet and is both analytically and technically different from the communication level. In Internet terms, communication or information exchange between hosts is established by means of applications such as the World Wide Web and e-mail. These applications use the Internet's interconnectivity to provide their services. The interconnection of hosts, in contrast, applies to the actual operation of the Internet as a worldwide, publicly accessible network of computer networks providing the preconditions for exchanging information on the Internet. The distinction between interconnection and communication, often characterized as a distinction between a connection level and a transportation level, equally applies to the non-Internet world. The public provision of railway carriages, for example, can be the result of government intervention at the level of transportation. In contrast, the national setting of gauge widths is an activity conducted at the interconnection level. Both functionalities are crucial to a well-functioning Internet. Without interconnection, exchange between hosts would be impossible. Without its ability to exchange information and ideas, the Internet would simply be useless. The distinction between fields of State influence however is not fundamental to this inquiry since both functionalities are relevant in terms of interdependency. The analytical distinction is merely used to ensure a variety in case studies because State interests also divide into concerns about communication and interconnection.

The *mode* of State influence concerns the way in which influence can be exercised. The mode of influence can be divided into *institutional* and *regulatory* influence, again a distinction that is fully compatible with modes of influence found in the non-Internet world. The institutional component allows for an investigation into the influence of States within transnational institutions. The regulatory component concerns the way in which States regulate private actors. Both modes allow for an in-depth investigation into consequences of transnational interdependency conditions on States in exercising their constitutional commitments and responsibilities.

The distinction between *fields* of State influence ensures that a variety of State interests are taken into account and, more importantly, provides insight into different manifestations of transnational interdependency between actors on the Internet. The distinction between *modes* of State influence concerns the method or ways in which States aims to exercise their influence and is relevant in that different modes of influence are likely to yield different conclusions concerning the effects of globalization on constitutional governance.

1.3.3   Case study overview

The use of the Internet as lens for examining the effects of globalization shows that this inquiry is designed to use limiting examples in order to study the phenomenon under extreme conditions. In order to identify the effects of increased transnational interdependence on the relation between the State and its subjects, also the State in question needs to be an extreme instance in order to be able to observe unequivocally a possible effect on the relation between the State in question and its subjects. Section 1.3.1 already limited the inquiry to Western States. For the purposes of this inquiry, the State under investigation in the case study component of the inquiry needs to have relatively high stakes in the Internet in order to be more inclined to influence decisions regarding the Internet on behalf of its constitutional commitments. This is why the central focus in the case studies is on the US.

From a constitutional point of view, the US is one of the first explicitly designed constitutional States in the world. Because its current constitution survived essentially in the same form from 1787 onwards, it has become a role model for political organization, exemplary to many subsequent constitutionalizations. Its constitutional developments form an important point of reference for fellow constitutional democracies all over the world.

In addition, the US has obtained a dominant position in political, economic and technological terms while maintaining its commitment to actively promote democratic decision making, a free market economy and individual rights. The US also fits the bill in terms of the interdependency requirements. The US world leadership in terms of connectivity, e-commerce and Internet technology (1) makes the US more susceptible to challenges implied by increased transnational interdependence, both in Internet terms as in the context of globalization. (2) Consequently, because there is more at stake for the US compared to other countries, it makes the US more inclined to use its power to influence decisions affecting the process in the light of its constitutional commitments. Given the US' stake in both globalization and informatization,[10] it is also likely to be one of the first countries to adapt to the changing circumstances.

Due to its hegemonic power and its role as a constitutional archetype for other nations, the US serves as *critical* element (case in point) in the inquiry. The similarities in the constitutional commitments of the US and other industrialized Western States, combined with the effects of the globalization process, which are similar for all industrialized States, allows for a generalization of the case studies in terms of the changes modern States face in the light of the globalization process. In other words, if changes brought about by the globalization process affects the US ability or manner of performing its constitutional commitments and responsibilities, it inevitably affects the other constitutional democracies as well. The research material used in the case studies designed to investigate the effects of the US attempts to influence key actors and issues on the Internet, is a combination of legal and policy documents on the one hand, and academic literature on the other hand.

---

[10] Informatization is the process of change that features (a) the use of information technology to such extent that it becomes the dominant force in commanding economic, political, social and cultural development; and (b) unprecedented growth in the speed, quantity, and popularity of information production and distribution; Wang, G., 1994, p. 5.

Figure 2 specifies the case studies in the context of the analytic framework based on the division between *field* and *mode* of State influence and the four areas of concern identified in the introduction, viz. (1) global governance, (2) global standard setting, (3) the promotion of fundamental values abroad, and (4) the development national (economic) policies.

FIELD OF STATE INFLUENCE

		COMMUNICATION	INTERCONNECTION
MODE OF STATE INFLUENCE	**INSTITUTIONAL**	CASE STUDY I: **DNS Management** (Global Governance)	CASE STUDY II: **Technical Standardization** (Global Standard Setting)
	REGULATORY	CASE STUDY III: **Censorship** (Exporting Values)	CASE STUDY IV: **Network Neutrality** (Economic Policies)

Figure 2. Case study overview

The first case study, 'Interdependence and Domain Name System management', concerns the State's institutional influence in the field of communication on the Internet. This case study deals with the organizational challenge for States to make global public policies in absence of a world government. The Internet's Domain Name System (DNS) enables hosts to exchange information using alphabetical names rather than Internet Protocol (IP) addresses, i.e., the numerical names used to identify individual hosts or computers. Because domain names play an important role in Internet navigation, the DNS has contributed much to the Internet's success. Since, in principle, only one name can be assigned to one unique IP address, names have become scarce goods. Whereas addressing and signposting are traditionally State responsibilities, on the Internet the composition and distribution of names is primarily in the hands of one single private organization, the Internet Corporation for Assigned Names and Numbers (ICANN). In addition, ICANN is also responsible for guaranteeing the protection of domain names against theft and abuse. By exploring the US role in the DNS, this case study investigates the development of one novel institution on the Internet that challenges the traditional role of the State as a guardian of property rights and critical (communication) infrastructures. One of the questions that arise in this context is what mechanisms hold ICANN accountable for its decisions and prevent the abuse of its powers as private organization acting in the public interest.

The second case study, 'Interdependence and technical standardization', concerns institutional State influence in the field of interconnection. As opposed to standardization processes in the telecom sector, the technical standardizations concerning Internet connectivity are primarily a result of a private organization called the Internet Engineering Task Force (IETF). Standardization processes are relevant to States since standards facilitate commerce. In addition, standards can be used as tool for the State to control its subjects. The US attempts to influence standard setting on the Internet is the topic of the second case study. The interesting question in relation to the overall topic of this inquiry concerns the objectives and influence of the US from a constitutional point of view and the effects of its attempts to influence global standardization processes.

The third case study, 'Interdependence and search operator censorship', concerns the regulation of communication on the Internet. It particularly investigates the role of the US in the regulation of search operators, which in addition to the DNS have become key players in Internet navigation. This case study, focusing on the US battle against Google's censorship activities in China, explores the challenge for States to promote their national interests by attempting to regulate private actors operating abroad in a world characterized by transnational interdependence. This is interesting in the light of this inquiry since 'extraterritorial regulation' shows how interdependence stimulates States to explore new ways for exporting their values. In addition, is also poses questions concerning State sovereignty and democratic legitimacy.

The fourth case study, 'Interdependence and net neutrality', concerns regulation of interconnection on the Internet. It particularly explores the effects of the possible US regulation on the issue of net neutrality, which is currently a much-debated issue within US congress. Net neutrality concerns the question whether State regulation of private parties is required in order to stimulate development of the Internet infrastructure in terms of access and innovation. A critical assessment of the issues involved provides insight into the fundamental choices States need to make in designing their national policies. The case in point concerns the development of the information infrastructure of the future. Within a world dominated by transnational interdependence, the question emerges how to stimulate innovation in a global context and what the effects of national innovation policies are on the global information infrastructure at large.

1.4   OUTLINE

Chapters 2 and 3 define the main objects of research. Chapter 2 describes the origin of the modern State as a constitutional democracy and describes the dynamic relation between the State and its subjects by using a conceptual model describing the interaction between government, the market and civil society. Chapter 3 outlines the effects of globalization on the State in terms of transnational interdependency and identifies the Internet as lens through which to examine the phenomenon. In addition, it highlights the essential features of the Internet as a communication and transaction medium characterized by an immanent transnational interdependency-imposing architecture.

The subsequent chapters (4 to 7) contain the case studies as outlined in the previous section. A central starting point in these case studies are various US attempts to influence decisions and actions on the Internet in the light of its constitutional commitments and responsibilities. In order of appearance, the case studies concern interdependence and DNS management (Chapter 4), technical standardization (Chapter 5), search operator censorship (Chapter 6), and network neutrality regulation (Chapter 7).

Chapter 8 contains the conclusions to the inquiry consisting of three parts. This concluding chapter consists of three sections. The first section summarizes the case study findings based on the investigation of US Internet policies. The second section provides a generalization of the case study findings. The third part of the chapter includes the implications of these findings and presents some recommendations for further research formulated as general hypotheses about the changing nature of constitutional governance.

Chapter 2
THE MODERN STATE

Constitutions provide a relatively neutral starting point for the inquiry from an ideological point of view because they capture the values and ideals of modern statehood in written commitments and responsibilities.[11]

This exposition explains how the constitutionalization of the relation between the State and its subjects marks the beginning of modern Statehood and uses early constitutional documents to induce the general principles and responsibilities underlying present-day democratic constitutional governance.

The first part of this chapter outlines the emergence of the constitutional democracy and its characteristics. The second part of this chapter develops a conceptual model as a heuristic device for describing its dynamic nature.

2.1 THE CONSTITUTIONAL NATURE OF THE MODERN STATE

On the face of it, the question 'What is a State?' seems a simple one to answer. The first thing to note is that it is primarily an empirical question. Careful observation and description generally tends to answer this type of question. One could survey a representative collection of States, describe their common features, and mould these findings in a theory encompassing all of those features in a coherent way. The myriad articles and books about the topic, however, seem to suggest that things are not this easy. One complicating factor is that States come in many guises. Because States vary widely in terms of political, legal and economic organization, it is hard to identify the common features in terms of organization, which, in turn, impedes the process of defining common goals. A second difficulty in defining the State is that it is studied by a variety of academic disciplines. Each discipline, ranging from sociology, politics, economics and legal studies to philosophy, has its own characteristic approach, methods and research questions. The result is a wide variety of academic literature on the matter. A third complicating factor is that the impact of the State on the daily lives of people is so comprehensive that in trying to answer the question, it is very hard to let go of all the preconceived ideas as to what the

---

[11] The expression 'ideology neutral' means 'ideology neutral' from a researcher's point of view. Constitutions themselves are not neutral with respect to ideology as we shall see and neither are their justifications.

R.W. Rijgersberg, The State of Interdependence
© 2010, T·M·C·ASSER PRESS, *The Hague, and the author*

State should be. Consequently, even in the literature that aims to describe the State 'as we find it' one often encounters ideological assumptions blurring the distinction between pre- and descriptive discourse.[12]

One of the first attempts to define the State was made by Aristotle in his Politics. Aristotle held that:

> '[E]very State is a community of some kind, and every community is established with a view to some good; for mankind always acts in order to obtain that which they think good. But, if all communities aim at some good, the State or political community, which is the highest of all, and which embraces all the rest, aims at good in a greater degree than any other, and at the highest good.'[13]

Typical for the vast amount of pre-twentieth century literature, Aristotle defined the State teleological, that is, in terms of its purpose or goal. Since Aristotle considered the highest good for people to live a virtuous life, he figured that it was the State's objective to make good citizens, capable of noble character.[14] One of the appeals of the Aristotelian approach is that by defining an entity in terms of its goals, one instantly obtains a framework for evaluating the entity's success in achieving the goal in question. As a definition though, Aristotle's approach is problematic in at least two respects. First, it is incomplete. A teleological definition rarely captures the full significance of the defined term in question, especially not of a complex phenomenon like the State. Secondly, a goal-based analysis is somewhat arbitrary since there are a host of other goals one could ascribe to the State, depending of one's personal beliefs, choice of scientific discipline and the space-time coordinates at which one is describing the State in question. In other words, a problem with goal-oriented definitions is that it is difficult not to bring in 'hidden' assumptions. This is exactly the point made by the political sociologist and historian of economics Max Weber when in 1918 he wrote the following:

> '[T]here is scarcely any task that some political association has not taken in hand, and there is no task that one could say has always been exclusive and peculiar to those associations that are designated as political ones; today the State, or historically those associations that have been the predecessors of the modern State.'[15]

Weber's solution to the problem was to abandon a teleological definition of State altogether. In order to avoid the subjective element in the definitions Weber put forward an alternative approach which has been very influential. He proposed a definition of the State in terms of its means, that is, the methods peculiar to the State that are used to pursue its ends. Taking this radically different approach, Weber was

---

[12] Classically put as the 'is-ought problem', this problem was first put forward in Hume, D., 1739, Book III, Part I, Section I.
[13] Barnes, J., 1984, Section 1252ª.
[14] Ibid., Section 1099ᵇ (30).
[15] Weber, M., 1919.

at once in the position to identify what he considered the distinguishing feature of the State as a political organization; the way it uses force to pursue its interests.

'A compulsory political organization with continuous operations will be called a State insofar as its administrative staff successfully upholds the claims to the monopoly of the legitimate use of physical force in the enforcement of its orders ... . [It] possesses an administrative and legal order subject to change by legislation, to which the organized activities of the administrative staff, which are also controlled by regulations, are oriented. This system of order claims binding authority, not only over members of the state, the citizens, most of whom have obtained membership by birth, but also to a very large extent over all action taking place in the area of jurisdiction. It is thus a compulsory organization with a territorial basis. Furthermore, today, the use of force is regarded as legitimate only so far as it is either permitted by the state or prescribed by it ... . The claim of the modern state to monopolize the use of force is as essential to it as its character of compulsory jurisdiction and continuous operation.'[16]

Weber's definition remains the most influential definition of the State to date. For example, in a well-established and much-used textbook on the modern State,[17] Pierson takes Weber's definition as a starting point and stresses that all the elements stemming from Weber's exposition of the mechanisms of the State to pursue its goals still form the core components of the discussions concerning the modern State. With the State as its central research object, various elements mentioned by Weber (its monopoly on the use of force, its territorial limitation, sovereignty, the rule of law, bureaucracy and citizenship) are also touched upon in this inquiry.

Despite the fact that Weber himself has been accused of slipping in values through the backdoor in his definition of State,[18] his remarks about the problems associated with teleological definitions raise an important point. Weber's solution, however, is too limited for the purposes of this inquiry. The reason is that the challenges posed to modern governance are not necessarily limited to a change in its mechanisms or means. For example, the implications of globalization on the modern State could consist of a change in the ability to achieve its goals effectively. A focus on means alone would not detect this. Thus, although abandoning a teleological definition is one way to avoid the value trap, this inquiry offers a more nuanced approach that steers a middle course between Weber and Aristotle. It tries to save the appeal of a goal-oriented approach by maintaining the Aristotelian intuition that the State, as a man-made construct, serves a purpose and is therefore definable in terms of its objectives, whilst taking on board Weber's remark on the value trap.

The question this inquiry sets out to answer concerns the implications of globalization for the modern State. An answer to this question requires both an idea about the nature of States, and a framework for evaluating the way in which globalization affects this relation. As the introductory chapter has already pointed out, the type of

---

[16] Weber, M., 1978, p. 54ff.
[17] Pierson, C., 2004.
[18] See for example Frohock, F.M., 1974.

State this inquiry is concerned with is the modern State. There are several ways in which to distinguish the 'pre-modern' from the 'modern'. In economics, one may hold the transition from a feudal to a free market economy to be constitutive of 'modernity'. In political theory, a prominent characterization of the modern State has been given by Quentin Skinner who has emphasized the modern State's doubly impersonal character,[19] the emergence of the State as distinct from both the rulers and its subjects. In political science, the birth of the modern State is often associated with the Peace of Westphalia (1648), marking the historical transition from a system of overlapping jurisdictions or spheres of influence (guilds, monarchs and clergymen) to a unified State with a sovereign ruling over a well-defined territory. This transition marks the beginning of international relations theory and has become a paradigm in much of the globalization debate. In contrast to the aforementioned avenues, this inquiry takes a legal approach. It takes the constitutionalization of values, commitments and responsibilities defining the relation between the State and its subjects as the defining feature of the modern State. This approach both minimizes the value trap whilst simultaneously providing a framework to assess the implications of globalization for modern governance.

There are several strategies for limiting the incorporation of values into the investigation. One strategy in order to increase objectivity in defining the State is to limit the domain of investigation into a more uniform type of State. Within this inquiry, the focus is on Western States. This choice follows from the nature of inquiry on the one hand and their stake in the development of both the Internet and the globalization process on the other hand. Due to their relatively open economies, Western States are likely to be affected rather strongly by the increased interdependency that is caused by globalization in general and the Internet in particular. A second strategy for minimizing the value trap is to be explicit about the particular perspective that is used to conduct the research since different scientific disciplines may yield different results. The legal starting point in this inquiry is the modern State as a specifically designed State. Whereas some constitutive elements of what in this inquiry is termed the 'modern' or 'constitutional' State were already in place before they were put down in writing, all modern States have constitutional documents in which the foundations and reasons for the State's existence are made explicit.[20] Assessing these documents in their historical setting will provide a relatively neutral basis for determining the purpose and role of the State. As a result, the starting point of the inquiry is the State understood as a constitutional or 'liberal' democracy.

Constitutions are particularly useful objects of inquiry. Without exception, constitutions require rather elaborate procedures for changing their contents, a proce-

---

[19] Skinner, Q., 1989.

[20] The United Kingdom of Britain forms an exception. Whereas it is built upon constitutional documents and possesses most features characteristic of the liberal democracy, it lacks an explicitly written constitution for the purposes of establishing a State. Consequently, constitutional documents are not clearly distinguishable from other laws by more stringent amendment procedures, a feature that makes it unsuitable for the purposes of this inquiry.

dural warrant distinguishing them from ordinary laws. This special position suggests that constitutions capture the more fundamental commitments of a community in need of protection from the political delusions of the day. The need to constrain today's majority[21] was already acknowledged by the framers of both the US and the first French Constitutions who incorporated additional barriers for changing the constitution as compared to generic laws and regulations. The current general practice is a two-third majority vote requirement to establish constitutional change,[22] this, in contrast to the majority vote required to pass generic laws.[23]

Constitutions capture the foundational values, commitments and responsibilities of political communities and are easily identifiable. In order to distil these values, responsibilities and commitments however, one needs to interpret constitutional texts. In order to avoid interpretative mistakes, this research interprets constitutions in their historical setting. The reason for this is twofold. First, it clarifies the circumstances and reasons why particular constitutional configurations have emerged historically. The second reason is that it emphasizes the dynamic nature of the modern State, a key assumption underlying this research.

The key to unveiling the meaning of a constitution in this inquiry is analogous to that of a written contract. In judging a contract objectively, one has to look at the publicly accessible meaning that a reasonable person would attach to the words in context. Consequently, only the intentions that the parties succeeded in manifesting to each other are relevant.[24] By looking at the intentions that parties have managed to preserve within an agreement in case of future disputes one obtains an objective way of determining the values, responsibilities and commitments of government that are 'locked in' into the constitutional documents that constitute the modern State.

The Constitution of the United States of America (1787) (US Constitution) occupies a very important place in the formation of the modern State. Where the Peace of Westphalia set the external paradigm of the State, namely that of a world order consisting of sovereign nation-States,[25] the US Constitution determined its

---

[21] Tribe, L.H., 2000, p. 18.

[22] See for example, Constitution of the United States of America (1787), Art. V. This article also leaves room for conventions amending the constitution at the request of the States. This however has never occurred. Because the US have a federal system, once the amendments are approved in Congress they need to be ratified by at least three-fourths of the states.

[23] Within the cluster of Western States, Germany is the only State that stands out in this respect. The atrocities of World War II (WWII) led to the incorporation of the so-called 'Eternity Clause' as Basic Law for the Federal Republic of Germany (1946), Art. 79(3). By stating that certain amendments to the German constitution are simply inadmissible, the German Constitution essentially hardwires Germany's federal structure and fundamental rights provisions forever into its legal foundations. The reason for this, of course, is historical. Since the cruelties committed in WWII were basically the result of a failing democracy allowing a chancellor (Hitler) to gain so much power as to transform the democratic German (Weimar) republic into a totalitarian State.

[24] Barnett, R.E., 2004, p. 103.

[25] The Peace of Westphalia established the rule of Kings over the Clergy as sovereign rulers over well-defined territory. The result was a division of Europe into clearly defined Protestant and Catholic sovereign States.

internal[26] paradigm by being the first State to capture its fundamental values, commitments and responsibilities within an explicitly designed legal framework. As today's archetype for political organization, it provides the basis for this inquiry. In order to understand the significance of the US Constitution and its objectives, it is therefore useful to pay tribute to a well-established legal research tradition and look at the historical setting that helped shaping the first (US and French) constitutions. The following sections show that today's State is a result of a historical process and prone to react to changing circumstances. In addition, it aims to determine the values, commitments and responsibilities of today's constitutional democracy.

2.2   PRE-CONSTITUTIONAL LANDMARKS[27]

Despite the US' exemplary role as explicitly designed State, it was not the first State to explicitly lay down the powers of government in constitutional documents. Its historical roots lie in two British 'constitutional' documents, the Magna Charta (1215)[28] and the Bill of Rights (1688). Whereas the United Kingdom (UK) does not have a written constitution, and many provisions regulating government behavior stem from case law, custom and convention rather than explicitly codified law, its history does contain some constitutional principles and documents limiting government power that form the basis for the US Constitution. In addition, many of the limitations on government found in other constitutions originated in the legal system as it developed in Great Britain.

2.2.1   The Magna Charta (1215)

When William the Duke of Normandy won the Battle of Hastings in 1066 and became King of the English, he firmly established feudalism in England. The king ruled as the top overlord and a system of contracts between the overlords and lords (or vassals) determined the rights and obligations attached to the use of a particular terrain. Whereas most of these mutual obligations were informal agreements, sometimes they were secured in a charter forced upon the king by powerful vassals. The Magna Charta is the most famous among these charters and establishes the mutual obligations between John of England and his most important vassals, his barons. The reason for setting up the document was two-fold. First John had lost a conflict with the pope that led him to give England and Ireland away as papal territories, effectively making the pope the top overlord. This unilateral decision by John had angered the vassals who indirectly lost autonomy over their territories (fiefs). The

---

[26] Tribe, L.H., 2000, on p. 23, 'Tribe characterizes the constitution as an internal device for achieving the desired mix of constraint and empowerment.'

[27] Lokin, J.H.A. and Zwalve, W.J., 2001; Turner, R.V., 2003; Vermeulen B.P., 2007; Prakke, L. and Kortman, C.A.J.M., eds., 2004.

[28] Magna Charta (1215).

second reason for setting up the Magna Charta was the disproportional tax increase by John onto his barons in order to finance his wars in France.[29] After a revolt in 1214, the Magna Charta re-established the barons' loyalty to the king in return for certain rights.

The document granted the barons some guarantees against the arbitrary use of Royal power. It also granted every free man the right to due process and the protection against unlawful imprisonment (*habeas corpus*).[30] It furthermore established a limit on certain duties and ascertained the approval of a council of noble- and clergymen before raising taxation on behalf of military purposes. It contained provisions regulating trade guaranteeing either consent or payment for takings by royal officials of corn, wood, horses and carriages[31] and forced the king to return any lands confiscated from a felon within a year and a day. In addition, it provided standard measures[32] and guaranteed the safety and right of entry and exit of foreign merchants.[33] Article 61 of the document even grants 25 barons the right to enforce the document using violence in case of a breach of contract by the king.

It is tempting to read the Magna Charta as the precursor for modern constitutions. The document seems to constrain the powers of the king by implementing some form of checks and balances since the judicial powers depended on freemen rather than the king's verdict. It also seems to contain the seeds of democracy in the establishment of the aforementioned council. In addition, the document appears to grant civil rights to the barons and guarantees a variation of free trade[34] and something akin to property rights, a prerequisite for a well-functioning market economy. Moreover, the explicitly stated right to take the law into one's own hands (Art. 61) in case of a breach of contract by the king even seems to justify a revolution on Lockean grounds.[35]

---

[29] The reason for these wars was because John of England desperately tried to acquire land on the Continent, the lack of which granted him the name John Lackland.

[30] Magna Charta (1215), Arts. 39, 40.

[31] Ibid., Arts. 28-30.

[32] Ibid., Art. 25.

[33] Ibid., Art 41: All merchants shall have safe and secure exit from England, and entry to England, with the right to tarry there and to move about as well by land as by water, for buying and selling by the ancient and right customs, quit from all evil tolls, except (in time of war) such merchants as are of the land at war with us. And if such are found in our land at the beginning of the war, they shall be detained, without injury to their bodies or goods, until information be received by us, or by our chief justiciar, how the merchants of our land found in the land at war with us are treated; and if our men are safe there, the others shall be safe in our land. Ibid., Art. 42: It shall be lawful in future for anyone (excepting always those imprisoned or outlawed in accordance with the law of the kingdom, and natives of any country at war with us, and merchants, who shall be treated as if above provided) to leave our kingdom and to return, safe and secure by land and water, except for a short period in time of war, on grounds of public policy-reserving always the allegiance due to us.

[34] Ibid., Art. 41.

[35] Locke, J., 1689. Locke advocated a contract theory of government that justified the executive power in government in exchange for protection of the people's property and wellbeing. The lack of such protection, or when the king becomes a tyrant and acts against the interests of the people in turn, grants the people a right, if not an obligation, to resist his authority.

The document however established nothing resembling the commitments inherent to our modern constitutional democracies. First, it did not establish the desired result at the time. King John renounced the charter immediately after the barons had left London on the basis that the contract was not made out of his free will and as such violated his royal rights. Furthermore, the lack of an independent judiciary disabled the barons to enforce their rights by court of law. In addition, the document did not establish rights for individuals per se, just privileges for members belonging to certain collective bodies (the church and the city of London) and to people as Estate members. The establishment of government based on a system of checks and balances, a sovereign power of the people to determine their own faith and the attribution of individual inalienable civil rights including those establishing a free market economy were not under discussion.

The value of the Magna Charta then, is not grounded in its achievements at the time. Neither is the document very relevant for today's legal practice. Still, its influence on the development of constitutional governance can hardly be overstated. After King John denounced the contract, the document reappeared in different forms until it found its final version in 1297[36] consisting of 37 instead of 61 articles. Ironically, whereas the 1297 version omitted the council provisions for tax increases and the barons' right to enforce the contract against the king by using violence, both these provisions were to play an important role in constitutional history. The council managed to develop into a council of dignitaries, the Great Council, which eventually developed into a bicameral legislative parliament in the 15th century. In addition, the Magna Charta's provision on taxation by consent was to play an important role in the constitution of the US.

The reason that so much attention is still devoted to the Magna Charta in relation to modern constitutions is 17th century legal scholar Sir Edward Coke, who rejuvenated the document by giving it an (rather) extensive interpretation. He considered the Magna Charta as a limitation of the king's power applicable to all its subordinates. In this interpretation it formed, in conjunction with the due process[37] and habeas corpus[38] provisions, an important source of inspiration for the English Bill of Rights (1689), the first document that can rightly be said to limit the power of government.

2.2.2   The English Bill of Rights (1689)

Despite the establishment of the court system in 14th century England and the development of parliament as a bicameral legislative body out of the Great Council in the 15th century, still the hereditary king remained in charge of the Executive branch and was much in control of Parliament since it only gathered at the king's request.

---

[36] Magna Charta (1297).
[37] Magna Charta (1215), Art. 39.
[38] Ibid., Art. 40.

The English Bill of Rights (1689)[39] was a result of the struggle between the king and parliament, which after the revolution of 1688 ended in a victory for parliament. The document formed a condition to the coronation of Mary and William of Orange to become King and Queen of England and Scotland (1689).

The English Bill of Rights did two important things. First, it explicitly bound government by law by granting William a conditional power to rule England subject to the provisions entailed in the document. Secondly, the Bill guaranteed a freely elected parliament as a legislative branch of government. This latter provision established a proto-democracy of sorts with parliament performing a legislative role within the State and the Crown performing the executive role whilst being accountable to parliament. The Bill forms a list of rights in respect of the people as represented in parliament, much in line with Locke's contract theory.[40] It firmly established regular meetings by a freely elected parliament for amending, strengthening and preserving the laws and required parliamentary consent regarding the execution of the law and in matters of taxation. In addition, the Bill guaranteed freedom of speech in parliament as well as free elections. It furthermore forbade the Crown to establish courts or perform as a judge effectively established the separation of powers in a legislative, executive and judiciary branch, a division of governmental branches later popularized by Montesquieu.[41] It also established the subject's right to petition the Monarch and the right to bear arms for defense, two rights that would also become part of the US Constitution through the US Bill of Rights (1791).

2.2.3   Conclusion

The UK can justly claim to have established the first political organization constrained by written limitations on the power of government through its (1689) Bill of Rights, which formed a constitution for William of Orange to ascend the English throne. Both the Magna Charta and the Bill of Rights form the historic building blocks for modern government since they formed conceptual precursors to both the US and Continental constitutional developments.[42] The exposition on the origin of the documents above also illustrates that political organization is a dynamic feature of society. Hence, it confirms the opening phrases of this inquiry that throughout history, both the nature and manifestation of political organization has continuously adapted to the specific needs of the age, a thesis that is confirmed by the following

---

[39] An Act Declaring the Rights and Liberties of the Subject and Settling the Succession of the Crown (1689).

[40] Locke, J., 1689. Note that whereas Locke published his work in 1689, it is generally held that the largest part of the work has been written before 1683.

[41] Montesquieu, C.D.S. and Varnet, J.J., 1748.

[42] However, the Magna Charta and the Bill of Rights did not culminate into an explicitly written constitution securing the foundations of government against the political delusion of the day. Whereas the lack of a constitution disqualifies the UK as a research object for the purpose of this inquiry, its does not disqualify the UK as a liberal democracy as such. In fact, most of the features attributed to the modern (that is constitutional) State are also found within the UK.

historical exposition of the constitutionalization of political organization. The next section identifies the emergence of the modern constitutional State in the light of two revolutions both rooted in a battle over taxation and privileges. Both the American and French revolutions constituted major breakthroughs in our constitutional development.

2.3   THE CONSTITUTION OF THE LIBERAL DEMOCRACY

Although the United States Constitution was perhaps not the first of its kind, it remained the most influential constitutions ever written. As one of the world's first explicitly designed States, it forms a textbook example for subsequent constitutional documents throughout the world. The US revolution and the resulting constitution illustrated the roots of the struggle for independence, liberty and democracy. As such, the US struggle had much in common with the revolution that led to the first European constitution, and indeed the history of both the US and France are highly interwoven as we shall see. The French Ancien Regime's[43] financial and military support to the colonies against the British played a decisive role in ending the American war for independence.[44] Ironically, the subsequent victory for the colonies led to the downfall of the very (Ancien) regime that had helped financing their war. The US struggle for independence resulting in its constitution served as an example for France in taking control of its own political future. The following description of the US and French experience, show how the constitutionalization of political life constituted a transformation in both political and in economic terms.

2.3.1   The US experience

The formation of the United States of America started with the Declaration of Independence from England originating in the seven years war between France and England (1756-1763) during which England conquered the French colonies in North America. The costs of war and territorial expansion had led the British government to tax the colonies in order to pay for the English administration of the overseas territories. At base, the increase in taxation was a result of the UK's mercantilist policies. Mercantilism essentially views the entire nation as one great commercial enterprise.[45] According to this doctrine, a nation's wealth consists primarily in the amount of gold and silver in its treasury. Consequently, an active colony policy was pursued in order to obtain cheap raw materials to the national economy and national shipping was encouraged to support the national merchant navy.[46] In addi-

---

[43] The term 'Ancien' or 'Old Regime' stems from De Tocqueville, A., 1856.

[44] The American War for Independence starting in 1775 ended with the Siege of Yorktown in 1781.

[45] Screpanti, E. et al., 2005, p. 34ff.

[46] The Navigation Acts (1651) prohibited the importation of goods by non-British ships, but also the monopolies granted by England to the East India Company by for example the Tea Act (1773) formed part of these mercantilist policies.

tion, protectionist measures were to decrease imports and increase exports at the expense of the colonies. The UK's mercantilist policies eventually led to a colonial boycott of British goods and eventually resulted in the Declaration of Independence signed on July 4 in 1776.

The Declaration of Independence (1776)

The 'Declaration of Independence from English rule by the thirteen united states of America' formed the precursor to the US Constitution and hence laid the foundation for the modern constitutional State. Thomas Jefferson, who drafted the US Declaration, had relied heavily on the Virginia Declaration of Rights (1776), which in turn was inspired by the English Bill of Rights (1689). The Virginia Declaration, containing sixteen articles, viewed government as the servant of the people and reaffirmed the natural rights of life, liberty and property following Locke's exposition in 'Two Treatises of Government'.[47] In addition, it put substantive restrictions on government power in terms of rights and as such formed an important inspiration for the US Declaration of Independence (1776), the US Bill of Rights that was later added to the constitution in (1791), and the French Declaration of the Rights of Men and the Citizen (1789).

The US Declaration[48] forms a turning point in history, not only by influencing subsequent constitutional documents, but also by forming the basis for the development of two fundamental principles elementary to all constitutional democracies. The first idea is that of constitutionalism, putting a judicial restriction on State power, and the second idea is that of self-governance by the people, also known as democracy. The US Declaration also reveals some political and philosophical ideas that have guided the development of the constitutional democracy. It refers to the law of nature as the basis for the inalienable rights and the idea of a social contract as the foundation for the State. In addition, it holds the sovereign power of the people as a guiding principle for justifying government and as an explicit justification of the rights of a people to resist unjust government.

The Constitution of the United States (1787)

After establishing their independence, the states sought to establish a government. The Articles of Confederation and Perpetual Union, accepted by the Second Continental Congress in 1777 and de jure ratified by all the states in 1781, formed the first constitutional document of the United States of America. This union however had serious drawbacks. Neither was there an executive, nor a judicial authority and the Confederation did not have any other means of enforcing Congress's will. The

---

[47] Locke, J., 1689. The document placed structural restrictions on government in terms of a system of checks and balances, an idea popularized in Montesquieu, C.D.S. and Varnet, J.J., 1748, in which he promoted a separation of the legislative, judicial and executive branch of government as a way of preventing tyranny and increasing liberty.

[48] The Unanimous Declaration of the thirteen United States of America (1776).

enforcement of decisions was left to the individual states themselves. One of the consequences was that Britain insisted on negotiating treaties with each individual former colony separately rather than with the newly established Confederation. The reason was exactly the Confederation's lack of power to enforce existing treaties. In addition, the Articles did not give the central government the power to prevent one state from discriminating against other states regarding foreign commerce.[49]

Hence, in order 'to form a more perfect Union' the 1787 Constitution of the United States tried to overcome these deficiencies. Its preamble reads:

> 'We the People of the United States, in Order to form a more perfect Union, establish Justice, insure domestic Tranquility, provide for the common defense, promote the general Welfare, and secure the Blessings of Liberty to ourselves and our Posterity, do ordain and establish this Constitution for the United States of America.'

The ideals expressed in the Declaration of Independence also informed the Constitution. 'We the People' for example, refers to the sovereign right of self-governance located in the people.[50] It also associates this sovereignty with justice and explicitly mentions liberty as a founding value of the constitution. The 1787 Constitution restricted government in two important ways. First, it established a system of checks and balances between government powers. On the one hand, it held on to federalism by stating that all powers not explicitly attributed to national government were left for the individual states or the people. Hence, decentralization established a vertical check on government power. On the other hand, it created a system of checks and balances between three distinct governmental branches (the executive, legislative and judicial branch) forming a horizontal check on government. In addition, it created a system of democratic representation.

The Bill of Rights (1789)

The explicitly stated powers in the constitution defined structural and procedural limitations to the governments' power. In the eyes of the anti federalists, opposing a federal structure, the limitations on government did not go far enough. After much deliberation and pressured by individual states to limit the federal powers of government further, ten amendments were added to the US Constitution. The 'Bill of Rights' limited the powers of government further, putting additional substantive limitations upon government. The basis for these limitations formed the inalienable rights of men, already expressed in the Declaration of Independence, the Virginia Declaration and the work of John Locke.

---

[49] For a more extended elaboration on the topic of the Articles of Confederation see, Jensen, M., 1970.

[50] Despite the ultimate natural rights justification is the fact that the people are God's creatures, it does place the emphasis on the fact that the people deserved a right to self-governance on the basis of equality.

2.3.2 The French experience[51]

The situation in France before the revolution of 1789 differed considerably from the situation in the pre-independence colonies across the Atlantic. One distinguishing element was the French feudal legacy, which had made society predictable on the one hand, but static and void of progression on the other hand. In addition, France suffered from a scarcity in land that was absent in the less densely populated English colonies. Whereas many elements in the political make-up of the colonies were left in tact after the Declaration of Independence and the subsequent constitutional establishment of the US, the structure of French society required a complete social transformation from top to bottom.[52]

Grounds for a revolution

The French Revolution marked a turning point in history by ending the Ancien Regime, that is, the monarchy of Louis XVI, characterized by an (near) absolute ruler obtaining its powers by divine ordinance. The Revolution was a turning point, despite the fact that France, similar to the English tradition, had a system of parliament in place in which the representatives of the three Estates (Clergy, Nobility and petty Bourgeois) formed a proto-democracy of sorts. However, this type of semi-representation had lost much of its splendor and effectiveness because they only gathered at the king's request. The last time the French king had called his General Assembly together dated back to 1614.

In the years of the monarchy, society still had many feudal characteristics. It had a strict hierarchical organization based upon three Estates. The First Estate, the Clergy had been rather powerful in France for over 800 years. Consisting of only about 150.000 souls, it held 10 to 15 percent of the land. The Second Estate, the Nobility, consisting of approximately 350.000 souls, owned about 30 percent of France's property and their most important source of income consisted of the collection of rents and dues (on salt, bread, wine, the use of mills amongst others) from the peasants living on their properties. The Third Estate comprised the rest of the population of about 25 million souls consisting of the bourgeoisie, the peasantry and the urban artisans. Whereas the Nobility and the Clergy were dependent on the king to a high degree, they did enjoy significant privileges (particularly in terms of taxation and public administration) over the Third Estate, which had to bring in most of the taxes. In the 1780s, the debt of the king had raised to such an extent that an increase of taxes was inevitable. By the end of the 1780s, the French State was facing bankruptcy, largely due to the lack of repayment of the debts caused by

---

[51] Part of this explanation is based on the exposition in: Kortman C.A.J.M., 2004, and Battjes, H. and Vermeulen, B., 2007.

[52] An exposition and full analysis of the differences and similarities of the background to the French and the US constitutions is beyond the scope of this inquiry. For the purposes of this inquiry, the main purpose of the French exposition is to emphasize the relevance of constitutionally guaranteed economic liberties as a foundation for a market economy.

previously fought wars. When the First and Second Estates refused to pay an increase in taxes debts and the Third Estate called for a decrease in taxation, the king was forced by the courts to call the General Assembly (of Estates) for a meeting in order to enforce a tax increase by law. In July 1788, the king complied. The meeting was scheduled for June 1789.

The Decree of the 4th of August (1789)

In the year following the king's call for a meeting of the General Assembly, the representatives of the Estates were chosen and lists of grievances and proposals for reform (Cahiers de Doléances) were set up containing proposals for increased representation and a written constitution. The consolidated list of the Third Estate featured loyalty to the king, loyalty to the Church and most importantly for our purposes; it also proclaimed the sanctity of private property.[53] This latter issue was particularly pressing for the Third Estate, of which the situation of the peasantry was particularly distressing. Although it did own 30 to 40 percent of the land, most of the arrangements were feudal in nature with severe restrictions on the use of its products. In addition, its members paid taxes to the king, the church, the lord of the manor and indirect taxes on wine, salt and bread. Understandably, the introduction of guaranteed inviolable private property rights was high on their agenda.

When the General Assembly gathered on May 5, 1789 a disagreement on voting rights led the Assembly of the Third Estate to declare itself 'National Constituent Assembly' (June 17, 1789). At this event, the Third Estate announced to represent 'the people' with the purpose of drafting a constitution, a plan not quite supported by the king and the vast amount of Nobility. Meanwhile, the tension in Paris was rising due to the need for reform combined with famine caused by a disappointing harvest. When the news reached Paris that the king had discharged his finance minister (Necker) due to his sympathy for the Third Estate, the people feared a counterrevolution and stormed the Bastille prison on the 14th of July. Whereas the events at the Bastille caused the king to recall his finance minister back into power, the peasantry outside of Paris was also becoming restless, had stopped paying taxes and started to burn down the houses of their landlords. Instead of fighting the peasants, the French aristocrats waived their privileges in the decree of the August 4th, which put a definitive end to the feudal legacy, the first step towards a new society.

The Declaration of the Rights of Men and the Citizen (1789)

The 4th of August was in many ways an important date in the constitution of a new France, not only because it was the day on which the feudal legacy ended, but also on this day, the Declaration of the Rights of Men and the Citizen, or the French Declaration for short, was established. The document formed the basis for the constitutional liberal democracy established in 1792, and has profoundly influenced

---

[53] An example regarding the call for the inviolability of the private property can be found in the Cahier of the Third Estate of Dourdon, Cahier des Doleances (1789).

subsequent constitutional democracies and international human rights frameworks. Today it forms a constituent part of the French constitution (1958) in addition to the preamble to the constitution of the fourth Republic established in 1946.[54] The preamble of the declaration reads the following:

> 'The representatives of the French people, organized as a National Assembly, believing that the ignorance, neglect, or contempt of the rights of man are the sole cause of public calamities and of the corruption of governments, have determined to set forth in a solemn declaration the natural, unalienable, and sacred rights of man, in order that this declaration, being constantly before all the members of the Social body, shall remind them continually of their rights and duties; in order that the acts of the legislative power, as well as those of the executive power, may be compared at any moment with the objects and purposes of all political institutions and may thus be more respected, and, lastly, in order that the grievances of the citizens, based hereafter upon simple and incontestable principles, shall tend to the maintenance of the constitution and redound to the happiness of all.'[55]

Consequently, the document contained the foundations for the new constitutionally warranted liberal democracy defining liberty as 'freedom to do everything not infringing the inalienable rights of others (Art. 4). With an emphasis on the equality of people within society and before the law (Art. 1), it provided the basis for democracy (Art. 6) and established an individual sphere free from governmental intrusion. In addition to the civil and political liberties like freedom of expression (Art. 14), is also contained a clause guaranteeing the inviolable right to private property (Art.17) an important characteristic of a market economy.

Whereas the US constitution clearly established an economic sphere free from interference from political actors, the value of this liberal principle can only be fully understood in the light of the French (or European) experience. Particularly this latter development shows the transition from a feudal to a market economy based on the free interaction between buyers and sellers unmediated by the arbitrary wishes of political actors like the State or privileged land owners. The French experience particularly shows that the creation of a government-free sphere of economic activity granted by the inalienable rights of private property. Its corollary 'freedom of contract' is a prerequisite for the effective allocation of goods and a pivotal element in the development of the modern State, an issue often underestimated by constitutional writers.

2.3.3   Two experiences compared

The constitutional development sketched above, shows that the history of the modern State was primarily driven by a need to restrict the powers of government and to

---

[54] Conseil Constitutionnel, July 16, 1971, Decision No. 71-44 DC; Conseil Constitutionnel, January 15, 1975, Decision No. 74-54.
[55] Declaration of the Rights of Men and the Citizen (1798).

redefine the relation between the State and its subjects. Simultaneously the transformation also constituted an economic transition.

Both experiences showed an appeal to inalienable rights and the laws of nature in order to justify their demands, ideas that are inherently connected to the ideals of the Enlightenment as expressed by thinkers like Locke and Rousseau. In addition, the objectives were largely the same. They justified a break with the old regime and aimed to secure (1) democratic representation by involving citizens in public decision making, (2) a market economy in order to free oneself from mercantilist strategies and (3) individual liberties to destroy the rudiments of feudal injustice.

The similarities between the two experiences are not coincidental. Characterized by its universality claim, the French Declaration was directly inspired by the Bill of Rights of Virginia (1776), which had also formed the basis to the US Bill of Rights. One influential link between the US and France was the French Marquis de la Fayette who headed the Editorial office that drafted the French Declaration. He had fought in the American Revolution and had personally experienced the emergence of the Declaration of Independence and the Virginia Bill of Rights. In addition, De la Fayette was a close friend to Thomas Jefferson, with whom he worked together whilst being the US ambassador in France. Thomas Jefferson was the principle drafter of the US Declaration of Independence and a former Governor of Virginia (1779-1781).

After the French Revolution and the American War for Independence both newly established liberal democracies showed some imperfections. The US had to wait until 1787 in order to obtain its current outlines due to the weakness of the newly formed union. The French constitutional history has even been described as a continuous experiment in political organization.[56] Today however, the French Declaration is a constitutive part of the French Constitution and the constitutional democracy forms today's archetype of political organization characterizing the modern State.

2.4   THE CONSTITUTIONAL STRUCTURE OF THE LIBERAL DEMOCRACY

The Constitution of the US confirms the ideals expressed in the Declaration of Independence. The values locked into the US Constitution form the basis of the modern State as we encounter it today.

---

[56] For example, the monarchy resulting from the French revolution (1791) was replaced in 1793 by the first French republic, which in spite of its democratic nature was never put into practice. The years that followed were also characterized by political instability resulting in the 1795 Constitution characterized by a strict separation of governmental powers until Napoleon seized power in 1799 and eventually became the absolute ruler of France. With little interest in constitution matters the principles of the Declaration were abandoned. The current French Constitution of 1958 however, has rehabilitated the Declaration by incorporating it into the document.

2.4.1   Democratic representation

The commitment to the central role of the people in public decision making, is firmly established in the US Constitution captured by the first three words of the Preamble 'We the People ...'. Whereas the theoretical underpinnings of the people as the sovereign power to enact government and create laws can be found in the work of Hobbes and Locke,[57] the US Constitution is the first document of its kind establishing a national government based on the consent of the governed.[58] The practical implementation of this principle is constitutionally warranted by citizen representation in government and a regular call for elections at predetermined intervals. Fundamental to a democratic electoral system is that it allows opposing forces to compete against each other and even to replace current office holders. As such, it provides feedback mechanisms for people in office and enhances the accountability of leadership. In addition, it legitimizes government in making decisions on behalf of the governed.

Whereas it took some time for the US Constitution to incorporate the views of every citizen into the formation of its public policies, regular elections have formed the basis for government ever since 1787 and currently, both Congress and the President are elected by the citizens. The House of Representatives consists of 435 members proportionally divided over the states according to the number of citizens. House members are elected every two years and eligible voters can only elect a representative residing in the congressional district that the representative will represent. The person with the highest number of votes wins. In order to counter the short terms the House members are in place, each state elects two senators to serve six-year terms. This process is staggered in that every two years one-third of the Senators is replaced. The election of Senators is not restricted to congressional districts but is state-based. As opposed to the congressional elections, the President is chosen for a period of four years indirectly. The parties choose their nominees at their national conventions indirectly. They are chosen by an Electoral College consisting of state representatives that are directly chosen by the citizens and who are pledged to vote for a particular presidential candidate and for a vice president, an act they perform after Election Day, after which the candidates are inaugurated on the 20th of January. Although not all constitutional democracies have implemented the democratic ideal uniformly, without exception they have all embraced the principle of democratic representation as a feedback and legitimizing mechanism for public decision making.[59]

---

[57] Hobbes, T., 1651; Locke, J., 1689.

[58] Whereas the Scottish Declaration of Abroath (1320) mentions the right of the Scottish people to choose their own king and explicitly connects the notion of freedom with laws, rule and consent, the Declaration of Abroath is not the forerunner of the US Declaration of Independence, neither did it form the basis for the US Constitution. Whereas it did establish independence from England, it merely affirmed assumption of a new king rather than establishing a new form of government. It certainly did not allude to modern democratic constitutional governance as we know it today.

[59] Compare: Prakke, L. and Kortman C.A.J.M., 2004.

2.4.2   Checks and balances

In addition to democratic representation, the second characteristic of the constitutional democracy is its system of checks and balances consisting of a system of
vertical (decentralization) and horizontal (separation of powers) principles for dividing governmental power.[60]

Vertical division of governmental powers

One of the first things the independent states needed to make clear was a division of
powers between the states and the union. This struggle, which continues to form an
important tension within American politics, resulted in a federal structure with clearly
defined roles for both national and local government. In principle, all the tasks that
are delegated to the national government are expressly stated in the Constitution.[61]
In addition to the important task of national security for example, the federal government also has an important role to play in the regulation of commerce. This
latter aspect is a logical consequence of the confederation which failed to establish
a unity strong enough to prevent unfair competition between the States, leading to
barriers to trade put up by the individual states effectively causing similar problems
to the barriers that the English put up to trade with the colonies. If one of the reasons for the Independence was to prevent this type of behavior and to stimulate
trade between the States, the federal regulation of commerce was a natural and
important role for the federal government to play.

The power of Congress, the legislative body of the national government, is limited to collecting taxes and borrowing money, regulating commerce, declaring war
and maintaining military forces. The US Constitution also forbids the states to issue
money, impose taxation on imports and exports, regulate interstate commerce and
impair the obligation of contracts. Despite this seemingly limitative enumeration of
national governmental powers, there is a constitutional provision by which these
areas can be extended, the so-called elastic clause.[62]

> '... Congress shall have power ... to make all laws, which shall be necessary and
> proper for carrying into execution the foregoing powers, and all other powers vested
> by this Constitution in the government of the United States, or in any department or
> officer thereof.'

In the course of history the elastic clause has formed the basis for a steady growth
of the federal government over the states, as will become clear later in this chapter.[63] Still, the federal structure of the US does limit the role of the central govern-

---

[60] Tribe, L.H., 2000, Section 2.3, p. 124 ff.

[61] Constitution of the United States of America (1787), Amendment 10.

[62] Constitution of the United States (1787), Art. I, Section 8(18).

[63] *McCulloch* v. *Maryland*, 7 US 316, 420 (1819) settled the scope of this clause in the light of the
federal government chartering a national bank in order to execute its duty controlling national eco-

ment considerably since the decentralization of public decision making enables the decisions to be made 'closer' to the individual[64] allowing for a more responsive government. Decentralization both increases democratic participation, representation and accountability on the other hand, while it also increases public policy and governmental effectiveness.[65]

Whereas not all modern States have a federal structure, all of the representative larger Western States have some form of decentralized structure limiting the central government in its sovereign power to enact and enforce legislation.[66] In sum, decentralization, albeit perhaps not the most important characteristic in the light of this inquiry, can safely be said to constitute an important feature of the modern State.

---

nomic policy. Chief Justice Marshall stated that a necessary and proper step to take since a government 'entrusted with such ample powers … must also be entrusted with ample means for their execution'.

[64] For an exposition of the pros and cons of federalism see, Erk, J., 2006.

[65] See for example the exposition in Chapter 7 in Norris, P., 2008.

[66] Prakke, L. and Kortman, C.A.J.M., 2004. From the larger EU countries, Germany, the UK and Spain all have a federal structure. Italy with five autonomous provinces has also sought refuge to decentralization as the most effective way of governing its territory. Even France, which is traditionally considered a unitary State ever since its revolution, is in fact a decentralized unitary State divided into four levels of local authority, communes (3600), departments (92) and regions (22). The fourth layer of authority is preserved for territorial units with a special statute like 'Corsica' that are relatively independent of the central government (see French Constitution (1958), Art. 75). The constitutional principle of subsidiarity (French Constitution (1958) Art. 72(2)) ensures that matters are handled by the smallest and lowest competent authority. The local and regional bodies have the power to organize local referendums; *LOI organique no. 2003-705 du 1er août 2003 relative au référendum local*, 2009, may experiment in policy making; *LOI organique no. 2003-704 du 1er août 2003 relative à l'expérimentation par les collectivités territoriales,* and have relative financial autonomy and share in local revenues; *LOI organique no. 2004-758 du 29 juillet 2004 prise en application de l'article 72-2 de la Constitution relative à l'autonomie financière des collectivités territoriale.* In addition they have responsibilities regarding economic development, tourism and professional education; *LOI organique no. 2004-809 du 13 août 2004 relative aux libertés et responsabilités locales.* The European Charter for Local Self-Government (1985) is signed by all European States with the exception of Andorra, San Marino and Monaco, France and Serbia. It allows local authorities within the framework of national law to regulate and manage a substantial share of public affairs under their own responsibility in the interest of the local population. It commits the European States to guaranteeing the political, administrative and financial independence of local authorities, which are to be elected by universal suffrage, and it is the earliest legal instrument to set out the principle of subsidiarity, that is, the principle ensuring decision making as closely as possible to the citizen. It also guarantees a constant check on the justification of governmental action at EU level in the light of the possibilities available at national, regional or local level. The principle of subsidiarity became an explicit part of the European body of law, Treaty Establishing a Constitution for Europe 2004/C310/01, Article 3b: The Community shall act within the limits of the powers conferred upon it by this Treaty and of the objectives assigned to it therein. In areas which do not fall within its exclusive competence the Community, shall take action, in accordance with the principle of subsidiarity, only if and in so far as the objectives of the proposed action cannot be sufficiently achieved by the Member States, and can therefore, by reason of the scale or effects of the proposed action, be better achieved by the Community. Any action by the Community shall not go beyond what is necessary to achieve the objectives of this Treaty.

Horizontal division of governmental powers

Where decentralization serves as a vertical power check among multiple layers of government and as such lowers the danger of power abuse by central government, the division of powers within government is also one of the essential elements of the liberal democracy. In addition to emphasizing the strength of decentralization as a force against despotism, Montesquieu's description of a system of checks and balances between branches of government[67] made him the father of one of the key concepts within constitutional theory. Whereas Montesquieu merely claims to describe the English situation at the time, his publication made it one of the guiding principles for the design of the US Constitution and subsequent liberal democracies. The idea is simply that one needs to attribute different tasks to different organizations (and people).

Constitutional democracies can be roughly divided into two types of government: Presidential and Parliamentary. The main difference is that in a presidential system the President is both chief executive and the head of State. In addition, he is neither part nor appointed by he legislature. Within a parliamentary system, the head of state and the chief executive are two separate offices, of which the head is often reduced to a ceremonial role. Since the Chief executive is chosen by the legislature the distinction between the legislature and the executive branch is somewhat less strict. In a Presidential system, Congress cannot select nor dismiss governments, and neither is the executive accountable to Congress despite their right of budget. In a parliamentary system, government is formed by assembly elections, based on the strength of party representation. The government officials are drawn from the assembly and are accountable to the assembly. Government rests on the assembly's confidence and can be removed if it loses that confidence. In both systems, the chief executive can be removed from office by the legislature. As we have seen in the previous sections, Britain is a good example of a parliamentary system whilst the US follows a presidential system. Whereas most European States follow the parliamentary system, France is the obvious odd one out. It has a hybrid system with a 'dual executive'.[68] For the purposes of this inquiry, there is no fun-

---

[67] Montesquieu, C.D.S. and Varnett, J.J., 1748.

[68] The current French system has a separately elected President who works in conjunction with a Prime minister and cabinet both drawn from and accountable to the National assembly. Central to the French system is the directly elected President, who generally determines the main lines of policy and personally appoints and dismisses the Prime Minister. He can dissolve the National Assembly (equivalent to the House of Representatives in the US system), and can take all measures required to in case of national emergencies. In addition, he can appoint the President and three members of the Constitutional Council and can have the Council to review international agreements on their constitutionality. The President also has shared powers that need the countersignature of the Prime Minister (PM) and main ministers involved in the preparation and execution of the decision. These concern the appointment and dismissal of ministers and state secretaries, the appointment of ambassadors, civil and military officials. The President promulgates statutes and has a right to veto ordinances and decrees that have been discussed in the Council of Ministers. Furthermore, the President declares war after parliamentary authorization and is responsible for negotiating and ratifying treaties. Regarding other foreign

damental difference between the two systems. Since the US forms the focal point of the case studies in this research and the US constitution has become the archetype for future constitutional democracies, the following sections focus on the US constitution. The conclusions regarding the constitutionally defined State-subject relation are applicable to all Western industrialized States.

The US has a presidential system of government. Its constitution reveals a rather strict division of government powers into a legislative, executive and judicial branch of government. Article I defines the bicameral legislative branch consisting of the House of Representatives (House) and the Senate, who both need to give their approval in order to enact a law. There is however a difference in task. Whereas the House has the sole power to originate revenue bills, the Senate alone approves presidential appointments. The bicameral system is an institutional constraint designed to provide a buffer against the temptation of the House to enact bills informed by short-term rather than long-term interests. The terms of office, six years for Senators and two-year terms for members of the House, reflect this stabilizing role of the Senate. One of the most important checks on the other two branches is the congressional power to appropriation, that is, that neither the Executive nor the Legislative branch can spend money without an act of Congress appropriating it. Congress also determines the size of the courts, including the Supreme Court.

The President is endowed with the Executive power to grant amnesty and convene Congress in special sessions. More important, however, he is responsible for foreign affairs in that he has the power to recognize other countries and negotiate treaties, which in turn have to be approved by the Senate. The President's most important check on the power of Congress is that he can veto legislation, which Congress in turn can undo by a two-third vote. His influence on the Judicial is that he appoints the federal judges.

The Judicial Branch[69] is vested in the Supreme Court. It consists of nine Justices that are appointed for life by the President and are approved by a majority vote in the full Senate. In addition to the ability to resolve conflicts between federal and state laws, it has the power to resolve interstate conflicts between citizens and it can determine at which level of government a power belongs. The Supreme Court also serves as a check on radical democratic impulses by guarding the abuse of liberty, property and the national government itself. The Supremacy Clause of Article VI[70]

---

policy decisions, including defense, the minister for foreign affairs assists him. Government consists of the PM, the ministers and state secretaries, who are appointed by the President after nomination by the PM. The powers of government are extensive, by setting the agenda in parliament it can favor the acceptance of government bills over bills proposed by individual members of parliament. In line the parliamentary system, the French government, unlike the head of State, is accountable to Parliament. Source: French Constitution (1958).

[69] Constitution of the United States of America (1787), Art. III.

[70] Ibid., Art. VI(2), the 'Supremacy Clause' states that '[T]his Constitution, and the Laws of the United States which shall be made in Pursuance thereof; and all Treaties made, or which shall be made, under the authority of the United States, shall be the supreme Law of the land; and the Judges in every State shall be bound thereby, any Thing in the Constitution or Laws of any State to the Contrary notwithstanding.'

and the Judiciary Act (1789) allowed the Supreme Court to check the consistency of state constitutions and laws concerning federal laws, treaties and the constitution. The landmark decision *Marbury* v. *Madison*[71] allowed the Supreme Court to rule on the constitutionality of legislative acts made in congress and treaties. As far as the check on the Executive is concerned, the Supreme Court has asserted judicial scrutiny over the President's power[72] at the same time however, the Supreme court has affirmed the President's unilateral power to declare individuals 'enemy combatants' possessing fewer rights than the average US citizen. Hence, the power of the President is firmly established. The Judicial Branch checks the Executive by issuing or refusing to issue warrants for searches and seizures.

2.4.3 Individual rights

The US Bill of Rights is the document that is solely concerned with the individual liberties of citizens. It guarantees a State-free private sphere in which citizens can move without being improperly infringed by government action. The Bill of Rights was designed to give each of the three branches of government clearer and more restricted boundaries in order to fulfill their purpose. Today it forms an integral part of the US constitution. The most important in the light of this inquiry are the following.

Amendment I, guarantees freedom of speech which is one of the most important elements in a society adhering to democratic values. It puts limits on Congress since it compels it to refrain from making laws abridging the freedom of speech, religion, press assembly or the right to petition freedoms. Amendments II-IV put limits on the Executive. The most important one is the requirement not to engage in search or seizure of evidence without a court warrant. Amendments V-VIII put limits on the Judiciary, the most important and famous one is the amendment V, granting immunity from testimony against oneself and being tried twice for the same offence. It furthermore guarantees that no property can be taken without just compensation. The last two amendments, IX and X, put limitations on National Government stating, that all rights not enumerated are reserved to the states or the people. The 17 amendments that have been made after 1791 extended voting rights,[73] changed the relationship between elective offices and the electorate[74] or amended the constitution to change the powers of government,[75] amendment XVI being perhaps the most important in this respect since it grants the national government the explicit power to tax income.

---

[71] *Marbury* v. *Madison*, 5 US 137 (1803).
[72] Lowe, T., et al., 2006, p. 29ff.
[73] Constitution of the United States of America (1787), Amendments XIV, XV, XIX, XXIII, XIV, XVI.
[74] Ibid., Amendments XII, XIV, XVII, XX, XXII, XXV.
[75] Ibid., Amendments XI, XIII, XIV, XVI, XXVII.

Also regarding individual rights, the US constitution is not alone. One of the prime outcomes of the French revolution is the Declaration of the Rights of Men and the Citizen (1789) (for short the French Declaration). The French Declaration is a liberal document par excellence and forms the basis for the substantive rights that are fundamental to French society. In the first article the freedom of the people and their equality in rights and the declaration that the only social distinctions may be grounded in the general good form the basis for French society as shown in its motto 'Liberty, Equality and Fraternity'.[76] The Declaration defines liberty as the freedom to do everything that injures no one else. The laws determine the borders of this freedom. The provisions in the Declaration determine these limits for government. Unlawful imprisonment (Arts.7-9), freedoms of expression and assembly (Art. 10-11), the right to require public accountability (Art. 15) and an explicit adherence to the rule of law and a division of government powers as conditions for a constitution (Art. 16) and last but not least the guarantee of private property as an inviolable and sacred right (Art. 17), all form part of the substantial provisions of the French Declaration as a reaction to the revolution. The Preamble of 1946, which also still forms part of the current French Constitution, establishes principles as a reaction to WWII, amongst which are the equality of men and women, a right to claim asylum for people facing liberty related prosecution, free education, government duties regarding health and material security. Interestingly we see a departure from the classical liberal freedoms expressed in the French Declaration and the US bill of rights, a topic at which we shall return later in this chapter. It shows an increase in governmental commitments and responsibilities.

More clearly, this trend is illustrated by the proposal for a constitutional document of the European Union. Whereas the original US bill of rights only contained 10 Amendments, and the French Declaration only 17, the Treaty that was to establish a Constitution for Europe[77] proposed in 2004 contained 53 articles in its Charter on Fundamental Human Rights. These articles in turn were divided into more than 90 provisions in total, many of which with a focus on positive rights, that is rights that are granted by government and need government action rather than abstinence in order to reach the goal. The integration commitment concerning people with disabilities,[78] and right of citizens to placement services[79] are two illustrative examples. Although both France and The Netherlands rejected the Treaty, they did not reject it because of Human Rights provisions. Today, all Western European States are committed to the 18 articles expressed in the European Convention on Human Rights.[80] Most constitutions also contain additional clauses tailor-made to their specific needs. Within the context of this research the individual rights can be distinguished into civil and political rights on the one hand, and economic rights on

---

[76] See, French Constitution (1958), intro to Art. 2.
[77] Treaty Establishing a Constitution for Europe 2004/C310/01.
[78] Ibid., Art. 86.
[79] Ibid., Art. 89.
[80] European Convention on Human Rights (1950).

the other hand. Additional aspects concerning human rights provision will be discussed when relevant in the chapters containing the case studies.

In addition to the substantial constraints to the privileges of government established by the Individual rights, all constitutions also guarantee procedural constraints. One important one already mentioned is the constraints on regulation and particularly on changing a constitution.[81] The other procedural constraints that are relevant concern the elective process, which is the topic of the following section.

Conclusion

The modern State is a constitutional democracy characterized by adherence to the rule of law based on the equality of the State's citizens and a general tendency to put stricter requirements on changes involving the more fundamental (constitutional) values of society. The previous sections showed that the early (French and US) constitutions were built upon democratic ideals and designed to limit governmental powers. These ideas still form the heart of all Western constitutions. They concern (1) democratic representation, (2) a constitutionally guaranteed system of checks and balances, and (3) substantial provisions guaranteeing individual rights establishing a private realm free from government interference.

As we shall see in the case studies that are central to this inquiry, all three aspects of the modern state as exemplified in the classic model of the State are challenged by the growing transnational interdependence between actors and activities.

2.5   CONSTITUTIONAL COMMITMENTS AND RESPONSIBILITIES

Sections 2.2 and 2.3 answered the question about the historical roots and context in which the modern State emerged. Section 2.4 answered the question as to what a State is in outlining the general constitutional characteristics of the modern State. Since the State's objectives follow from the constitutional documents under investigation, they are relatively stable and identifiable. If the circumstances change, States have to adapt in order to continue to achieve their objectives.

In order to show the dynamic nature of the State-subject relation to date, it is within this inquiry sufficient to focus on three fundamental objectives that can be constitutionally induced and are aims in themselves; democratic decision making, welfare and securing individual rights.[82] The following sections show the changing role of the State-subject relation in the transition of the liberal democracy into today's welfare State by developing a conceptual model based on three forces within the State: government, the market and civil society.

---

[81] Within the US constitution this provision can be found in Constitution of the United States of America (1787), Art. V.

[82] It is not claimed within the context of this inquiry that the identification of three main state objectives covers the role of the modern State in all its complexities. It is merely a heuristic device, designed to set the changes in constitutional governance in context.

2.5.1   The liberal democracy

Constitutions form the basis for the State-subject relation since they define the relation between government on the one hand and the citizen on the other hand. Central
to the constitutionalization of the relation between government and the citizen is
the concept of individual liberty or freedom from governmental constraints. This
freedom materializes constitutionally though the provisions protecting individual
or fundamental rights. Although strictly speaking, individual rights also form the
basis for the democratic deliberation, it is heuristically useful to distinguish between two private spheres within the State based on fundamental rights. The first
private sphere is the realm constituted by civil (and political) liberties, of which the
freedoms of expression, association and religion are the most important. The second private sphere is the realm constituted by economic liberties and consists of
guaranteed private property rights and its corollary, freedom of contract. Civil rights
(or sometimes called civil and political rights) form the basis for civil society and
stimulate the organization and deliberation of individuals free from government
interference and free from economic constraints. The economic liberties, on the
other hand, form the basis for the market economy,[83] which, in contrast to the
feudal system in the French pre-revolutionary era, is based on individual property
rights rather than on dependency relations between lords and vassals.

Government, civil society and the market

Figure 3 depicts the important relation between the three constitutionally defined
sources of influence in a conceptual model labeled 'triangle of liberty'. The figure
distinguishes between a private and a public realm. The public realm is the realm of
government influence and is characterized by regulation. The private realm consists of the two private spheres, which allow the market economy and civil society
to flourish. The three competing forces within the State (government, the market
economy and civil society) are interrelated.[84] On the one hand, they form a system
of checks and balances; on the other hand, they reinforce one another.

---

[83] Private property, freedom of contract and self-interest are the pillars of the market economy and
the basis of our current wealth. For a more elaborate exposition of this system see, Smith, A., 1776.

[84] The triangular model in order to distinguish forces of influence in a society has been proposed
before. Particularly the model developed in: Zijderveld, A.C., 1999, may look somewhat familiar. In
contrast to the distinction made here, between government, the market and civil society, Zijderveld
distinguishes between the State, the market and civil society. The purpose of his distinction is to show
that within a well-functioning democracy, the ideological traditions associated with each element in the
model (the State as the focus of a socialist tradition, the market as the focus of a liberal tradition and
civil society as the focus of a conservative tradition), need to keep one another in check. Within this
inquiry however, the triangle illustrates the changing dynamics between the State and its subjects. This
relation is largely characterized by the interplay of government, the market and civil society, which
have constitutional foundations. Zijderveld's 'Democratic Triangle' and the triangle used in this inquiry are quite different, both in setup as in heuristic value.

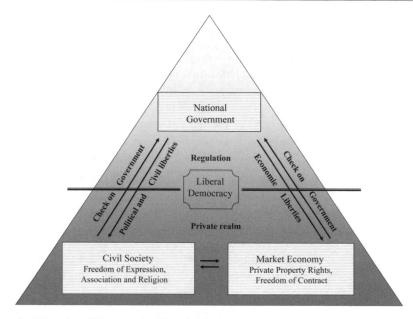

Figure 3. Triangle of liberty – the liberal democracy

The constitution defines the relation between State and it subjects by setting limits to the way in which government can interfere in the private lives of its citizens. This enables government to make decisions on behalf of the public and constitutionally guarantees the parameters within which civil society and the market economy can develop and flourish. A market economy is characterized by the free negotiation between buyers and sellers constitutionally guaranteed by private property rights and its corollary freedom of contract. Free negotiations ensure an effective alloca-tion of resources because supply and demand determine prices that form an indica-tion of the product's scarcity as a result of individual action. This scarcity in turn, can inform government to take decisions in the public interest, promote invest-ments, offering tax relief etc. The success of the (market) economy directly affects the treasury. This makes government and market actors dependent on one another. Market actors need government to ensure a stable economic environment (guaran-teed property rights and freedom of contract). Government on the other hand needs the income generated by taxing market actors in order to finance its activities. In one sense they reinforce one another, on the other hand, they also form a check on each other preventing the other to increase their powers too much.

Civil society also has an ambivalent relation with government. On the one hand, a flourishing 'marketplace of ideas' is a necessary prerequisite for informed demo-cratic decision making in the public interest.[85] It allows politicians to take the opin-

---

[85] Although he used the term 'free trade in ideas' instead of 'marketplace of ideas', the concept is generally attributed to Justice Holmes in his dissenting opinion in *Abrams* v. *U.S.*, 250 US 616 (1919). In his opinion Holmes stated that the theory of the Constitution is that 'the ultimate good desired is

ions of its citizens into account in a rather direct manner and hence forms a tool for prudent decision making. On the other hand, it keeps government in check since it allows for a civil opposition to government policies. Civil society also forms a counterbalance to market players by informing the public and organizing pressure groups that influence the behavior of market players. In addition to the pricing mechanisms, civil society can serve as additional tool for corporations to allocate their resources. In return, the private capital raised by entrepreneurs enables individuals to become relatively independent from government, reinforces independent deliberation and enables the private funding of civil society groups, think tanks, etc.

In more general terms, the freedom from government constraints established by guaranteed civil and economic liberties also forms an essential prerequisite for democracy. Without a sphere of economic independence, the notion of civil and political liberties would be meaningless since voters would simply be inclined to vote for the interests of their landowner, as the discussion of the French feudal system has illustrated. Without guaranteed civil liberties like freedom of speech and association, the development of novel ideas would significantly decrease, which in turn would prevent the development of new political ideas and hamper government to act upon the wishes of its subjects.

Civil society and a well-functioning market economy depend as much on the individual liberties outlined above, as they are needed for government to fulfill their constitutional obligations to foster these liberties. Individual liberties empower citizens in their role as independent judges of government, a prerequisite for genuine democratic decision making. Without the formal freedom (civil rights) and actual ability (through private property) to deliberate freely, there is no genuine choice to be made in terms of representation.

A prerequisite to a well-functioning democracy and a flourishing market economy and civil society is the existence of a relatively strong government. Government is needed in order to guarantee private property rights over a longer period in order to accomplish the necessary trust and stability to establish a flourishing market economy. The same holds for civil society since without a stable government today's freedom of speech and organization could easily become tomorrow's government's target for oppression. Democracy also requires a relatively strong government, able to organize reliable elections, generate transparency in decision making and maintain feedback and accountability mechanisms. Constitutions provide the democratic basis for a relatively strong government but more importantly, it provides government the powers necessary to live up to these commitments and responsibilities. By granting government the monopoly on the legitimate use of force it effectively grants government the power to provide security at two levels by protecting its citizens (1) from one another, preventing people from infringing the rights of others, for

---

better reached by free trade in ideas (…) that the best test of truth is the power of the thought to get itself accepted in the competition of the market, and that truth is the only ground upon which their wishes safely can be carried out'.

example by sentencing criminals to jail and keeping mentally deranged persons in mental hospitals. (2) The second level of protection is from foreign intrusion. Whereas this type of security has many aspects, its most obvious exponent is the fact that States maintain standing armies. The globalization process has important implications for the State's ability to provide its citizens with basic security, as the subsequent chapters will show.

2.5.2   The development of the welfare State

Section 2.3 showed the development of political organization and the constitutionalization of the State-subject relation. Also *within* the context of the constitution, the relation between State and its subjects is dynamic in nature. The rise of the welfare State in the 20th century has extended the way in which States carry out their constitutional responsibilities and commitments towards its citizens resulting in an increased government influence in the daily lives of its citizens and the economy.

The liberal democracies established by the early constitutions were designed to satisfy two needs. Politically they were to establish a limited government expressed in the emphasis on individual liberty. Economically they were designed to promote welfare[86] by laying down the foundations of a market economy. The characteristics of the constitutional democracy, democratic representation, a system of checks and balances and fundamental liberties, all form tools to establishing welfare and liberty. Within the US context this resulted in the Congressional authority to regulate commerce by the so called 'commerce clause'.[87] In addition to the free economic sphere constitutionally granted by the acknowledgement of private property rights,[88] the power to regulate commerce is an important constitutional feature since it includes the power to regulate interstate commerce and its channels and instrumentalities.[89] Currently the clause permits Congress to regulate intrastate economic activities provided they have a substantial effect on interstate commerce[90] The powers

---

[86] 'Welfare' here is to be interpreted as 'prosperity'.

[87] Constitution of the United States of America (1787), Art. 1, Section 8(3) states that Congress had the power to specify rules (1) to govern the manner by which people may exchange or trade goods from one state to another, (2) to remove obstructions to domestic trade erected by states, and (3) to both regulate and restrict the flow of goods to and from other nations (and the Indian tribes) for the purpose of promoting the domestic economy and foreign trade, for a more elaborate exposition of the commerce clause see, Barnett, R.W., 2001.

[88] Some relevant legislative clauses concern Amendment V US Constitution ensuring that no one will be deprived of property without due process of law and adequate compensation. Another task of governments are set out to do is to secure the enforcement of the duties resulting from freely made contractual agreements. A corollary to the constitutional commitment to a market economy captured by Art. I, Section 10 US Code, ensures that no state shall impair the obligations of freely made contracts.

[89] See, *Gibbons* v. *Ogden*, 22 US (9 Weath.) 1, 193-198 (1824).

[90] See, *United States* v. *Darby*, 312 US 100, 118-119 (1941); *Wickard* v. *Filburn Heart of Atlanta Motel* v. *United States*, 397 US 241, 257-258 (1964); *Katzenbach* v. *McClung*, 379 US 294, 298 (1964); *United State* v. *Lopez*, 14 US 594, 559-560 (1995).

granted to regulate commerce formed an important basis for a substantial increase of government interference in the economic affairs of the individual states and hence the economic freedoms of individual citizens.[91]

Throughout the Western world States have assumed additional responsibilities since the 18th century, reaching far beyond the 'minimal' or 'night watchman' State of the classic liberal era in the 19th century. The current French Constitution provides an interesting example of this shift in perspective. Its preamble refers to the utterly liberal French Declaration that considers the aim of all political association to be: 'the preservation of the natural and eternal rights of man, that is, to secure the following rights; liberty, property, security and equality.'[92]

The same preamble also refers to the provisions captured in the Constitution of the Fourth Republic established just after the war in 1946. This provision establishes France's commitment to social rights ensuring positive liberties, the most prominent of which are the rights to work and the right to enjoy state facilities in the areas of health care, education, leisure and culture. Again informed by history this preamble was established after the victory of the allied forces, which was effectively a victory for democracy over fascism. The preamble states as much when it reads: 'In the morrow of the victory achieved by the free peoples over the regimes that had sought to enslave and degrade humanity. (...) being especially necessary to our times.'

In the US, a similar transition occurred. The Declaration of Independence[93] held that the purpose of government was to grant its citizens at least the inalienable rights of life, liberty and the pursuit of happiness.[94] In the course of the 20th century the State has gradually assumed more powers, particularly due to a broader interpretation from the so called 'welfare clause'.[95] From welfare as 'prosperity', the State has evolved into a State that translates welfare as 'social responsibility'.[96] The consequences are significant. Within the US context, Roosevelt's New Deal can be seen to mark a turning point in the development of the US into a welfare State.[97] Reacting to the Great Depression of 1929, Roosevelt sought to reform the

---

[91] The barriers put on trade characteristic to the mercantilist era artificially distort the free exchange of goods and hence lower the welfare (in the sense of prosperity) of the people. At the end of the 18th century, however, the liberal economic theory of *laissez-faire* politics was only partially applied leading to tensions threatening the domestic tranquility within the confederation. In fact, the transition from a confederation to a federal State was partially motivated by individual states following the same mercantilist practices as their former rulers. As a result, a stronger federal State was created in order to lower the trade barriers between the states. This power became an important provision and incentive for government to expand its power and to gain a more significant role into the lives of its citizens.

[92] Declaration of the Rights of Men and of the Citizen (1789), Art. 2.

[93] Unanimous Declaration of the Thirteen United States of America (1776).

[94] Locke, J., 1689.

[95] Constitution of the United States of America (1787), Art. I, Section 8, empowers Congress to levy taxes and pay debts in order to provide for the country's general welfare.

[96] The US Supreme Court has broadly interpreted this clause to allow congress to create, for example the social security system, source: Black, H.C. and Garner, B.A., 1999, entry 'General Welfare Clause', p. 694. See also, Tribe, L.H., 2000. § 5-6, p. 833ff.

[97] Friedman, L.M., 2002, p. 176ff.

US economy, eventually resulting in more powers to the central federal government. One of its most important achievements was the Social Security Act of 1935 which made 'taking care of the poor' a federal responsibility, an act that was later expanded to include healthcare and is currently codified in the title 42 USC.[98] Many functions however are still held by the states and in practice and like most other States today, the US has a pluralistic system in that there is both private and public schooling, insurance and healthcare. In 1937, the Supreme Court abandoned the use of the freedom of contract provisions (US Constitution, Amendment XIV) in order to protect the economic liberties of corporations and individuals. In addition, a broader interpretation of the 'commerce clause'[99] allowed congress to regulate virtually anything that potentially can travel across state lines.[100] This transition from a *laissez-faire* policy regarding economic affairs to an era allowing more regulation on behalf of the general welfare has made a considerable impact on the relation between the State and its citizens.[101] In the words of the Nobel Prize winner and economist Hayek, 'all modern States have made provision for the indigent, unfortunate, and disabled and have concerned themselves with questions of health and the dissemination of knowledge.'[102] Consequently, States have expanded their grip on the daily lives of their subjects considerably in the course of the 20th century.

This influence and protection is not without cost. More government interference has lead to an increase in taxation and hence a loss in the freedom to allocate one's private property. In addition, the market has become increasingly regulated as the rise of consumer safety and antitrust regulation show. The rise of the welfare State has considerable effects on the fundamental liberties as they were conceived in the early liberal democracies.[103] The effect of the rise of the welfare State is a declining private realm free from government interference, a development that is common to all Western States. Figure 4, illustrates the essential difference between the liberal democracy and the welfare State by showing that the level of government influence (regulation) has increased significantly at the cost of the individual freedoms in the private realm.

In Figure 4, the horizontal line marking the distinction between public and private realm is (light) grey in color while the situation characterizing the situation in the welfare State is depicted in black. The arrows pointing downwards on both sides of the triangle show the direction of the transition. Economically the most significant effects of the increase in State control concern the intrusions with re-

---

[98] United States Code, Title 42.

[99] Constitution of the United States of America (1787), Art. I(8), reads, 'Congress shall have the power (…) to regulate Commerce with foreign Nations and among the several states, and with the Indian Tribes (...)'.

[100] Chemerinsky, E., 2002, p. 256.

[101] Ibid., p. 584ff.

[102] Hayek, F., 1960, p. 257.

[103] See Figure 3 'Triangle of liberty – the liberal democracy', p. 40 *supra*.

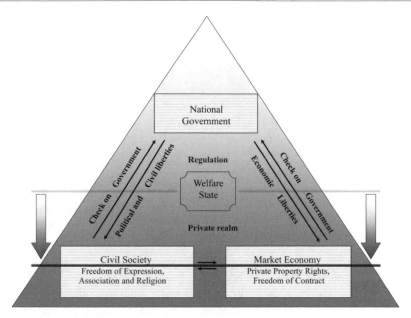

Figure 4. Triangle of liberty – the welfare State

spect to private property and the interference in the freedom for individuals to determine their contracts voluntarily. Whereas of course the increased taxation on
income is one of the most striking developments that distinguish the welfare State
from the early liberal democracies, the interference in markets is the most important aspect of transition. Particularly the rise of antitrust legislation marks a transition from a constitutional obligation of government to protect its subjects against
itself to a governmental responsibility for the State to protect the citizen to any form
of monopoly power. In the 'civil' realm perhaps the most significant development
is the relatively recent effect on the right to privacy, a corollary to freedom of expression. The availability of monitoring techniques combined with the developments after 9/11 shows a tendency to infringe this right considerably.[104] This increase
in State power also has its effect on the way in which States try to regulate, or
influence events and actors in a world characterized by transnational interdependence between actors and activity, as we shall see in subsequent chapters. Whereas
in the old Westphalian world of sovereign independent States, one could achieve
the result simply by enforcing national regulation, in a globalizing world, this in-

---

[104] *Meyer* v. *Nebraska*, 262 US 390 (1923) interpreted the 'liberty' interest of the Due Process
clause of the 14th amendment as guaranteeing, among other things, a right to the pursuit of happiness,
and, consequently, a right to privacy. USA Patriot Act (2001), Section 215, allows federal investigators
to access library and bookstore records. It allows FBI agents to (secretly) obtain a warrant from the US
Foreign Intelligence Surveillance Court for library or bookstore records of anyone connected to an
investigation of international terrorism or spying, a provision that has become know as the 'library
provision'. The provision needs a 'reasonable cause' as opposed to a 'probably cause' which was
commonly used within the context of criminal law.

strument is likely to become less effective. Consequently, alternative routes need to be explored, as the following chapters shall show.

2.6   CONCLUSION

This chapter set out to describe the State as a historically determined dynamic entity responsive to the needs of the day by showing how two specific developments have shaped today's modern State. The first essential development was the codification of the State-subject relation in constitutions designed to limit the powers of government and establish a market economy. This turning point in State history culminated in the 'mother of constitutions' as the US Constitution can rightly be called. The second development to shape today's State was the transformation of the modern State into a Welfare State, accompanied by a partial infringement of the rights that were designed to protect against government interference. A conceptual triangle was developed as a heuristic device to illustrate the changing relation between the State and its subjects over time. It showed that the modern State has taken up additional tasks either in order to protect the citizen (from the State, each other and foreign intrusion) or to increase (social and economic) welfare. The result is a significant body of law varying from consumer rights, the setting of minimum wages and antitrust laws, to healthcare and social security programs.

A second objective of this chapter was to create a framework in order to determine the nature of the modern State. This question has been answered by defining the modern State as a Western liberal democracy operating under a specifically designed constitutional umbrella. The characteristics of the modern State were identified accordingly as the following governmental commitments and responsibilities: (1) democratic participation in public decision making (2) a constitutionally guaranteed system of checks and balances (3) substantial provisions guaranteeing inalienable civil rights establishing a realm free from government interference, and economic freedoms in the form of private property rights.

A prerequisite to maintain these commitments and responsibilities is a relatively strong government. Constitutions provide government with the necessary powers to (1) provide security and protect individuals (a) from internal threats, that is, from violations of rights by other citizens and (b) from external threats, that is foreign intrusion. In addition to security, two further objectives can be distinguished from a constitutional point of view, (2) the provision of welfare and (3) securing individual liberties.[105] The second objective is welfare, which was initially interpreted as 'pros-

---

[105] The equality objectives mentioned in the French Declaration (and also informing the Declaration of independence) can be subsumed under the two objectives since gross inequalities between citizens endanger the stability of the State (as the French and American experience illustrated) and hence threaten the liberty and welfare objective. In addition, equality in the sense of 'equality before the law', and equality in democratic participation are guiding principles of a well-functioning democracy and indeed a constitution prerequisite to limit the powers of government.

perity' within a constitutional context, but became in the 20th century increasingly associated with additional tasks requiring more government action, particularly at the costs of individual economic liberties (private property and freedom of contract). In addition to the US and French constitutions all larger States on the European continent have gone through this transition. They all have adopted 'general welfare' provisions, which have been interpreted extensively over the course of the 20th century and many have even taken this development one step further by allowing social rights a central place in their constitutions. The shift from the early liberal democracy into the Welfare State has had significant consequences on the State-subject relation. Perhaps the most striking consequence of which is that the Welfare State gradually impeded the traditionally strong individual liberties, particularly in the economic realm (private property and freedom of contract). In order to investigate how globalization affects constitutional commitments and responsibilities, the next chapter identifies the essence of the process in the growing transnational interdependence between actors. In addition, it shows that the Internet as a transnational medium forms an ideal testing ground for studying the effects of interdependence on constitutional governance in an interdependent context.

Chapter 3
GLOBALIZATION, INTERDEPENDENCE AND THE INTERNET

Globalization brings with it increasing levels of transnational interdependence between actors in social, economic and political terms. This chapter introduces the Internet as a global communication, transaction and transportation infrastructure. It shows that its very architectural characteristics create a type of transnational interdependence that is similar in key respects to the type of transnational interdependence that characterizes the globalization process. Since the Internet takes the notion of transnational interdependence to its extreme, it provides the ideal laboratory conditions for examining the effects of globalization. In particular, the Internet provides the means for (1) clarifying the challenges posed by the globalization process and (2) investigating its effects on democratic constitutional governance.

The first part of this chapter explains the phenomenon of globalization and uses the conceptual triangle developed in the previous chapter to illustrate the fundamental changes this poses for the State in the light of three sources of influence: government, the market and civil society. After identifying the essential character of the globalization process, the Internet is introduced as a communication architecture by means of three principles, (1) its packet switching transmission technique, (2) the end-to-end design principle, and (3) its layered design model. The latter part of this chapter uses a model developed by David Held[106] to justify using the Internet as instrument for examining the effects of globalization on democratic constitutional governance.

3.1   THE INTERDEPENDENT STATE

The challenge for today's State is globalization defined as a process increasing the level of interdependence between cross-border actors and activity. The concept of globalization of course denotes more than just a stretching of social relations and activities across regions and frontiers. It suggests a growing magnitude or intensity of global interaction.[107] Consequently, States and societies become increasingly enmeshed in worldwide systems and networks of social interaction, or, as David Held put it,

---

[106] David Held is the Graham Wallas Professor of Political Science at the London School of Economics.

[107] Held, D., 2000, p. 4.

R.W. Rijgersberg, The State of Interdependence
© *2010, T·M·C· Asser Press, The Hague, and the author*

'Globalization is a process that embodies a transformation in the spatial organization of social relations and transactions, generating transcontinental or interregional flows and network of activity, interaction and power.'[108]

The most significant effect of this increase in spatial reach is the transnational nature of the social relations and organization. The territorial nature or our traditional political organization based on States combined with the lack of a truly global and effective world government, poses challenges for the State in order to deal with this transnational reorganization of social life. In writing on the connection between rights and globalization for example, David Law describes it as follows:

'Across the political spectrum it [globalization] evokes a sense that largely uncoordinated action by faceless actors is changing political, social and economic life in ways that we have yet to realize, and that we cannot truly prevent. [Globalization] is a word coined to describe a future that we have created yet cannot fully control.'[109]

Law's description emphasizes globalization as an inevitable process that has already been set in motion. As a reaction to this process, States are in the process of change in order to find a new equilibrium that will enable them to address the problems associated with globalization. This reorganization of social life on a transnational scale[110] has important consequences, as this inquiry will show.

The conceptual triangle introduced in the previous chapter distinguishes three central forces within society: civil society, the market and government.[111] Whereas Chapter 2 showed the transition of the modern State from a liberal democracy to a welfare State, the globalization process shows another transition to the way in which those three forces relate to one another. Figure 5 below, depicts the situation in what has been labeled the 'Interdependent State'. In order to do this adequately, the presentation of the model has been slightly amended. Where in the previous models (Figures 3 and 4), the governmental force of influence within the State was depicted at the top of the triangle with the private realm containing the market and civil society forces at the bottom end, in Figure 5 these forces in the triangle are depicted upside down. The reason for this amendment is that the role of the State seems to have changed. Like the models before, the three forces maintain the same principal relation. The governmental force is also still the most dominant one in the interdependent State. The major difference with the previous model is that the State is not depicted as an isolated unit anymore but is increasingly open to foreign influences as the dotted lines marking the boundaries of the State indicate.

---

[108] Held, D. and McGrew, A.G., 2000, p. 3.
[109] Law, D.S., 2008.
[110] Keohane, R.W., 2002.
[111] See specifically Figure 3 'Triangle of liberty – the liberal democracy', p. 40 *supra*, and Figure 4 'Triangle of liberty – the welfare State', p. 45 *supra*. The two figures depict the transition of the constitutional State from a classic liberal democracy into a welfare State in which the classic liberties have increasingly become pressurized.

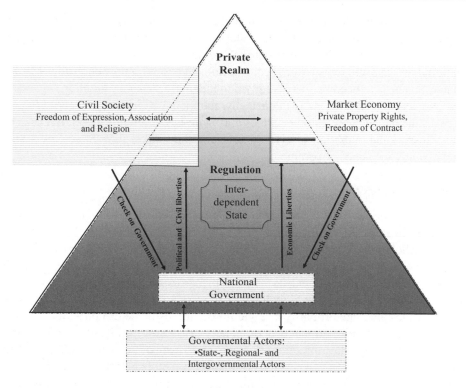

Figure 5. Triangle of liberty – the interdependent State

In Figure 5, the State is depicted as a permeable State in which the accent of government is foundational rather than (top-down) comprehensive in nature, the visualization of which is achieved by putting government at the bottom of the triangle.[112] As the figure indicates, markets have increasingly become regional or global in nature. Similarly, civil society has undergone an organizational globalization. The State itself has also become increasingly dependent on other transnational actors since foreign events and decisions increasingly affect national policies. Vice versa, national decisions increasingly have transnational effects. Hence, the next phase in Statehood is a transnationally interdependent State that is increasingly subject to external influences. Whereas the national influence of government is declining, the potential transnational influence of average individual States can said to be on the increase since national decisions increasingly have transnational effects.

---

[112] As the two other representations outlined in Chapter 2, Figure 5 does not claim to sketch the full picture of the impact of the globalization process on the State in relation to other States, transnational markets and civil society. It merely serves as a heuristic device in order to clarify the conceptual shift of major changes in society.

Figure 5 shows the interdependent State as a novel constellation of political organization and influence. The interdependent State is a permeable State, subject to outside influences. (1) Economically, States are increasingly dependent on non-national markets and transnational corporations in order to make decisions. (2) Socially, States have become increasingly dependent on stronger, globally organized civil society forces (NGOs). (3) Politically, the increased interdependence also increases the dependency on other States and State-based organizations. Because of the transnational operation of civil society and the market, non-State actors also increasingly influence governments.

Three approaches to globalization

The State under transnational interdependence is increasingly influenced by a variety of political, social and economic actors operating transnationally. Many globalization scholars have emphasized the effects of this process. They can roughly be categorized as hyperglobalists, skeptics or transformationalists.[113] The first approach is advanced by the hyperglobalists. Their explanatory model is primarily economic in nature. They consider the globalization process a result of economic processes and consider the State primarily as a victim of circumstance. Empirically they see the emergence of transnational economic networks that increasingly dominate decision making regarding production, trade and finance. Hyperglobalists tend to emphasize globalization as a new era dominated by a global market place and hence see the power and role of State eroding as an inevitable consequence of this process. Ideologically, they are inclined to evaluate the present developments in the light of a global market ideal. Hyperglobalists tend to promote a limited government coupled to a strong belief in the fruits of private initiative stimulated by widespread capitalism.

The second approach is advanced by the skeptics. Their explanatory model holds States to be the prime movers of the process. For example, they consider the (neo-liberal) political decisions to lift international restrictions on capital in the eighties and nineties the basis for the latest spur in what they merely call 'a heightened process of internationalization'. They deny the globalization process as a novel historical epoch and their empirical data show the formation of trading blocks as strongholds of national governments and the uneven distribution of economic development. This data seems to justify the thesis that several aspects of the process have actually enhanced the position of particular States rather than weakened the position of the State as such. Ideologically, they evaluate the current transitions in the light of the ideal of a global civilization. They are skeptics as to the benefits of the process and tend to focus on the rise in inequality between States and economies. Skeptics maintain that States still form the driving force behind processes of internationalization, and as such have certain responsibilities regarding the current trend.

---

[113] Held, D., 1999, p. 5ff.

Both strands present their view on globalization historically. Where the hyper-globalists envision a linear process towards global unity rooted in economic integration, the skeptics see periods of heightened internationalization because of national State policies. For both strands, their historical emphasis (economics v. the State) also determines their ideological outlook. The hyperglobalist emphasis on economic integration stresses the role of transnational markets in determining the social processes underlying the current transformation of society. The skeptics on the other hand, stressing the importance of State policies, are more conservative and hold that current transformations are primarily the result of State policies, a position that is in line with their realist outlook on international politics.[114] Hence, States have a role to play in order to bring about global justice.

For the purposes of this inquiry, however, the normative stance and the explanatory component regarding the origins of the globalization trend are not relevant. Here, it merely suffices to acknowledge that globalization increases the level of transnational interdependence between actors all over the world and that this trend is likely to continue. Both the hyperglobalists and the skeptics could accept this thesis although they differ on the causes and their valuation of the process. The third strand of thinking about globalization holds a less idealized view on the process, more in line with the major assumptions underlying this research.

The transformationalist's approach holds that globalization is the central driving force behind the rapid social, political and economic changes that are reshaping modern societies and the world order.[115] Thus rather than an explanatory model and a valuation they just emphasize a general change in social relations and point out that transformation of social relations is due to an increased transnational interdependence between actors and activity. For transformationalists, globalization is changing societies and individuals at all levels of their existence. Unlike the hyperglobalists and the skeptics, they do not have a particular conviction regarding the origin of the process nor do they have an ideological bias concerning a global market or a global civilization. They admit that the current transnational flows and interconnectedness are unprecedented in history and acknowledge both processes of integration and fragmentation. Whereas the hyperglobalists see a declining role for the State and the skeptics see the State primarily as a cause for globalization, transformationalists see the globalization process as a driving force of social transformation.[116] They hold that the new economic, political and social circumstances transform State powers and the context in which States operate. The strength in this approach is that it neither claims a particular historical root to the process, nor brings in ideology to evaluate the current state of play in the process.

---

[114] Realism in the context of international relations theory is a strand of political conviction that shares a belief that states are primarily motivated by the desire for military and economic power or security, rather than ideals or ethics and is often used interchangeably with power politics.

[115] See for example, Giddens, A., 1990; Castells, M., 1996.

[116] Held, D., 1999, pp. 7-9.

The transformationalist's approach is particularly interesting in the context of this inquiry because it allows for a more neutral empirical inquiry free from strong ideological preconceptions. It allows acknowledging a historical development of the process without having to jump to the hyperglobalist conclusion that the State is trading places with global institutional arrangements. Neither does it compel a commitment to the primacy of the State as the prime mover in guiding the process. Furthermore, it allows for a broader conception of globalization with a wider range of effects, some enhancing and some diminishing the role of States concerning particular aspects of social life. For example it would allow for a conclusion that civil society, as an autonomous force, is a driving force in transforming constitutional governance. The transformationalist approach allows for a more nuanced and broader view on the process as a whole. In addition, this approach also allows us to acknowledge that the world has never yet experienced the levels of interdependence and interconnectivity that it faces today, an assumption that seems realistic considering the level of cross-border flow of goods, services, people and information. In sum, the transformationalist approach towards the globalization process seems the most open and neutral starting point for this investigation.

This research differs in two important ways from vast amount of globalization literature. First, the object of this study is neither to establish empirical evidence for globalization nor to explain the causes that are responsible for this process. It simply assumes that there is a process of intensification of transnational interaction between actors, creating transnational interdependence on various levels of social interaction whether cultural, economic or political in nature. Secondly, contrary to much globalization research that focuses on the State as a political organization, the focus of this research is on the State as a constitutional (that is legal) entity. The effects of globalization have caught the attention of legal studies since the beginning of the nineties. Particularly within the confinements of international law, the emerging relevance of non-state actors within the international legal order has become a fruitful object of inquiry.[117] Another focus of attention for legal scholars, particularly within the international legal context, is emergence of self-regulation and its implications.[118] One of the novelties of this inquiry is to take the constitutional commitments of the modern State as a starting point in order to investigate the effects of globalization on the State-subject relation. With the nature of globalization defined as a process increasing the level of transnational interdependence between actors and activity, the transformationalist framework provides ample room to investigate this relation on the basis sketched above.

---

[117] A good example of this approach can be found in: Kreijen, G., ed., 2002.

[118] An example within the context of the Internet, including an extensive bibliography can be found in: Mifsud Bonnici, J.P., 2008.

3.2   THE INTERNET ARCHITECTURE

Similar to the State described in the previous chapter, the Internet is a dynamic entity that has developed in response to the challenges and demands from a variety of stakeholders and circumstances. From a small initial community of interlinked military and academic organizations it has advanced into today's global network with over 1.7 billion users.[119] Whereas its initial design was to work at one document from several physical locations, today it forms the basis for a significant share of the world's daily transnational activity whether political, economic or social in nature. Its tripartite role of being a global communication, transaction and transportation infrastructure has given rise to a variety of new technical applications and modalities of communications like e-mail, on-line video conferencing and real-time gaming. In this light, it is hard to deny the Internet's dynamic and fast changing nature. In contrast to the developing State, the Internet allows for considerably less interpretation as to its workings, role and purpose. The challenge in this chapter then is not in defining the Internet but in locating its significance in relation to the continuously developing and hence changing State in the light of globalization.

According to Tanenbaum, one of the worlds leading experts in the field and successful author of an authoritative introduction to networks, the term 'Internet' refers to a network of interconnected computer networks that use certain protocols and offer certain types of services like e-mail, the ability to transfer files and the ability to link websites.[120] The key to the universal interconnectivity between the computers and computer networks is the standardized Transmission Control Protocol over Internet Protocol stack (TCP/IP for short). This protocol is a layered architecture designed to exchange information between computers in which the TCP transport is used to deliver data across the IP network. A second characteristic is the packet-switching technique, a specific way in which information are cut up in packets and are sent over the web. In sum, the definition that shall be used throughout this work is the following:

'The Internet is a worldwide, publicly accessible network of interconnected computer networks that transmit data using packet switched transmission technique[121] and the standard Internet Protocol.'

A functionally defined five-layer model generally explains the Internet architecture. The technical expertise required for the purposes of this investigation how-

---

[119] Nielsen/Netratings, 2009. The usage of the Internet in these statistics is defined as anyone currently in capacity to use the Internet. That is: (1) the person must have available access to an Internet connection point, and (2) the person must have the basic knowledge required to use web technology.

[120] Tanenbaum, A.S., 2003, p. 50ff. Much of the explanation about the workings of the Internet is based on Tanenbaum's exposition.

[121] The packet switching transmission Technique (or packet switching for short) is discussed in Section 3.2.1.

ever, allows for a less thorough exposition. Within the context of this inquiry it suffices to distinguish two layers; one layer establishes the interconnection between hosts,[122] and the second layer establishes the communication between hosts. Before explaining this design model more extensively, however, more needs to be said about the two other key principles that enable us to gain insight into the revolutionary workings of the Internet in contrast to previous information and communications media; the packet switching transmission technique and the end-to-end design principle.

3.2.1   Packet switching transmission technique

In contrast to the traditional ways of information transmission like radio contact or telephone systems, the Internet uses packet switching instead of circuit switching. As opposed to circuit switching, the packet switching technique does not require a dedicated connection between two communication points (or nodes) that remains established during the time of the communication. Instead, as Figure 6, 'The Internet architecture', shows graphically, packet switching cuts up the information in tiny packets, labels them with the receiver's (unique IP) address in order to send the packets off independently. It does so over a variety of links or paths (designated by the black lines) and through a variety of servers or nodes, i.e., transmission points through which the information is routed to the intended receiver. The communication software available at the receiver's end of the connection enables to reassemble the packets in the right order and compile the intended message.

The packet switching transmission technique was crucial to the development of the Internet. The advantage of this technique is twofold is that it is far more robust than circuit switching techniques. Since the packets are sent off independently and can use different routes to arrive at their destiny, the effect of errors during the information transmission is minimized. Packet switching allows for re-routing particular pieces of information when a certain connection between different servers or nodes fails. In contrast, when the open connection used to establish information exchange using circuit switching fails, the information exchange simply stops. This advantage enhancing the reliability of communication was the reason for the Department of Defense to stimulate the Internet's development; the idea was to develop a communications structure that would be immune to precision bombardments. In addition, the packet switching technique is much harder to intercept as Figure 6 immediately reveals.

The packet switching technique is not without consequences for individual States. As much as an enemy is unlikely to own all the servers in order to intercept a complete message, this also creates difficulties for home countries to intercept Internet traffic. Even under complete control of the nodes, the packet switching

---

[122] A *host*, in computer science, is a computer containing data or programs (applications) that other computers can access by means of a network or modem.

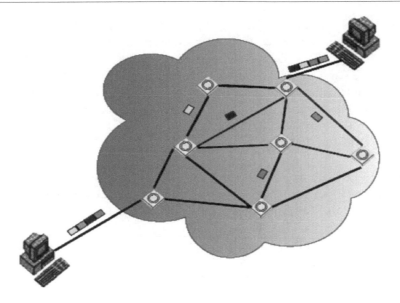

Figure 6. The Internet architecture

technique of cutting up information would significantly complicate the reconstruction of the message at an arbitrary point in the network. Hence, the interception of
information is most likely to occur at the ends of the network, close to the information receiver or sender. This hinders both intercepting and filtering information
considerably more than the old-fashioned opening of envelopes somewhere at the
trajectory from A to B. In addition, the network character of the Internet has increased the mobility of the users. The ability of users to access applications from a
variety of locations, also makes interception considerably more difficult than putting taps on phone lines. A more detailed way in which States have tried to address
this problem can be found in Chapter 5 'Interdependence and Technical Standardization' and Chapter 6 'Interdependence and Search Operator Censorship'.

If reliability is the first advantage of the packet switching technique, the second
advantage is that it is more efficient in terms of bandwidth. Whether the transmission medium is phone/cable, wireless or satellite connection, due to the fact that a
user does not have to reserve a line in order to communicate, the transmission line
is never occupied for a long time. Whereas circuit switching has the advantage that
indeed the communication does not suffer from congestion once the connection has
been set up, it may suffer from congestion before the line is set up. For example, if
someone is already engaged in a telephone conversation or the network is down
due to an overload of users for example in case of a regional panic attack caused by
terrorist activity or a natural disaster. A related advantage is that packet switching
minimizes the time it takes for data to pass across the network, since a host does not
have to wait for a line to be 'free' in order to be able to transmit the information.
The packets are simply sent independently over an available route.

To conclude, the packet switching technique has significant consequences for social relations on the Internet. It connects all users through a system of interconnected nodes forming a transnational infrastructure of connected computers and hence users. It particularly has significant consequences for the ability of States to fulfill their constitutional responsibilities since single States are no longer capable of controlling the exchange of information to the same extent as they used to.

3.2.2   End-to-end design principle

As Figure 6 illustrates, the actors sending and receiving information over the Internet are conceptually located at the edges of the network. These computers at the edges of the network also form the locus of the applications that enable specific user services like the World Wide Web or e-mail. Figure 6 shows a clear division between the end points of the network and the links and nodes within the 'cloud' at the centre of the network. The idea is that (1) the network (cloud) only provides the very basic service of interconnectivity between the computers at the edges, (2) that the more sophisticated applications of the system are conducted at the end-user computers, and (3) that this is the result of a deliberate design principle, the e2e design principle. Saltzer, Reed and Clark, who coined this term, called it a kind of 'Occam's razor' when it comes to choosing the functions to be provided in the network.[123] Phrased as a plea for the e2e approach they point out that since applications are often not known before the subsystem (read 'network') is specified, a designer might be tempted to put more in the subsystem than necessary. Due to limited imagination and idiosyncratic view on possible applications, this might result in a design that is less open to unforeseen needs and applications. In effect, combined with a designer's lack of omniscience it might lead to designs that actually prevent certain applications from being developed. The idea is to keep the prime functionality of the Internet simple.

The textbook story to the Internet attributes its success largely upon its e2e design base. It has allowed new applications to develop at its edges that were never envisioned in its early history. A few of its well-known success stories are the World Wide Web, e-mail and MSN. The possibility to transfer money on line safely and cheaply has enabled the development of the Internet as a global market place facilitating the success of on-line auction houses like ebay.com and on-line stores like Amazon.com. Also from a social network point of view the textbook version holds that the end-to-end design enabled the development of unforeseen applications, network sites like LinkedIn, and Face book, peer-to-peer networks and the development of on-line gaming portals are all said to be consequences of the Internet end-to-end structure.

---

[123] Saltzer, J.H., et al., 1984. They pointed out that most features in the lowest level of a communications system have costs for all higher-layer clients, even if those clients do not need the features, and are redundant if the clients have to re-implement the features on an end-to-end basis. The end-to-end principle is also found in: IETF RFC 1958.

Similar to the packet switching transmission technique, the e2e design of the Internet has had some consequences for the State-subject relation. The traditional telephone system was essentially an intelligent telecommunications network with 'dumb' devices (telephones) connected to it. The e2e design has reversed this. A 'dumb' network with 'intelligent' applications located at its edges encourages people to innovate and develop new applications and devices. Again, as with the circuit switching technique, it lowers the type of control that States can exercise on the developments in the market. In effect, the e2e design principle in combination with the packet switching transmission technique has encouraged individual initiative and liberated the citizen to an extent. Whereas the adequacy of the e2e roots of the Internet network will be questioned later in this inquiry,[124] it is safe to say that the Internet's architectural design appears to prevent the development of central network control.

3.2.3   Layered design model

The Internet roughly works as follows. Big chunks of information are translated into protocols, subsequently (1) cut up in smaller pieces, (2) labeled with (a) the destination address, (b) addressee and (c) a way to reassemble the cut-up information by the receiving computer. Subsequently, the packets are (3) sent over the nodes of the Internet in bites of electrical, optical or radio signals. At base, the Internet consists of a wide variety of computer networks glued together by the TCP/IP protocol stack[125] that enables a fruitful interaction between hosts and computer networks. There are several ways of modeling the workings of the Internet. Technicians generally use a layered model, the principles of which are simple. Each of the layers consists of a type of functionality, and each layer relieves the adjacent layer of certain technical details. Most textbooks explain the workings of the Internet using a model of five different layers of functionality (application, transport, network, data and physical).[126] The following sections describe a two-layered model sufficient for the purposes of this inquiry. The model divides the Internet functionally into a communication layer and an interconnection layer.[127]

The communication layer establishes the mutual communication between applications. At this layer, the wrapping of information into chunks is performed so that they can be sent over the web as packets. It also facilitates unpacking the chunks of information into the desired format, suitable for the particular application and un-

---

[124] See Chapter 7 'Interdependence and Network Neutrality'.

[125] A protocol stack is a particular software implementation of a computer networking protocol definition.

[126] Tanenbaum, A.S., 2003.

[127] These categories naturally follow from the Internet architecture since within the Internet architecture connecting computers, that is enabling computers to exchange date, is functionally distinct from the use of the Internet as conducted on the communication level. They also form the basis for structuring the case studies used in this inquiry, see also Figures 1 and 2, 'Case study framework and overview', pp. 9 and 12 *supra*.

derstandable to the user. Within the context of this layer, application-specific protocols define the way in which the information is handled by means of computer programs. In addition, they transfer the data in a uniform manner to the adjacent connection layer, which enables the transportation of the packets and establishes the connections between hosts. The communication layer ensures that a message sent by say, Pegasus mail can be easily read in another e-mail program, say Mozilla. The protocol responsible for this is the Enhanced Simple Mail Transfer Protocol (ESMTP). Other applications use other application specific protocols. The Post Office Protocol version 3 (POP3) for example, is the standard to retrieve e-mail from a remote server over a TCP/IP connection. The File Transfer Protocol (FTP) is used for transferring certain types of files over a TCP/IP connection. Other often-used applications on the Internet are web browsers. In order to enable these browsers to surf web pages, the Hypertext Transfer Protocol (HTTP) was developed, enabling the transfer of information on the World Wide Web displayed as a system of interlinked documents using hyperlinks to quickly move from one document to the next.[128] Hence, the communication layer in the model defines the way in which end users receive and disseminate information using particular Internet applications. This layer is also called the content layer[129] since at this level the exchange of information, understandable for the end user takes place. This distinguishes it from the role of the connection layer at which the content of the information in principle does not serve a role. In e2e terms, the interconnection layer relates to the outer ends of the network, the realm of the Internet users.

The role of the interconnection layer is to establish interconnectivity between hosts. It also enables the transmission of the packets of information over and in the network. Within the interconnection layer a physical and a non-physical component can be distinguished. The physical components are computers serving as routers (nodes) and communications channels (sometimes called pipes) forming the physical basis of the Internet. The physical basis for the Internet varies and can for example consist of fiberglass cables, copper wiring, but also satellite connections. The non-physical components consist of the protocols managing the reliability of the transfer, the addressing of the packets and the transmission of the packets between two nodes. The most important protocol that is used to get the information across the network is the Internet Protocol (IP), which provides the service of communicable unique global addressing amongst computers by using unique numbers that are assigned to computers, the so-called IP addresses. Chapter 4 'Interdepen-

---

[128] Notice the difference between the Internet and the World Wide Web (www). Whereas the Internet refers to the architecture of connectivity enabling one to perform tasks involving the transfer of information over a network of interlinked computers using the TCP/IP protocol stack, the www on the other hand, refers to the particular type of connecting information. It contains a protocol that is primarily concerned with the form of information exchange, it is a specific way of retrieve, display and connect information. The www is therefore a way of communicating. It uses the connectivity of the network in order to establish the connections.

[129] See for example, Benkler, Y., 2000.

dence and Domain Name System Management' discusses this IP addressing system in more detail since it is intimately connected with the DNS, one of the few Internet areas that require some form of central coordination. As opposed to the communication layer, the interconnection layer mainly arranges the simpler or more fundamental features of the Internet; its actual infrastructural component. The general textbook view is that the 'intelligent' components of the Internet are end-user protocols employed at the outer edges of the network.

3.3   TRANSNATIONAL INTERDEPENDENCE

The previous section defined the Internet as a worldwide, publicly accessible network of interconnected computer networks that transmit data by packet switching using the standard IP. It explained the workings of the Internet by means of the packet switching transport technique, the end-to-end design principle and the layered design model, consisting of an interconnection layer and an intercommunication layer. This section links the Internet with the globalization process through the concept of transnational interdependence. By applying a model for determining the level of globalization at a certain period in time, it shows that the Internet is extremely suited as lens for investigating the State-subject relation under conditions of transnational interdependence.

3.3.1   The Internet as a catalyst for globalization

The Internet's contribution to the increase in global communication can hardly be overrated. The way in which it connects over 1.7 billion users is a social revolution in itself. Indeed, where the telephone in principle established long-distance communication for the masses, it has never remotely established an actual level of transnational interconnectivity the Internet provides. The Internet has caused a reduction in communication costs in general but it has also made communicating fully location independent, i.e., exchanging information with a neighbor is as costly as exchanging information with someone at the other side of the world. In the light of other traditional media, the Internet is a revolution. Whereas the printing press, radio and television contributed significantly to the establishment of mass education and the exchange of ideas on an unprecedented scale, the fact that nearly every teenager in the Western world is personally able to broadcast his or her message to a world audience is an unsurpassed revolution in the development of communication. Thus, the decrease in communication costs has not only intensified the information exchange worldwide, it has also changed the nature of communication by allowing anyone connected to the Internet to exchange information on a one-to-many basis, a type of information exchange that has long been reserved for professionals only due to its capital intensive nature.

The increased interconnectivity combined with the possibilities offered by a one-to-many exchange of information and a decrease in communication costs, affects the relation of the State and its subjects. In principle, it is much harder to control information as aspect pointed out when discussing the packet switching technique above. Moreover, the sheer quantity of information exchanged also complicates State control over information flows considerably. The possibility of one-to-many type of communication by individual citizens has empowered the citizen with respect to the State since it is more difficult for States to control millions of individuals engaged in broadcasting than it is to control, say, hundred large broadcasting agencies.

The Internet also has important economic implications. It has given rise to completely new industries. It has created markets for services and devices that are necessary for the Internet to operate adequately, e.g., Internet Service Providers (ISPs), router services, domain names, and applications. It has also provided a market for the 'informatization' of society, that is, the transition or parallel development of traditionally non-Internet industries on the Internet, of which the digitization of public information, market research techniques and marketing devices are but a few examples. The most important economic aspect however is that the Internet has become the world's first truly global transaction platform. It facilitates location-independent contracting, payment and delivery. The invention of secure on-line banking and direct payment systems has contributed significantly towards this development which were, similar to e-mail and the World Wide Web, unforeseen spin-offs from the network as it was originally intended. Another success story is the development of on-line auction houses and web stores, of which ebay.com and amazon.com are arguably the most famous. Note that the role in delivery and transport is not limited to banking matters. All types of information can be transported over the web, whether they consist of text, music, video or software applications.

The Internet is more than simply an additional medium for information exchange. On the one hand, it serves an important social function by lowering communication costs. On the other hand, it has important economic implications. As a mere information medium, it supports transparency of markets regarding supply, quality of products, availability and pricing. As a global transaction medium, it has generated new markets and has become a global marketplace in itself. Both social and economic aspects of the Internet mirror important aspects of the globalization process, as we shall see in the next section. In addition, both aspects have important ramifications for the State in the light of its constitutional commitments in an interdependent context.

Globalization is not a new phenomenon. Already in medieval times, the union of city-states into trade leagues had created a form of interdependence between otherwise sovereign territories.[130] Whereas, for example, the Hanseatic League was mainly limited to the social and economic realm, it also had political implications. The colonialization period from the year 1500 onwards, also created an increase in

---

[130] The Hanseatic League is one of Europe's most famous trade leagues. For more information see: Braudel, F., 1979.

transnational economic, political and social mutual dependency between home countries and their colonies. From the beginning of the 20th century, people have increasingly become interdependent on actors and actions operating beyond the
confinements of their national territories as the emergence of international and regional organizations from the latter 19th century onwards shows. In other words,
many periods in history have seen an increase in transnational interdependence
between people in terms of economic, social and political activity. Particularly in
the 20th century, there has been a continuous increase in transnational interdependence, especially after WWII.

In sum, the Internet, as a relatively new global communication, transaction and
transport medium, is a pivotal catalyst in today's phase in the globalization process.
Since the Internet is simultaneously a communication, transaction and a transportation infrastructure, it stimulates the exchange of ideas and helps to integrate markets and increase transparency. In addition, the Internet enables the transportation
of information services and related artifacts to such a degree that it increases the
overall transnational interdependency between people and societies. First, as a novel,
cheap and more diversified information exchange platform the Internet stimulates
the transnational exchange of ideas location-independent since distance on the
Internet is cost-independent. Secondly, it stimulates the mutual interdependence of
people and societies by making markets more transparent. As opposed to a marketplace limited to advertisements in regional newspapers, the Internet immediately
displays information about markets and products globally. Consequently, the rules,
practices, customs, and prices are increasingly determined transnationally. In short,
the Internet has stimulated transnational interdependency between actors and activities and remains to do so in economic, social and political terms. As a catalyst
for globalization, the Internet is a pivotal element in the process.

3.3.2   The Internet as instrument for examination

The most interesting aspect of the Internet in the light of this inquiry, however, is its
architecture. The Internet's very design imposes a type of interdependency upon
Internet actors that surpasses the level of interdependency created at this stage in
the globalization process in both immediacy and comprehensiveness. In order to
understand the relation between globalization and the Internet on the one hand, and
its relevance to the State-subject relation, the model developed by Held (see Figure
7)[131] is particularly insightful.

Although originally developed in order to distinguish between different types of
globalization in various historical periods, the model gives us more insight into the
nature of globalization since it identifies criteria by which to identify the level of
globalization at a given point in time. Applying these criteria to the Internet conceived as an independent research object enables one to see that the Internet takes

---

[131] Held, D., 1999, 'Introduction', pp. 1-31.

Key Dimensions	Key Characteristics
Spatio-temporal Dimension	•*Extensity of Global Networks* •*Intensity of Global Networks* •*Velocity of Global Flows* •*Impact propensity of Global* *Interconnectedness*
Organisational Dimension	•*Infrastructure of Globalization* •*Institutionalization of Global Networks* *and the exercise of Power* •*Pattern of Global Stratification* •*Dominant modes of Global Interaction*

Figure 7. Forms of globalization – an analytic framework

the level of transnational interdependence to its logical extreme. Since both States and individuals have identical needs both off line and on line, and constitutions do not lose their value in an on-line environment, the Internet can serve as a testing ground for examining the effects of increased levels of transnational interdependence on constitutional governance as the following paragraphs will explain.

Held distinguishes two key dimensions of globalization, the spatiotemporal dimension on the one hand and the organizational dimension on the other. The spatiotemporal dimension is designed to measure the reach of interaction between networks, flows and relations at a particular period in time. The organizational dimension in the model refers to the degree of institutionalization of the global networks, flows and relations. Both dimensions of globalization interlink and reinforce one another. The larger the spatiotemporal reach, the easier it is to adequately organize these networks, flows and relations. Reciprocally, the better one's organization, the further the spatiotemporal dimension can be developed. As such, they form two sides of the same coin.

The spatiotemporal dimension

The spatiotemporal dimension concerns the level of links and expansion of human activity. Held distinguishes four elements that are crucial to the spatio-temporal dimensions of globalization: extensity, intensity and velocity and impact propensity. The extensity criterion involves the degree in which the social, political and economic activities stretch across political frontiers, regions and continents. It concerns the reach of the activities employed and their effects. The intensity concerns the magnitude of interconnectedness and flows of trade, finance, culture and cetera.

It reflects the interconnectivity and interdependency established between actors and activity between and within networks. The velocity in turn, expresses the speed in which the global flow, i.e., interaction and processes increase as the world-wide systems of transport and communication speed up the diffusion of ideas, goods, information and capital spread throughout the world. The impact propensity is the degree in which the global and the local enmesh. In other words, how non-local actors and actions affect local actors and actions and vice versa.

Concerning the spatiotemporal dimension of the model, both the Internet's reach (extensity) and interconnectivity (intensity) are put to their logical extremes. Since the number of linked computers defines the extensity of the Internet, and the interconnectivity of those computers effectively defines the Internet, the extensity and intensity of the spatiotemporal is total. In addition, due to the Internet's nature as an electronic information platform and marketplace, particularly regarding information transfers, banking activities and the sale of applications, the velocity of exchange is in principle, immediate, only matched by the cash and carry exchanges conducted at local markets in the non-Internet world. Regarding the impact propensity, the information that is or is not made available at one part of the network, immediately affects all other users on the network. Similarly, censorship activities, the offering of products, implementations of new protocols or the compulsory use of electronic signatures somewhere on the web all have these effects.

The organizational dimension

The second dimension in Held's model is the organizational dimension. This dimension is also divided into four key elements (1) the infrastructure forms a precondition for globalization since it forms the precondition for interconnectivity needed in order for flows (whether this concerns information, people, goods or services) to establish.[132] (2) Institutionalization concerns the frameworks used by the governing powers to control and regulate the networks. Institutions facilitate exchange, they provide stability and trust for expansion. (3) Stratification is the means through which one may identify the organizational changes operated throughout the networks after being included in a global system. (4) The modes of interaction, in turn, deal with the way in which different networks interact.

Also concerning the organizational dimension of the model, the Internet takes the globalization indicators in terms of connectivity and interdependency to its logical extreme. Designed in order to find limitations in the adequate functioning of the (interconnected) networks, the four key organizational characteristics defined in

---

[132] In Held's framework, the infrastructural element can refer to anything that facilitates or hampers the spatio-temporal dimension of globalization. The absence of saleable sea routes for example may hinder the exchange of flows (goods, information or people) between physical locations. In addition, legal barriers might hamper the exchange of flows. Held even considers symbolic qualities to have infrastructural qualities, like mathematics as a common language for science or, as is the case with the Internet, the common availability of protocols enabling the interconnection between computer hosts.

Held's model are practically non-existent as limiting factors on the Internet. In principle, they simply do not pose constraints to the Internet's reliability and stability for information and transactions going from a to b over the network. This holds for the level of the infrastructure as well as for the level of institutionalization, stratification and modes of Interaction. Since the Internet was developed to evade the vulnerability of previously existent networks, all four possible obstructions to the level of interdependence outlined in Held's model are minimized in the network. Considered as a network in itself the Internet constitutes a realm that is both immediate in terms of interconnection and potential transaction and transportation velocity. It is comprehensive in that its structure is its reach.

3.4   CONCLUSION

The process of globalization defined as a process of increasing transnational interdependence of actors and activities, affects all aspects of our daily lives. It affects the State in that the transnational transformation of both civil society and the market economy create powerful transnational influences on the State that serve as additional checks on government. It also affects the sovereign power of States in that foreign actors increasingly affect both the domestic political agenda and foreign affairs policies. It affects the State in its ability to adequately promote its constitutional values, commitments and responsibilities. Consequently, globalization is likely to have significant impact on modern governance in the public interest.

The Internet relates in two important ways to the globalization process. As a pivotal catalyst, the Internet accelerates and reinforces the globalization process. The availability of a cheap and user-friendly global communication and transaction medium stimulates transnational interaction and hence increases transnational interdependence between actors and actions. More importantly, however, as a prototype to the globalization process in terms of interdependence, the Internet serves an instrumental role in studying the challenges and effects posed by the process, particularly to the changing role of the State. Transnational interdependency concerns the level of cross-border reciprocal dependence characteristic of the globalization process and affects the whole range of social-, economic and political relationships. The Internet, as a global communication-, transaction and transportation infrastructure, has predictive value concerning the State-subject relation because its very architecture imposes a level of transnational interdependence upon Internet actors that is yet unmatched in the non-Internet world. In terms of both immediacy and comprehensiveness, the Internet takes the notion of transnational interdependence to its logical extreme. Without assuming that the level of overall globalization will ever reach this level of enmeshment, the Internet does enable the identification of trends since it forms a magnifying glass, or lens, through which to view the subtle changes in the State-subject relation that gradually emerge as a consequence of the globalization process. As such, it forms a promising research object in studying the globalization phenomenon. The Internet serves as a precursor to the developing State-subject relation due to globalization.

The following chapters consist of four case studies based on the model developed in Chapter 1. They cover the following aspects of State influence: global governance (Chapter 4 'Interdependence and Domain Name System Management'), global standard setting (Chapter 5 'Interdependence and Technical Standardization'), the promotion of fundamental values (Chapter 6 'Interdependence and Search Operator Censorship'), and the development of national policies (Chapter 7 'Interdependence and Network Neutrality').

Chapter 4
INTERDEPENDENCE AND DOMAIN NAME SYSTEM MANAGEMENT

The Internet blurs the paradigmatic divide between State and market coordination. Its decentralized architecture does not appear to allow for central planning in the public interest as typically conducted by States and State-based organizations. Yet, the Internet Corporation for Assigned Names and Numbers (ICANN) sets public policies in managing the Internet's Domain Name System (DNS) without the traditional limitations on power characteristic of modern States. Its central coordination of the global DNS does not appear to fit a market model either since its alleged DNS monopoly seems to have deprived the Internet user from the free choice that characterizes market coordination.

This chapter sets out to identify the effects of globalization on the execution of constitutional responsibilities and shows that private governance in the public interest can be a viable alternative for State-based institutions. This inquiry into the DNS shows that the inextricable bond between the State and its subjects created through the State's monopoly on central coordination in the public interest has lost its self-evident status. In addition, it shows that, contrary to the prevalent scholarly view on the matter, ICANN is primarily kept in check by market mechanisms and has developed a governance model well suited to fit the economic reality underlying its operations.

4.1 INTRODUCTION

The key to global interconnectivity on the Internet is the Internet's unique IP addressing system. In order to facilitate navigation on the Internet, a DNS was developed as application to the Internet, allowing the use of unique strings of letters (domain names) instead of unique numerical IP addresses to navigate the Internet. Names help Internet users to remember people, products and services. They also allow users to find the required host simply by guessing the name of the company site or e-mail address. Due to the intensity with which the DNS is used by both end users and applications, the DNS is to the Internet's communication level what the IP is for the Internet's interconnection level; an indispensable device for reliable, effective and smooth exchange of information over the Internet.

R.W. Rijgersberg, The State of Interdependence
© *2010, T·M·C·ASSER PRESS, The Hague, and the author*

The DNS is relevant to the overall topic of this inquiry for the following reasons. First, it is the most successful and widely used Internet application to date. Whereas it is strictly speaking not a necessary requirement for a network to perform its essential function, establishing interconnectivity, both end users and applications such as e-mail and the World Wide Web, rely to a great extent on the DNS, either to find their hosts or to enable their services. As such, the DNS has contributed significantly to the Internet's worldwide success. Since names are easier to remember than numbers and since names allow for association with the relevant people, products and services, the DNS, still today, forms a critical tool in facilitating global interaction over the Internet.[133]

Secondly, the DNS is also relevant to this inquiry in terms of (transnational) interdependency. Since domain names require uniqueness in order to maintain a reliable exchange of information over the Internet, a name used at one end of the network cannot be used in another part of the network. By the same token, failure of a particular domain name to reliably represent its associated IP address at one end of the network directly affects the ability of a host at the other end of the network to access the information labeled by that particular name. As such, it directly relates to what chapter three identified as the most important feature of the globalization process and the Internet architecture: transnational interdependency between actors and activity.[134]

Thirdly, the DNS is relevant to States in promoting the interests of their citizens. Traditionally States have borne the responsibility for public infrastructures and associated operations like signposting (compare the road system) and addressing (compare the telephone system). Given these responsibilities, one would expect the State to play various roles in DNS management, for example in maintaining the infrastructure and in coupling domain names with IP addresses (uniform resolvability). Since DNS users have vested interests in names, also the allocation of domain names seems to imply State involvement in the public interest. The private nature of DNS management challenges the traditional role of the State concerning infrastructure related activities and property rights. As such, it has profound implications for the State in performing its constitutional role as a promoter of its citizen's interests providing security, welfare and individual rights.

It particularly sets out to shed some light on the effect of globalization on constitutional governance. This chapter aims to identify ICANN's DNS responsibilities and the way in which ICANN's power is limited in the light of its public responsibilities. In addition, it aims to establish the extent in which this example of private global governance affects the State in its classic role as a promoter of its subjects' interests.

---

[133] NRC, 2005, p. 26ff.

[134] Confined to the economic realm this phenomenon is called '(transnational) spillover effect', which are externalities of (economic) activity on foreign actors who are not directly involved in the specific activity.

4.2   The Domain Name System

In order to appreciate the ICANN's role as a DNS manager, this section first sets out to explain the workings of the DNS system in view of its technical characteristics. In addition, it explains that the US decision to privatize the DNS management was largely due to accommodate for the transnational interests of US corporations. The third part of this section points out some particular State interests related to the DNS in the light of its traditional responsibilities towards its subjects.

4.2.1   The technical characteristics of the DNS

Technically, the DNS is characterized by a decentralized or distributed database system that is hierarchically organized and centrally managed in order to guarantee uniqueness. The DNS uses the network architecture of the Internet to ensure uniqueness of the domain names. The key to the system is the division of names into several class names separated by dots. The name *bbc.co.uk* for example consists of three different classes or levels. The *.uk* part of the name for example, denotes the Top Level Domain (TLD) 'uk', the two letter abbreviation 'co' used to establish *.co.uk*, is a Second Level Domain (SLD) name designed to cluster the names and therefore domains of companies within the UK. This second level domain in turn can be divided into subsets of third level domains, again defining sub categories within that particular second level domain name.

Instead of distributing a single list to every computer on the network, the current DNS uses servers to store the information. Servers are computer devices that provide services to other computers, applications and end users. They run computer programs that respond to service requests by sending back responses. The advantage of using a service system is that not all computers connected to the Internet need to obtain a listing of all the possible names and associated numbers individually. Instead, a system of servers stores the information independently from the end-user computer. Because domain names are divided into different levels, the server system allows the information of each level to be stored at different servers. The servers containing name-number information of a particular top level domain and the servers containing the relevant information of the sub level domains are by means of this distributed database system operated on different locations, using different registry operators. The use of (different) servers to store the information to identify IP addresses considerably decreases the number of errors in the registries by spreading the risk. In addition, since domains are registered at different servers, the system allows for amendments in the IP-name relation at the lowest possible (decentralized) level of the DNS.

The division into de-centrally managed sub domains and servers forms an efficient and reliable way of translating the names into the particular IP addresses necessary to establish the connection between the hosts. Dividing the traffic over various servers prevents unnecessary congestion by reducing the traffic per server. The system also makes a more efficient use of names since identical strings of letters can denote different hosts under different higher-level domains. For example, the letters 'cia' denotes the US's Central Intelligence Agency registered as *.cia.gov* (IP address 198.81.129.100) and denotes Britain's Chemical Industries Association when registered as *cia.co.uk* (with the IP address 89.145.68.28). Using decentralized servers instead of lists proved a very successful way of using names for numbers on the global Internet. The system invented in 1983 still serves today's demands.

In addition to using a distributed database system, the DNS is also hierarchical in nature. This feature is particularly relevant to the system in order to maintain uniqueness of the names. As outlined above, class names represent different levels within the hierarchical naming structure. At the top of the naming hierarchy are the TLDs. Since each TLD is managed by a different server at a different location as outlined above, its hierarchical nature suggests the existence of yet another level within the structure necessary to ensure the uniqueness of TLDs. The ultimate key to the domain name universe is the root zone file. It consists of an index of TLDs (*.com, .org, .uk*, etc.) and a number of IP addresses of servers that are able to perform the next step in translating the composite domain name into final destination's IP address. The file itself is not part of the domain name servers system but is located on a 'hidden' server which itself is not accessible for resolving domain names. The 'hidden root' is copied by 13 root zone servers, which are part of the DNS and enable the distribution of the information enclosed in the root zone file. These root zone servers are called 'authoritative' since they receive their root zone information directly from the (hidden) root zone server. Since the root zone file is the master file from which the DNS gets its data, presence in the root determines which (top-level) domains are available on the Internet. The overall control of the root zone file and server therefore amounts to substantial economic and political power since 'control over names and numbers effectively means control over the mechanisms of visibility on the Net.'[135] Controlling the root can be said to equal controlling the Internet since additions and deletions to this file affect the top of the Internet's naming universe and affects (eventually) all underlying domains and servers. This poses considerable responsibilities for the DNS's governing body.

Domain name resolving

When a domain name is used in a specific application like an Internet browser or an e-mail program, it needs to be translated into a specific IP address. This process is called 'resolving'. The resolving process mimics the hierarchical decentralized naming system by resolving the domain names level by level as Figure 8 shows.

The resolving process starts by sending a query to the resolver. A resolver is a piece of software running on the host's computer that transfers the query to a name server and waits for an answer to return. Name servers are computers running name-serving software that is used to perform the actual resolving of the domain

---

[135] Weinberg, J., 2000, p. 189.

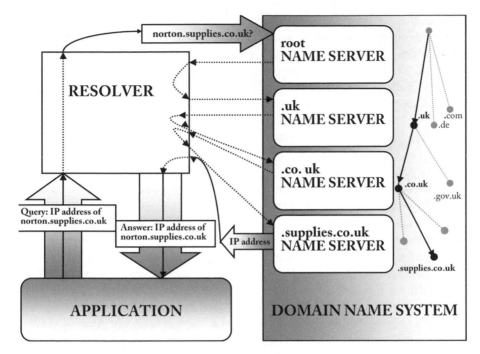

Figure 8. Domain name resolving

names.[136] The DNS and the way of resolving domain names can be conceptualized as an inverted tree of servers containing a series of tables, linked like the branches of an inverted tree springing from a single, common root (cf. right-hand side of Figure 8). A search for an address starts at the root or top of the tree, and works its way downwards through the successive branches, or lower tables, until the table that holds the desired address is found. When posing a question to a particular root zone server the server neither 'knows' where to find specific content, nor whether the content is available.

The server replies by sending the address of the server that is able to perform the next step. In our example, the name server puts the query to the DNS root. It is able to find the root name server since the IP addresses of the name servers for the root were manually entered into a (hint) file on the ISP server. The root name server replies to the query *norton.supplies.co.uk* by returning the IP address of the server managing the *.uk* TLD. This server contains a list of second level domains and the

---

[136] Note that the procedure outlined in figure 8 is extremely simplified. There are quite a number of variations to this procedure possible. For example, there are different types of revolvers, some with and some without built-in storage devices. In addition, the example also assumes that the query is conducted from a host located outside the sub-tree supplies.co.uk, and also that it is the first time such a query is conducted. Since the purpose of the example here is merely to demonstrate how the DNS works and to determine the role of the US (and States in general) within the DNS, this simplified version suffices for the purposes of this chapter.

corresponding IP addresses of the servers handling these second level domains. Hence, putting the same query to the *.uk* name server, the server replies by returning the IP address locating the *co.uk* name server, which in turn on being queried, returns the IP address of the *.supplies.co.uk* name server. This last server in turn replies with the IP address of the host maintaining a website on which to find the parts and supplies for your favorite motorcycle.

4.2.2   Globalization and the DNS

When the Advanced Research Projects Agency (ARPA) launched the world's first packet switched network in 1967, it did not use a naming system. It established its connections between hosts solely by using numerical addresses. When the network grew, a simplification was needed in order to facilitate the identification of the hosts on the network. Particularly since within ARPANET's architecture the numerical addresses of the hosts changed regularly, user-friendly names provided stability to the system. This proto-DNS operated by maintaining a HOSTS.TXT file listing all the names and (IP) numbers that was distributed and stored in each individual computer.[137] At base, this file was a large telephone directory that was sent to every host in the system in order to be able to contact host X at number *n*. When the Internet expanded, this system became increasingly difficult to handle, particularly since with every change to HOSTS.TXT, the whole document needed resending to every computer on the Net, which consequently led to an increased number of errors over time. In 1983, the current DNS, initiated by Jon Postel[138] and developed by Mockapetris[139] solved the problem by inventing the distributed database described above.

The Internet's success also created additional challenges. When in 1983 the Internet split into a civilian and a military part (MILNET), this also created a shift in responsibilities and costs. After the US National Science Foundation (NSF) had taken over the responsibility and funding for the civilian part from the US department of Defense, it contracted a private company called Network Solutions Incorporated (NSI) to take over the registration services for many of the TLDs. By the early nineties however, the Internet was growing nearly exponentially and private corporations became increasingly interested in the network to explore the commercial opportunities that the Internet offered. Particularly its transnational opportunities, worldwide communications, transactions and transportation of information, led to a call for an internationalization of DNS coordination, which was, up to this point, fully controlled by the US government.

Accordingly, an International Ad Hoc Committee (IAHC) was set up in order to investigate how to incorporate the interests of both business and the international

---

[137] NRC, 2005, p. 40ff.
[138] IETF RFC 819.
[139] IETF RFC 882; IETF RFC 883.

community into the development of the Internet. In 1997, they issued their findings in which they proposed a framework for a governance structure.[140] Emphasizing the public nature of the DNS, the IAHC proposed a public oversight committee consisting of two United Nations organizations, (1) the World Intellectual Property Organization (WIPO) and (2) the International Telecommunications Union (ITU), in addition to the International Trademark Association (INTA), one administrative and some technical organizations.[141] Whereas the proposal did involve non-State stakeholders, the UN, ITU and WIPO involvement clearly showed a bias towards an Intergovernmental public policy framework.

The Clinton administration however, displayed a profoundly different view on the development of the Internet and the DNS whilst acknowledging the need for internationalization. In a policy document issued in July 1997, it put the following five principles forward with a strong emphasis on private initiative to lead the way in the development of the Internet. More particularly the document expressed the specific objective to pre-empt commerce-inhibiting governmental actions regarding Internet commerce.[142] The principles expressed were the following: (1) The private sector should lead and (2) governments should avoid undue restrictions on electronic commerce. (3) If necessary, governmental involvement should be limited to support a simple minimalist legal environment for commerce. (4) Governments should recognize the unique qualities of the Internet (characterized by bottom-up decision making and its decentralized structure) and (5) electronic commerce over the Internet should be facilitated on a global basis (stressing the Internet's role as a global marketplace).[143]

This 'Global Framework for Electronic Commerce' explicitly recognized the profound implications of the Internet infrastructure for both civil society and the economy. It mentioned that the Internet empowers people and democratizes society by offering an additional, easy to use platform for the exchange of ideas. It also emphasized the Internet's profound effects on business models and trade[144] and that its success and development was primarily due to private initiative. The Clinton Administration considered State involvement to be prone to constrain the development of commerce. States were the source of taxes and duties, restrictions on information, control over standards development, licensing requirements and rate regulation of service providers, all inhibiting a free and unconstrained development of private conduct. In addition, States were generally considered slow decision makers. Consequently, the Internet's fast changing technological environment would

---

[140] IAHC, 1997.

[141] The technical organizations are, Internet Architecture Board (IAB), the Internet Assigned Numbers Authority (IANA), and the Internet Society (ISOC), which is concerned with the promotion of the development and availability of the Internet and its associated technologies and applications. The administrative organization involved was to be the Council of Registrars (CORE).

[142] See, A Framework for Global Electronic Commerce (1997), 'background'.

[143] Ibid., 'principles'.

[144] Ibid.

not be suitable for governmental control or supervision. This general attitude concerning the Internet, outlined in the Electronic Commerce framework, also informed the Clinton Administration regarding the management of the DNS.

Recognizing the transnational interests in the Internet, the Clinton administration issued a Green Paper in which the Department of Commerce's plan within the Global Framework for Electronic Commerce regarding the DNS was unfolded.[145] The idea was to increase competition, promote international participation and privatize the DNS. The tasks suitable for being performed though a competitive system (registration of domain names for example) should be transferred to the market. The tasks in need of coordination (DNS, root server system and protocol assignment) were to be transferred to a representative not-for-profit corporation. The Green Paper outlined a transition trajectory after which the influence of the US would gradually be withdrawn. After a period for public comments on the Green Paper, the US Department of Commerce issued its (White) paper on DNS policy.[146] In line with the proposals made in the Green Paper it was held that a new not-for-profit company was to be established that would oversee the management and assignment of domain names and IP addresses with the task to ensure stability, competition, private and bottom-up coordination, and fair representation of the Internet community.[147] Accordingly, the National Science Foundation transferred its administrative authority regarding the cooperative agreements concerning domain name registration services to the US Department of Commerce (USDoC), and a group led by Jon Postel proposed a set of bylaws and articles of incorporation of the 'to be established' ICANN. The signing of the Memorandum of Understanding (MoU) on the 25th of November 1998, between the USDoC and ICANN marked the beginning of a new era in DNS management,[148] initiating a process in which the US was to transfer its DNS responsibilities to ICANN.[149]

4.2.3   State responsibilities and the DNS

Since addressing systems require uniqueness, they benefit from central coordination in the public interest; a task that, in the non-Internet world is traditionally conducted by States and State-based organizations. The fact that the DNS is globally managed by ICANN, does not seem to relieve individual States from their responsibilities towards their subjects. The DNS in this respect poses additional responsibilities since unlike the names used in off-line addressing and signposting systems, domain names can meaningfully refer to content represented by the name in question. This latter feature has made them valuable property to their owners.

---

[145] NTIA, 1998a.
[146] NTIA, 1998b.
[147] Ibid.
[148] USDoC and ICANN, 1998b.
[149] After a period of US oversight, see, USDoC and ICANN, 1998b; 2003, the privatization of ICANN was finalized on September 30, 2009, see, ICANN, 2009b.

The following three examples of DNS related State responsibilities illustrate the particular interests of individual States in the DNS.

Security

Traditionally States are responsible for the development and maintenance of critical public infrastructures and associated operations (signposting and addressing).[150] The DNS poses a challenge for States from a national security point of view because it creates a dependency on a DNS manager for the national information provision and in securing a critical communication, transaction and transportation medium serving as an important role in the nation's economy. One striking example of State interests regarding national security is the State's interest in country code (cc)TLDs. The TLD universe is functionally organized and can roughly be grouped into two classes. Generic (g)TLDs consist of twenty, three or four-letter abbreviations and denote general categories. The *.org* TLD for example, stands for 'organization' and is reserved for non-commercial enterprises. The *.com* domain on the other hand stands for 'commerce' and hence is reserved for commercial enterprises. The TLD system also caters for a functional ordering on the basis of geography through a second class of names, the ccTLDs. They consist of two-letter codes that are functionally organized to represent geographical organization (*.uk* for example, stands for United Kingdom, *.de* for Germany and *.eu* for Europe).[151] Despite the fact that private corporations manage many ccTLDs and servers, the ccTLDs associate a particular State with a particular TLD. This in turn causes many entrepreneurs and individuals alike to buy domain names falling under specific ccTLDs, to indicate the territorial reach or geographic origin of their services. Individual States, however, cannot guarantee the maintenance of a particular ccTLD. The responsibility to determine and maintain particular ccTLDs is up to the root zone file manager. Whereas large parts of the national economies depend on these TLDs, the ICANN-ruled DNS appears to prevent States from securing their critical communication infrastructure independently.

Welfare

In addition to preserving national security, States also seem to have an interest as promoters of their citizen's interest to secure the uniform resolvability of the Internet. Domain names require uniqueness to maintain the reliability of the DNS. In case of discrepancies between names and numbers, a server could return two different addresses for the same domain name. Ensuring predictable results from any place on

---

[150] Moteff, J. and Parfomak, P., 2004.

[151] In addition to the ccTLDs, there are four geographically limited gTLDs: *.asia* is regionally limited and reserved for the Pan-Asia and Asia Pacific region. In addition, *.gov* can only be used by US government organizations, *.mil* is reserved for the US military and *.edu* is reserved for accredited US institutions for postsecondary education. These latter three gTLDs are the relics of the DNS's US roots. For a complete list, see, IANA, 2002.

the Internet (uniform resolvability) is the key to a well functioning DNS. Although all Internet users have a stake in the uniform resolvability of the Internet, States as central coordinators in the public interest seem the right candidate to ensure this uniqueness. Off line they manage signposting and addressing, but also, for example, serve as land registers etc, all in order to maintain and protect the economic order. States also have interests in uniform resolvability as consumers. With ICANN's private management of the global DNS, States seem to have given up this traditional role.

Intellectual property rights

Ever since the transition of a feudal system to a market economy, States have had an important role in the distribution and maintenance of property. When the US was first being occupied by immigrants for example, the administrations of the Colonies arranged the allocation of private property in the public interest.[152] Securing private property rights forms a traditional State responsibility in maintaining the economic and social order. In discussing the constitutionalization of the US and France, Chapter 2, identified the maintenance of property rights as one of the fundamental constitutional tasks of the modern State in order to guarantee a well-functioning market economy. Since domain names represent vested interests both on and off line, they have become very valuable to both its owners and users. ICANN's DNS seems to prevent States from performing their role as national securers of private property rights.

4.3   ICANN's Alleged Accountability Problem

The previous section established that States traditionally have interests in the DNS in terms of national security and maintaining the economic order. The US decision to internationalize the DNS by transferring the central coordination of the DNS to ICANN has not relieved States from these traditional responsibilities in the public interest. In fact, particularly the privatization of the DNS management has been the source of great concern to both States and scholars alike. The source of the problem is ICANN's control over the root zone file since this is one of the few points of central control on the decentralized Internet. The intense use of the DNS and the apparent inextricable link between the Internet infrastructure and the DNS application has led many to conclude that ruling the root equals ruling the Internet.[153]

On the one hand, ICANN's monopolistic coordination of the DNS appears to prevent users from exercising the free choice that characterizes the allocation of the

---

[152] The allocation of land to private parties in the public interest was primarily done though auctions or by allowing citizens to claim unsold surveyed land, see, Merrill, T.W. and Smith, H.E., 2007, p. 121ff. A more detailed exposition of the division of land in early America can be found in; Price, E.T., 1995.

[153] This is the central thesis in Mueller, M., 2002.

means of production by the market. The lack of alternative domain names forces the Internet users to depend on ICANN for the allocation and use of domain names. On the other hand, ICANN as a private enterprise does not have the safeguards in place against power abuse that characterize modern States in exercising their coordinative tasks in the public interest. One particularly pressing debate in the academic literature concerning the DNS touches upon perhaps the most fundamental problem that haunts ICANN ever since its inception, its accountability deficit. The following example illustrates why accountability is deemed so important in managing the DNS.

Suppose that, by accident or on purpose, the ccTLC of the Islamic Republic of Iran, .ir, is deleted from the root zone file. The authoritative root zone servers would automatically copy the new list from the root zone file without the IP addresses of the relevant referring (name) servers. Consequently, any query from a resolving program asking for the IP address of the server containing the list of servers able to resolve the addresses falling under the .ir domain, would return an error. Since DNS servers are frequently updated by obtaining their information from the authoritative servers, eventually, none of the TLD servers containing the address of the .ir TLD server would be able to direct the resolving software. Eventually, the TLD .ir and all its underlying addresses would be lost to the Internet community.[154]

If the example mentioned above may seem somewhat far-fetched, this is exactly what happened one level down from ICANN's responsibility, on the 2nd of October 2007. On this day the US government, responsible for the authoritative domain name server handling the .gov domain pulled the plug on California's .ca.gov domain.[155] This action was triggered at the third domain name level when the authoritative domain name server handling the domain of the Transportation Agency of Marin County, tam.ca.gov, was illegally modified by hackers and directed queries to porn sites rather than to the requested Transportation Agency's site. Since the ISP responsible for TAM's authoritative domain name server was unable to solve this problem, the responsibilities concerning this server were transferred to the state of California. This action made the state of California responsible for the authoritative domain name server operating at the level of tam.ca.gov in addition to its traditional responsibility at the ca.gov level. As a result, third parties, presuming the problems retrieving the tam.ca.gov host were due to a hacked domain name server, were likely to assume the problems also occurred at state level, i.e., at the domain name server handling the ca.gov domain. The Federal Government agency, responsible of the authoritative domain name server for the .gov domain in turn, decided

---

[154] This example is a simplification of reality. 'Caching', that is, storing the IP addresses in on the ISP server level or at the hosts computer, makes it possible to access content directly avoiding the use of authoritative name servers. The data in the caches however needs to be updated regularly in order to guarantee the validity of the information and avoid the expiration of the data in question. Eventually then, also caches will not suffice to preserve the information that is lost by the deletion in the root zone file.

[155] McMillan, R., 2007.

to remove the *.ca.gov* domain as a valid address on the *.gov* authoritative root zone file. As a result, several state Web sites were inaccessible and e-mails were reported not to get through. Fortunately, since it takes some time for DNS servers to update their information, the federal government's quick response prevented a major disaster. If the problem had not been resolved within 24 hours, Web access and e-mail to all state agencies using the *ca.gov* domain would have been cut off.[156] What this example shows is that the power over DNS is not mere theory. Ruling the root zone content effectively means deciding over life and death on the Internet.

Managing the DNS however, entails more than determining the size of the Internet. According to Klein and Mueller, ICANN sets public policies in a number of ways.[157]

> '... It makes competition policy by controlling business entry into the domain name registry market and by determining the market structure of the US$ 2 billion industry. It engages in rate regulation, setting the base price for the majority of the worlds wholesalers and retailers of generic domain names. It makes intellectual property policy by defining and enforcing global laws regarding rights in domain names. Indirectly ICANN affects freedom of expression because its trademark protection in domains makes set limits to public use of words, and its rules regarding registrant data are intended to make anonymous expression on the Internet impossible... Finally, ICANN's powers are open ended; the entities it regulates must commit to implementing any further policies the organization should promulgate. ICANN's regulatory and supervisory activities constitute global public policy of a type usually exercised only by governmental (or intergovernmental) entities.'[158]

Klein and Mueller seem to have a point. The power to set public policies is indeed generally a task that is delegated to (inter-)governmental agencies. Traditional communication infrastructures, including associated addressing and signposting tasks, are generally controlled by (inter-)governmental agencies that are ultimately backed by democratic representation, a system of checks and balances and guaranteed fundamental rights. ICANN lacks such mechanisms, as the following sections will show. First of all, despite its inclusion of interest groups into its formal decision making procedures, ICANN's board is not chosen democratically and certainly not by adequate representation of the affected community. Secondly, both the rules ICANN sets regarding the number and nature of the TLDs in the root zone file and the conditions under which registries can perform the administration of the TLD servers combine what in State terms would be called the legislative and executive task. The registries implementing these policies are picked by ICANN to conduct these tasks based on their ability and consent to ICANN-set conditions. In addition, ICANN's ombudsman, put in place to resolve complaints about staff or board deci-

---

[156] Ibid.

[157] One of ICANN's decisions regarding the domain name universe that gained a lot of attention was its decision not to issue the .xxx TLD, a TLD that was to function as an online red-light district; Mathiason, J., 2009, p. 93ff.

[158] Klein, H. and Mueller, M., 2005.

sions, actions or inactions, does not serve as a sufficient check upon ICANN's power either[159] since his judgment mainly concerns unfair treatment based upon rules that are not democratically justified. Whereas the ombudsman has the power to investigate policy decisions, and can make use of alternative dispute resolution (ADR) techniques to resolve problems, he does not have any power to make, change or set aside a policy, an administrative or Board decision, an act or omission.[160] In other words, there is no judicial check upon ICANN within its structure either. Also fundamental liberties (property, contract and speech for example) are not guaranteed by ICANN. Whereas it does not formally put restrictions on the names that can be used on the Internet (SLD names), the fact that it limits the Internets domain name universe by its refusal to admit additional TLDs can be explained as a limitation on speech.[161] ICANN's Uniform Dispute Resolution Policy (UDRP)[162] violates the 'first-come, first serve' principle that usually guides the appropriation of property rights. According to Klein and Mueller, since the UDRP promotes the vested interests of (real-world) trademark owners, it diminishes rather than strengthens the security of the established property rights held by non-trademark owners. In short, ICANN's organizational structure does not establish the traditional accountability mechanisms we associate with decision making in the public interest. Its structure simply does not seem to establish a sufficient limit on public decision making powers in the light of its pivotal public responsibilities that are at stake in managing the DNS.

4.3.1 Solutions to a problem

When ICANN was founded in 1998, its board consisted of nine technical experts, nine user representatives and a president, none of them elected by the Internet users.[163] The transfer of the DNS management responsibilities from the US government to the not-for-profit corporation ICANN soon raised questions regarding its policy setting power and led to a variety of proposals to overcome its democratic deficit.[164] Two exemplary solutions stand out: (1) the implementation of a global elections system in order to appoint ICANN's board of directors, and (2) a familiar solution, intergovernmental supervision. Both solutions need to be seen in the light of ICANN's well-documented legitimacy problem.[165]

In 2000, answering to intense lobbying pressures, the board decided to have five out of nine user representatives directly elected by the Internet community,[166] hereby

---

[159] ICANN, 2009c, Art. 4 concern the provisions for the Ombudsman.
[160] Ibid.
[161] Klein, H. and Mueller, M., 2005.
[162] ICANN, 1999b.
[163] See, Weinberg, J., 2000, note 130; Froomkin, M., 2000.
[164] There are a number of sources available that describe the emergence of the Internet and the history of ICANN in more detail than is relevant to this inquiry. A few useful sources are: Mueller, M., 2002; NRC, 2005; Mathiason, J., 2009.
[165] Weinberg, J., 2000.
[166] Hunter, D., 2003.

in effect creating a half-baked bottom-up approach in order to partly overcome the accountability deficit.[167] Despite its promising outlook, the project failed miserably. Of the estimated 375 million Internet users at the time, less than 0,001 percent actually voted.[168] Failure of the experiment led ICANN to abandon the idea of direct elections altogether in 2002.[169]

The second proposal that has been put forward, intergovernmental supervision, offers another route to overcoming the legitimacy problem. It tries to solve the problem top down, by gaining international as opposed to democratic legitimacy. Much in line with the initial proposition made by the IAHC, this solution would make ICANN accountable by the international community of States. The cluster of proposals presented by the UN working Group on Internet Governance (WGIG) for example, formed an initiative to this end.[170] This type of proposal is mainly rooted in the widespread concern regarding the alleged unilateral US power over the root zone, in combination with a strong belief that internationalization of Internet governance is a first step in overcoming the digital divide.[171] Despite pressures from countries like Brazil, Russia and China at the UN World Summit on the Information Society (WSIS) in 2005[172] where the internationalization of ICANN was at the top of the agenda, an agreement was reached to maintain the *status quo*.[173]

Democratic representation is designed to avoid governmental power abuse and legitimizes decisions taken in the public interest on behalf of the people. In ICANN's case, this principle underpinned the election experiment and formed the basis for the supervision proposals. Intergovernmental supervision influences decisions by holding the organization accountable to the international community, represented by State officials. In sum, both mechanisms are based on the same objectives: (1) constraint of the decision-making powers, (2) influence outcomes, and (3) legitimize public decision making though democratic representation. Representation through elections provides the 'bottom-up' means and intergovernmental supervision provides the 'top-down' means to achieve these goals. None of the attempts to overcome ICANN's accountability problem by the efforts to implement traditional democratic accountability succeeded. An investigation into the reasons why these efforts failed however is beyond the scope of this inquiry. The more interesting

---

[167] Klein, H., 2001.

[168] Palfrey, J.G., 2004.

[169] ICANN, 2009c.

[170] WSIS, 2005a.

[171] Note that the residual power of the US over the root zone file originates from the IANA contract: USDoC and ICANN (1998a). While NSI continues to operate the primary root servers, it shall request written direction from an authorized US government official before making (or rejecting) any modifications, additions or deletions to the root zone file: USDoC and NSI (1998), see also: Mueller, M., 2005a.

[172] See for the UN's comments; WSIS, 2003a.

[173] Also Europe has shown concern about the US' position ever since the nineties; at the WSIS 2005 meeting, Europe held an intermediate position pleading for an independent forum which would act as a platform for all stakeholders; Reding, V., 2005.

question from our perspective is whether democratic accountability is actually *required* in order to control, influence and legitimize ICANN's DNS decisions.

Ultimately, the reason why people require limitations on public decision-making powers is relative to their degree of dependency.[174] Democratic theory requires citizen participation exactly because citizens lack alternatives to the decisions made in the public interest. This is the reason why democratic accountability mechanisms and a limitation on government powers by a system of checks and balances and fundamental rights are built into our constitutions. In ICANN's case, however, this analogy breaks down on closer inspection.

4.3.2 Two misconceptions

The previously mentioned UN proposals and the more recent 'G12 proposal' put forward by EU Commissioner Reding,[175] have one thing in common. They essentially strive to put the DNS under intergovernmental supervision. The main reason is the general feeling in the international community that US has too much control over ICANN and the ICANN-managed root zone file. Not surprisingly since the US government still has the last say in the additions and deletions regarding the root zone file,[176] despite the official finalization of the transfer of DNS responsibilities to ICANN on September 30, 2009.[177]

Since the Internet is a transnational medium, affecting the global public interest, our democratically informed sense of justice tells us that uniform control by one nation is not fair. Indeed, since every user is affected, every user should be able to participate in DNS decision making. In the eyes of many players, the US seems to have a disproportional amount of power over the root zone file. The fact that 10 of the 13 authoritative root zone servers are located on American soil, three of which are even run by the US government, seems to strengthen the dominant position of the US.[178]

Appearances however are deceptive. The US power over the root zone file is rather overrated. As stated in Chapter 3, one of the characteristics of the Internet is that it empowers the Internet end users. First of all in its capacity to facilitate the exchange of ideas over a large base of users on a grand scale, allowing them to develop applications largely independent from powerful players on the network. Secondly, for the first time in media history, the devices by which the distribution of information is conducted, within the Internet context these are the servers operating as 'nodes' in the network, are essentially the identical to the end-user equip-

---

[174] Post, D., 1999.

[175] See for example, Goldsteinreport, 2009, in which EU Commissioner Reding advocates a split in the DNS responsibilities divided into a technical component and a policy component.

[176] See, USDoC and ICANN (1998a), and the associated contract between the USDoC and Verison, (successor of NSI); USDoC and NSI (1998).

[177] For more information on the transition of DNS responsibilities see, ICANN, 2009b.

[178] NRC, 2005, p. 103.

ment, namely computers. In sum, the combined availability of both DNS knowledge and essential equipment (computers) allow private actors to set up their own alternative DNSs effectively limiting US' (and ICANN's) power on the Internet. From a political point of view, the most interesting alternative DNS in this respect was the European Open Root Server Network[179] (OSRN), a privately operating root server network consisting of 13 independently operating root zone servers. It provided a European alternative counterbalancing US' (and ICANN's) power.

The ORSN had two operating modes. The ICANN-based operating mode was the normal mode and involved daily synchronization with the ICANN-based system with one exception: removed TLDs were not removed from the ORSN root. If ICANN (or the US), were to move a certain cc-TLD in ICANN's root zone directory, this TLD would not automatically be removed from the OSRN root. The second operating mode was ICANN-independent that did not synchronize automatically. This mode would be activated whenever the political situation requires this, for example, in case of a possible modification or actual or expected downtime of ICANN's root.[180] The servers of this network were primarily placed in Europe. The interesting point about the existence of this alternative is that possible US power abuse by deleting TLDs, for example, the .ir domain from the Internet universe, would not prevent the ORSN users from reaching the deleted domains. The moment that the .ir TLD name would be deleted from ICANN's root zone file, the ISP could and, pressured by their customers, probably would switch to the OSRN-operated DNS servers enabling their users to reach the Islamic Republic of Iran without difficulty. Due to a lack of funding however, the OSRN stopped its activities on December 31st, 2008 after having been on line since 2002.[181]

In addition to alternative DNSs, there are many so-called satellite servers in place routing our daily Internet traffic.[182] As opposed to the 13 authoritative root zone servers obtaining their information directly from the root zone file, a host of satellite servers distributing root zone information are in operation obtaining their information by copying the authoritative servers' content or by copying the information on copies of these servers. It is highly unlikely that all operators responsible for these servers would copy unwanted US deletions in their copy of the root zone file.

The US power over the root zone file, however, is not the only overrated issue in the current debate on Internet governance. There is an even more persistent and fundamental assumption. It concerns ICANN's alleged monopoly over the DNS. The issue at stake is (again) the determination of the root zone file content. In this case, however, the question is not so much the above-mentioned security argument, that is, the fear for deletions, but it merely concerns the opposite, ICANN's determination of additions to the root zone file.

---

[179] De Vey Mestdagh C.N.J. and Rijgersberg R.W., 2007.
[180] Ibid.
[181] This chapter will address the reasons for abandoning the OSRN project at a later stage.
[182] NRC, 2005.

In order to retain uniform resolvability, i.e., guaranteeing that every connection, whether in Spain or Alaska, has access to identical information, maintaining one single root zone file is elementary. Currently, ICANN manages 20 gTLDs and 252 ccTLDs.[183] The hardware and the technological expertise on how to set up a DNS, however, are widely available and ICANN has not been very fast in expanding the domain name universe with additional TLDs.[184] As a result, from 1996 onwards, several alternatives have been developed catering for the increased demand for new TLDs.[185] The most important commercial TLD providers simply offer an alternative system of root zone servers that include ICANN's root zone file similar to the OSRN discussed above. On their own root zone server system, they offer registration for additional TLDs and complete domain names. In order to increase access to the newly registered names they contract ISPs, thus providing access to ICANN-independent TLDs.

One of these companies, New.Net had contracted Tiscali (7.4 million users), EarthLink (4.8 million active subscribers) and Tutopia (2.7 million subscribers), claiming to have over 174 million New.Net enabled users in 2007.[186] Currently they claim to have sold over 25.000 domain names.[187] New.Net is but one of many companies offering alternative domain name services on the TLD level. Other companies offering alternative root servers systems are, for example, UnifiedRoot[188] and Public-Root.[189] In addition, China as a country also operates on this market since it has launched alternatives to .com domain names in Chinese characters.[190] Whereas these Chinese addresses are directly accessible to 110 million Chinese Internet users, they are not accessible outside China.[191]

In effect, the assumptions informing the proposals to implement traditional State-based democratic accountability mechanisms in order to control, influence and legitimize ICANN's decision-making power are based upon factual misconceptions. Neither the US power over the root zone file, nor ICANN's power regarding the DNS are strong enough to justify the implementation of classic State-based ac-

---

[183] For an overview, see, IANA, 1998; 2002.

[184] As Paul Vixie, one of the Internet's key architects told in the interview held by Rhoads, C., 2006.

[185] AlterNic, eDNS and Iperdome for example, were early alternative DNS providers.

[186] New.Net Domain Names, available at <www.new.net/about_us_partners.tp> and <www.new.net> (retrieved October 1, 2007) (website has since been updated).

[187] New.net, available at <www.new.net> (retrieved December 31, 2009).

[188] UnifiedRoot's site is available at <www.unifiedroot.com/en/about_unifiedroot> (retrieved on December 31, 2009). UnifiedRoot also works on a commercial basis in order to promote the liberalisation of the domain name market. It has also contracted Tiscali in order to provide access to their extended universe, see also <http://hothardware.com/News/Dutch-tech-firm-wants-to-rid-the-Web-of-the-com> (retrieved on December 31, 2009), also published in *TechRepublic*.

[189] Public Root (<http://public-root.com>, retrieved on December 31, 2009) offers its global root zone servers system in addition to alternative domain names. It has also launched a TLD system in Turkey; Palmer, J., 2005; TDN Staff, 2005.

[190] PDO Staff, 2006.

[191] BBC Staff, 2006; McKinnon, R., 2006.

countability mechanisms. Interestingly enough, the alternatives that have been and are available are provided by *private* as opposed to *governmental* actors despite the classic State tasks that are involved in ICANN's DNS governance. The next section proposes an alternative frame of reference in order to assess ICANN's conduct and power.

4.3.3   Market accountability and the DNS

The availability of alternatives causes the State frame of reference to break down as a viable model to assess and design ICANN's accountability mechanisms. The availability of alternative server systems and competing TLD providers renders the need for traditional political accountability mechanisms superfluous. This breakdown of one classic accountability model does not necessarily imply that everything is new about DNS-governance and the way in which it is held accountable for its actions. There is another widely accepted, traditional accountability model available that does seem to fit ICANN's situation rather well as the following exposition will show. The market model is able to provide us with a better understanding of the economic reality, i.e., the expanding competitive environment, in which ICANN operates. The accompanying notion of accountability might shed a new light on ICANN's accountability requirements and its curious hybrid organizational structure.

In a market situation the notion of accountability to the public takes on a completely different form. The traditional State-based principle of accountability to the public gives way to an accountability mechanism through which citizens influence decision making not by representation but by voting with one's feet. As opposed to political accountability, market accountability is based upon informal decentralized economic mechanisms rather than highly formal hierarchical control types of accountability. On a marketplace, the ability of a company to attract and maintain customers is the main indicator of the company's accountability to the public. On a market, the principle of political accountability is replaced by a company's ability to respond to its consumer needs. Actual customer choices are the key constituents of the main accountability mechanism of the market. On the Internet, the actual competitive character of the TLD-and root servers system markets forces a shift in conceptual frame of reference upon us. Consequently, ICANN needs to be assessed using a market rather than a State frame of reference. In the previous sections, the focus has been on an adequate description of the DNS and the supply side of the services involved. The next section focuses on the demand side of the DNS services and shows that ICANN's current stakeholder model is a new organizational arrangement based on market principles and a variety of consumer demands.

4.3.4   State participation in ICANN

The analysis thus far established that ICANN can be considered a market party. Instead of using a normative model in order to examine the adequacy of ICANN's accountability mechanisms, this section provides a description of ICANN's actual accountability to the public by focusing on the role that States and private Internet users play within ICANN's organizational structure. The latter part of this section explains ICANN's hybrid structure in the light of the market model.

Figure 9 'ICANN's Organizational Structure' shows that ICANN's board is its central policy making body.[192] It consists of a President and fourteen directors that decide by a majority vote. The (board-independent) Nominating Committee (NC) appoints eight directors based on the criteria of geographical diversity and technical skills.[193] The Address Supporting Organization (ASO), the Generic Names Supporting Organization (GSNO) and the Country Code Name Supporting Organization (CCNSO) appoint two directors each.[194] These directors in turn, annually elect the President.[195]

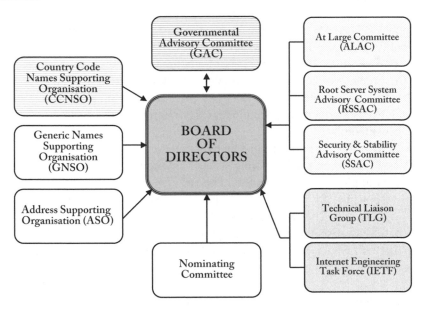

Figure 9. ICANN's organizational structure[196]

Within ICANN, the Internet users are represented in a variety of ways. ICANN's prime provision for empowering the global individual Internet users is the At Large Advisory Committee (ALAC).[197] Operating on the same level as the technical advisory committees (the Security and Stability Advisory Committee, the Root Server

---

[192] ICANN, 2009c, Art. II, Section 1.

[193] Ibid., Art. VII, Sections 4 and 5.

[194] Ibid., Art. VI, Section 2(1).

[195] Ibid., Art XIII, Section 2.

[196] This picture is a simplification of the picture found at ICANN's website <www.icann.org/structure>.

[197] See the ALAC's homepage at <www.atlarge.icann.org>.

System Advisory Committee, the Technical Liaison Group and the Internet Engineering Task Force), the ALAC used to be purely advisory in nature, informing ICANN's board directly about the Individual user's concerns. Recently, ALAC's status has been upgraded somewhat as ICANN's board has approved to grant the ALAC one (voting) director in ICANN's board.[198]

Similar to the ALAC, the governmental concerns are addressed by the Governmental Advisory Committee (GAC)[199] consisting of representatives of national governments, governmental organizations, and regional bodies like the European Commission. Its task is to provide advice on public policy issues affecting governments[200] and like the ALAC, the GAC's influence is primarily advisory and informative. ICANN's recent privatization through the expiration oversight contract with the US Department of Commerce relieving ICANN from US oversight has strengthened the role of the GAC in the development of the review processes in the light of public policy concerns.[201] Unlike the ALAC, the GAC is not represented in ICANN's board, but ICANN board's commitment to search for mutually acceptable solutions in cases of diverging views between board and the GAC does give the GAC some influence, as does its recently acquired role in the development of ICANN's review procedures.[202] The scope of its advice, however, concentrating on the interaction between ICANN's policies and national laws or international agreements, limits its powers considerably.[203]

The ALAC is not the only way in which the Internet users are represented. Within the NC they occupy half of the voting seats[204] giving the ALAC a large say in the appointment of eight ICANN directors. The NC also appoints half of the CCNSO's Council responsible for developing ccTLD policies, which in turn appoints two ICANN directors.[205] They are represented by nine out of twenty-one voting members in the GSNO, responsible for developing generic (g)TLD policies[206] and again, the appointment of two ICANN directors. In short, the Internet users are directly involved in the appointment of ICANN's directors and the development of TLD policies.

The inclusion of both users and State representation within ICANN poses difficulties for the State frame of reference since organizations involving States (like the United Nations or the European Union) are traditionally *limited* to States or State representatives and do not provide for additional mechanisms incorporating private

---

[198] ICANN, 2009a.

[199] See the GAC's homepage at <www.gac.icann.org>.

[200] Bettinger, T. et al., 2005, p. 15.

[201] ICANN, 2009b.

[202] ICANN, 2009c, Art. XI, Section 2(1)(j).

[203] For example, one of the public policy issues concerned law enforcement cooperation of the potential .xxx registry; GAC, 2005.

[204] ICANN, 2009c.

[205] Ibid., Art. IX, Section 3(1).

[206] Ibid., Art. X, Section 3(1).

interests in other ways.[207] From a market perspective, the inclusion of both governments and private users is also unusual, but it does allow for a natural explanation. The reason is that both governments and private parties are domain name consumers and are in this capacity similarly affected by ICANN's policies.

As was noted before, on a market, the accountability to the public is simply constituted by the organization's capacity to attract customers and its ability to maintain to serve them according to their needs. Since States are customers in the ccTLD business and since they are more likely to foresee conflicts with their national legal frameworks affecting national citizens, they obtained a specific status within ICANN. The inclusion of both government and individual stakeholders is very natural if viewing ICANN from a market perspective. A market perspective immediately makes clear that ICANN, in order to maintain market share in the Domain Name market and in order to avoid Internet splits[208] needs to incorporate both private and Stately actors in its organizational structure. Since on the Internet decisions regarding the DNS can have implications for national legislation and existing treaties, the inclusion of States for keeping in line with the legal frameworks poses several advantages. It improves ICANN's responsiveness to the governmental needs and consequently reduces the emergence of premature splits of the Internet along territorial lines, hence maintaining market share.

Inclusion of individual consumer representation (as private stakeholders) within ICANN's organizational structure is also in line with the market model since it provides the most direct way to monitor consumer needs. Historically the inclusion of private parties is justified by the Clinton administration's conviction that the Internet should be developed by private initiative rather than by State control. In fact, the incorporation of both private users and governmental organizations as customers within its formalized organizational structure actually takes the notion of responsiveness one step further. Instead of the traditional sales monitoring, relying on market surveys and customer satisfaction reports (generally outsourced to other companies), customer participation in company decision making is quite a revolutionary way of keeping in line with the customer's needs. In effect, ICANN has taken the market's prime accountability concept, responsiveness, to a higher level in its need to maintain and increase its market share. In this sense, judged from a market frame of reference, ICANN's accountability mechanisms are quite advanced and sophisticated. Moreover, judged by its market share, ICANN is a rather effective organization.

4.4   THE STATE AND THE DNS REVISITED

The previous sections have established that ICANN's organizational structure does not allow for significant State participation in ICANN's public decision making in

---

[207] See, United Nations Charter (1948), Art. 2(1). See also newly established treaty-based organizations (such as NAFTA, EU, etc.).
[208] See for example Mueller, M., 2001.

the public interest. The incorporation of the GAC only marginally incorporates States in their classic role as protectors of critical infrastructures. By means of the ALAC, States can participate, but identical to the State's involvement in the technical committees, they are not appreciated for the interests they represent but on the merit of their ideas. Notwithstanding, ICANN's governance of the world's prime DNS does not necessarily deprive States from their responsibilities towards their subjects as has been pointed out in Section 4.3. In the light of these considerations, the following sections explore the consequences private global governance for the classic State roles identified in Section 4.3; national security, uniform resolvability and intellectual property rights.

4.4.1   Security

Protection from external and internal threats is a well-established State task. The State's role in the GAC is not enough to secure the continuation and reliability of the national Internet infrastructure. The reason is that the GAC's limited advisory role only allows for advice on possible conflicts between ICANN's policies on the one hand, and national law and International treaties on the other hand.[209] Within the context of the review procedures its advice is not binding either. As such, the GAC could complain about power abuse when ICANN pulls the plug on a certain domain but it doesn't have the power to prevent such an event from happening. Consequently, the GAC is by no means powerful enough to ensure the security and reliability of the critical infrastructure Internet has become. The US as a hereditary ruler of the Internet still occupies a special place in this regard since it made sure, before transferring the DNS responsibilities to ICANN (a process that took more than ten years to complete), to established that any change to the root zone file would be subject to approval by the US Department of Commerce (Internet Assigned Numbers Authority or IANA contract).[210] Since, thus far, this clause has not been tested in practice, it is not completely clear what this power actually amounts to although it has been identified as performing a key role in securing the Internet as critical infrastructure from a US point of view.[211]

In addition to the IANA contract, ICANN has additional legal ties to the US as not-for-profit corporation under Californian state law. In terms of national security, this incorporation commits ICANN to charitable and public purposes enforceable under Californian law. The additional commitments under this law mean that ICANN's Board directors are legally responsible for upholding the four duties under this law: (a) a duty of care; (b) a duty of inquiry to make informed decisions; (c) a duty of loyalty; and (d) a duty of prudent investment which entails amongst others avoidance of speculation.[212] The final way in which the US is able to influence

---

[209] See ICANN webpage at <www.icann.org/en/about/>.
[210] USDoC and ICANN (1998a), and USDoC and NSI (1998).
[211] See for example the provisions in; Cybersecurity Act (2009), connecting the IANA contract to cybersecurity provisions in its Section 8.
[212] ICANN, 2008.

ICANN's decisions is by means of the authoritative root zone servers. Of the 13 servers, 10 are situated on US soil, three of which are in the hands of the US government. Particularly though these latter three servers operated by the National Aeronautics and Space Agency, US Department of Defense and the US army Research Laboratory, guarantee a degree of State-guaranteed national security in terms of Internet robustness. Although the three servers operated by the US government can be used to counter root zone file decisions, and provide more direct means for securing national security, not even the US can control the Internet and ensure its reliability single-handedly. Whereas the three US servers may sufficiently secure the national infrastructure directly, there are ten other root zone servers (and a large number of satellite servers) that could be affected by irregularities and which in turn might affect the visibility of US and non-US information.

For non-US residents however the national situation is even less secure. In Europe for example, governments do not own a single root zone server. The most important initiative that indeed formed a serious protection to ICANN's possible power abuse or failure to the system was the European Open Root Server Network that served as check upon ICANN's possible power abuse by operating a complete alternative root server system to counterbalance ICANN's US-dominated root zone file. The list of sponsors, however, shows that the money received in order to set up and maintain the infrastructure necessary to set up such an alternative system, was not a government initiative but was funded by private corporations. Although governmental initiatives could possibly form a European counterbalance to ICANN's US dominated root zone server system, there are no public sources confirming this. This despite the openness of secret services on their activities related to the Internet. Whereas certain secret service reports, for example, mention protection against malign attacks on servers[213] and the Internet as a tool for radicalization of Muslims,[214] they do not mention anything about DNS security at the level of the root zone. Since security services are fairly open about possible national threats and the way they plan to fight it, it is reasonable to infer that national security is no longer an affair solely run by States. The OSRN example in particular seems to suggest that national security in terms of a well-functioning Internet has become a private affair in an interdependent world and the State's role has become marginalized in this respect. The crux of this case study is not that everything changes under conditions of interdependence. It does show however that interdependence gives rise to new forms of governance, even at the level of our most pivotal national security concerns.

---

[213] See for example, Her Majesty's Government, 2006; 2009. The German Intelligence Service (*Bundesnachrichtendienst*) also mentions its dependency on the critical information infrastructures but only emphasizes this in the context of 'Information Warfare', i.e., the fact that information has become a critical element in protecting national security. There is no mention of its dependence on the DNS and associated threats. See their website at; <www.bnd.de/nn_1366028/DE/WirUeberUns/WirUeberUns__ node.html?__nnn=true>.

[214] See, Her Majesty's Government, 2006, p. 12.

4.4.2   Welfare

Maintaining the reliability of a critical infrastructure is important for States. Both as protectors of their subjects and as consumers, the States have important stakes in the reliability of the information infrastructure. States have both security and welfare interests. An ill-functioning Internet would ruin the trust necessary to exchange information and hence would discredit the Internet as a reliable transaction medium. The uniform resolvability of the DNS is a crucial factor in this. Despite these interests, States hardly have any means for enforcing uniform resolvability upon the Internet users. The reason is the Internet's decentralized structure. ICANN's relation to the registrars of both the TLDs and the SLDs consists of private contracts. These private contracts do require the registries to ensure the universal resolvability of the level in question by requiring the registries to issue a particular name only once, but States hardly play a part in it. If a registrar would refuse to comply, ICANN would simply employ a new registrar. Also regarding their own ccTLD, States hardly have any control other than the control they exercise on not-for-profit corporations acting on behalf of the public interest. The most important way in which States can guard the process of universal resolvability is through their say in ICANN and by putting pressure on ICANN informally through the ITU, a subsidiary of the United Nations. The global character of the Internet also makes it more difficult for individual States to prevent private actors from using their computers as alternative DNS servers. Similar to the example regarding national security the role of the State is rather limited, and again it is up to private actors and technical experts to maintain reliability of the DNS.[215]

4.4.3   Intellectual property rights

There has been one way in which States have been rather more successful maintaining their classic responsibilities. It concerns the way in which they have been able to incorporate previously established property rights, notably trademarks into ICANN's Universal Dispute Resolution Policy (UDRP) which was adopted soon after ICANN's establishment in 1998 and was to achieve two important goals. First it was to establish a system to resolve disputes between trademark holders and domain name registrants, an issue that particularly in the early days of ICANN's existence was a very important issue since invariably registrants bought domain names with the sole intent to sell them to companies with vested interests in the names. In addition, the UDRP provided an effective remedy since registries are contractually held to implement panel decisions within ten days of the verdict.

Through serious lobbying and pressured by the established enterprises that had already made serious investments in their trademarks, the UDRP incorporated the

---

[215] See also Chapter 5 'Interdependence and Technical Standardization' on the State's role in technical standard setting.

advice of the WIPO, a specialized agency of the UN dedicated to developing a balanced and accessible international intellectual property (IPR) system. WIPO is an organization designed to promote the protection of IPR throughout the world through cooperation among States and in collaboration with other international organizations.[216] The idea to incorporate WIPO's advice in developing the UDRP originates from the White Paper issued by the Clinton administration. This paper stated that the US government would ask the WIPO to conduct a consultative study into the trademark issues involved in the DNS.[217] Whereas WIPO's advice contained a proposal for subjecting DNS management to intergovernmental oversight,[218] the Clinton administration decided to transfer the DNS management to ICANN. Despite this decision, ICANN did implement much of its dispute resolution recommendations concerning the implementation of established trademark interests in order to fight cyber squatting. Consequently, ICANN implemented a policy that is followed uniformly by all registrars in the *.biz, .com, .ifo, .name, .net,* and *.org* gTLDs.[219] Currently the UDRP allows for arbitration by a small number of non-governmental arbitral bodies[220] and is quite successful. The strength of it, next to its relative low cost and fast decision making ability, is that both the domain name holders and the registrars are committed to the UDRP for arbitration.[221]

The general policy guiding the UDRP is that it is up to the complainants to prove (1) that the disputed domain name is identical or confusingly similar to a trademark or service mark in which the complainant has rights, (2) that the registrant has no rights or legitimate interests in respect of the domain name, and (3) that the domain name has been registered and is being used in bad faith. The UDRP identifies tests of 'bad faith' and grounds for demonstrating a registrant's 'rights and legitimate interests' in a domain name. In short, the interests of trademark holders are well established through the arbitration conducted based on the UDRP. Although non-governmental arbiters (as opposed to government employed judges) conduct the UDRP, the State has managed to maintain and promote the vested interests in names fairly well. In the current employment of the UDRP however, the State has only a rather limited role to play: namely of that as an ultimate remedy concerning financial redress in case of domain name disputes.

ICANN's incorporation of trademark law poses an interesting break with the classic first-come first-serve principle traditionally associated with the acquisition of private property. By means of its UDRP, ICANN accommodates previously established 'real world' trademark interests in order to fight the occurrence of cyber

---

[216] Source: WIPO's website available at <www.wipo.int/about-wipo/en/what_is_wipo.html>.

[217] NTIA, 1998b.

[218] IAHC, 1997.

[219] See the resolutions passed and discussed in: ICANN, 1999a.

[220] ICANN, 1999b.

[221] Fast and cheap dispute resolution generally acknowledged to be the characteristic advantage of most private dispute resolution procedures over State based arbitration. See, Mifsud Bonnici, J.P., 2007, p. 212ff.

squatting, that is 'buying' Internet domain names with the purpose of selling the name to a company with established 'real-world' trademark claims.

ICANN's incorporation of the real world trademark interest can genuinely be said to constitute one of the few success stories for the State in the interdependent world of the Internet. The justification of which is that specific commercial (private) interests were supposed to guide the further development of the Internet. It again confirms that in the context of the DNS the role of the State as a protector of private property is changed. No longer is the State the sole guarantor of private property. Nor are States the organizations that set the rules unilaterally. At base, only as ultimate remedy and safety net, the role of the State remains fully unaffected.

4.5   CONCLUSION

In the light of the general analysis of the effect of globalization on the constitutional governance, this chapter set out to identify the effects of global DNS management on the changing role of the State in terms of its traditional constitutional responsibilities. Several conclusions can be drawn from the DNS case study.

(1) Transnational interdependence can form an important ground for privatizing operations in the public interest.

Both the decentralized structure of the DNS and the privatization of its management are consequences of the Internet's success as a transnational communication, transaction and transportation infrastructure. The interdependent nature of the Internet had convinced US corporations that an internationalization of the DNS was needed in order to build the confidence needed to use the Internet as vehicle for expanding their horizons beyond the territorial borders of the US. With the transnational commercial opportunities of the Internet in mind, the US government realized that its unilateral management of the DNS was not a viable option anymore in the second half of the nineties. As a result the Clinton administration decided to privatize the DNS management and transferred the DNS responsibilities to the private not for profit corporation ICANN. Thus, the transnational nature of the Internet combined with the national interests of the US to internationalize its DNS management led to the privatization of the DNS. In effect, the DNS case study shows that the transnational interdependence created by the Internet led to the privatization of the DNS.

(2) Operations in the public interests do not necessarily require constitutional accountability mechanisms.

Whereas the US' ability to influence ICANN's allocation of private property (domain names) in the public interest is undeniable, as is the absence of perfect competition in the TLD and root server market, the DNS is neither run by the US, nor is there a strict monopoly on the DNS market. Due to its technical qualities the Internet's DNS servers are at base end-user devices designed to facilitate the use of the Internet by other end users. This feature facilitates the creation of alternative roots and despite the State's interests in DNSs both the maintenance of an integral part of the public infrastructure and the allocation and maintenance of private property have become primarily private responsibilities. This private initiative even goes as far as to provide a private counterweight to ICANN's public powers inherent to its control over the root zone file.

The interdependency-imposing nature of the Internet in combination with its transnational reach, make classic State-based accountability mechanisms superfluous. The end of the ORSN adventure on December 31st of 2008, due to a lack of funding, indicates that the sponsors render the current ICANN situation sufficiently safe to stop funding this alternative root server system and confirms that operations in the public interests do not necessarily require constitutional accountability mechanisms.

(3) The need for global coordination gives rise to novel hybrid governance structures that diminish the role of the State and liberate citizens to a certain extent from coercive State monopolies.

ICANN's stakeholder model presents a novel and effective way in which to organize policy makers operating in a global environment. As such, it may well serve as a viable alternative for territorial government in the light of globalization. Its hybrid governance structure may turn out to be a natural and even desirable form of decision making in an interdependent context. The case study also shows that new ways of organizing classic State tasks break up the State's monopoly as a mouthpiece for voicing their citizen's needs. Consequently, the interdependence created by the Internet has partially untangled the traditionally inextricable link between the State and its subjects. The case study examined in this chapter has shown that governance, i.e. the continuous exercise of political authority, has ceased to be a purely State-run affair, even regarding critical infrastructures.

(4) The national State still serves a role, however limited.

Within the context of ICANN it provides ultimate remedies in case dispute between parties and in providing the necessary preconditions to a well-functioning civil society and market economy.

States, despite the incorporation of State interests through the GAC and the incorporation of the WIPO-advice concerning vested interests in names, have hardly any influence on the way in which the DNS is run despite their traditional role. This also holds for the US despite appearances. Both institutionally and instrumentally, the role of the State has diminished significantly. Even the three essential tasks in the public interest mentioned in the previous chapter (security, welfare, and provision of individual rights) have become primarily private affairs at a global level.

Despite the influence of some traditional organizations, like the WIPO and to some extent the ITU, the role of the State in the DNS remains weak. The most significant 'Stately' contribution to the DNS is the security of previously established trademark interests. Ascribing this outcome solely to Stately efforts however, underestimates the vested interest of commercial enterprises pushing for an internationalization of one of the most important applications to the Internet, its DNS.

Ultimately, however, the State serves as the final safety net for legal security. Even domain name disputes can ultimately be put before traditional courts and even ICANN's decisions can be put before Californian law. Still, the DNS is mainly constituted by private contracts and private dispute resolution. Within the context of the DNS, the State simply serves as a fallback or security net for some of the traditional State tasks related to critical infrastructures and property.

Chapter 5
INTERDEPENDENCE AND TECHNICAL STANDARDIZATION

States play an important role in standardization processes and even the early (US and French) constitutions contained provisions explicitly stating State responsibilities for the standardization of currencies and weights and measures. Today's State involvement reaches far beyond to include, for example, health and safety standards.[222] In addition to their legislative capacity, States are also involved as developers, investors, end users when exercising procurements, and as lobbyists within Standard Setting Organizations (SSOs). Traditionally the standardization of critical infrastructures, such as railroad and telecommunications systems, form important areas of State concern. Since both States and citizens have become increasingly dependent on the Internet, State interests have increased accordingly.

On the Internet, standards facilitate communication and interconnectivity between hosts, systems and applications. In addition to facilitating communication and commerce, standards also determine the amount of control or protection that can be exercised. Since Internet standards concern individual liberties as well as security concerns for States, this chapter aims to gain some insight into the methods and the effects of State-attempts to influence Internet standard-setting processes on the global Internet. It takes the US attempts to influence standard setting in the telecommunications sector as a starting point to provide more insight into the State's ability to maintain its traditional (constitutional) commitments and responsibilities towards its citizens.

5.1   INTRODUCTION

Within the context of this inquiry, the Internet serves as a precursor for what globalization may have in store for us in terms of transnational interdependence and its consequences for constitutional governance. Chapter 3 showed that the transnational interdependence on the Internet is a consequence of its architecture. The Internet's

---

[222] For standardization processes in public health and safety issues, see for example, Water Quality Standards and Implementation, 33 USC § 1313, and; Federal Motor Vehicle Safety Standards, 49 USC, Part 571. Within the EU the legal equivalents are; Council Directive 98/83/EC, and; EC Regulation No. 661/2009 of the European Parliament and of the Council, concerning type-approval requirements for the general safety of motor vehicles, their trailers and systems, components and separate technical units intended therefore.

R.W. Rijgersberg, The State of Interdependence
© 2010, T·M·C·ASSER PRESS, The Hague, and the author

architecture is largely determined by technical standards called protocols. Whereas the physical network architecture can vary from twisted-pair and coax cable to glass fiber cables, protocols form a uniform element in establishing communications and interconnectivity between nodes, hosts and applications in the network. Without technical standards like the IP addressing system or the Simple Mail Transfer Protocol (SMTP) used in the exchange of e-mails, the Internet would simply not be able to function. Both the transmission of information over the nodes of the network and the processing and handling of information conducted by means of applications are established by standards. Hence, the first reason why Internet standard setting is relevant to the overall topic of this inquiry is that the Internet essentially is a collection of standards.

Standards not only determine the functionality of the Internet medium in terms of its primary goals (communication and interconnection); they also affect the information freedoms enjoyed by the individual users. Both effects are of interest to States in the light of their traditional responsibilities. The technical standards used on the Internet require a uniform implementation in order to ensure interconnection between hosts and interoperability[223] or communication between applications. The Internet is a global medium. This combination imposes an immediate transnational interdependency between actors that changes the unilateral ways in which individual States have traditionally designed and regulated their (national) critical infrastructures. Without uniform standards, Internet connectivity and communication is not possible. Hence, the topic touches the core of the Internet. The second reason that Internet standard setting is relevant to the general investigation, then, is that it allows us to investigate global decision making under full interdependency conditions.

Internet standards also affect the State in its constitutional capacity. In addition to facilitating commerce (welfare), standards also enable governmental control (security). This latter aspect makes global Internet standard setting particularly interesting from the perspective of this investigation, because unlike classic international SSOs, the most important Internet SSOs are private organizations. This raises questions about how States exert their influence in global standard setting processes and what the consequences are for individual States to fulfill their constitutional commitments and for example, in terms of protection and security.

In the light of the general analysis of the effect of globalization on constitutional governance, this chapter attempts to answer the question concerning the effects of transnational interdependence in terms of global standard setting. This chapter does so by identifying the standard setting role of the US in the development of standards related to its critical communications infrastructure.

---

[223] Interoperability is the ability of two or more systems or components to exchange information and to use the information that has been exchange; IEEE, 1990.

5.2   STANDARDS

Standards come in many guises. The two most influential international technical SSOs are the International Organization for Standardization (ISO)[224] and the International Electrotechnical Commission (IEC).[225] The ISO is the world's largest developer and publisher of international standards.[226] The IEC is responsible for the publication of international standards for electrical, electronic and related technologies, including telecommunication and multimedia. In conjunction these organizations have developed the following definition of the term standard.

> 'A standard... is a document, established by consensus and approved by a recognized body that provides, for common and repeated use rules, guidelines or characteristics for activities or their results aimed at the achievement of the optimum degree of order in a given context... Standards should be based on the consolidated results of science, technology and experience and aimed at the promotion of optimum community benefits.'[227]

Standards, in this view, are primarily ordering devices designed in the public interest, providing stability and hence reinforce trust. The French report to the Organization for Economic Cooperation and Development (OECD) uses a slightly different definition. It defines standards as constructs resulting from reasoned, collective choice enabling agreement on solutions of recurrent problems.[228] In this report, standards are held to strike a balance between the technical possibilities on the one hand and the interests and constraints imposed upon those standards by users, producers and government on the other hand. In this context, one might add the lobby of civil society groups as an additional autonomous factor in this balancing of interests. Standardization then, strikes a balance between the technical possibilities on the one hand and the interests of governments, markets and civil society actors on the other hand.

Whereas the two definitions outlined above view standards as the result of collaborative processes, standards in turn, also determine social processes to a significant extent. Scholars such as Brunsson and Jacobsson[229] emphasize this normative feature of standards and view them as autonomous sources that order, or coordi-

---

[224] ISO's website at <www.iso.org>. Since the acronym of the International Organization for Standardization is different in various languages, the organization has 'standardized' the short form of its name. ISO is derived from the Greek word *isos* meaning 'equal' and serves as the worldwide short name for the organization.

[225] IEC's website at <www.iec.ch>. It has published over 5000 international standards to date and its operating costs reach nearly USD 20 million.

[226] ISO has published over 16.500 international standards since its foundation in 1947. Its operating costs (excluding the costs of running the technical committees) reach over USD 25 million; Ibid.

[227] IOS/IEC, 2004, p. 8.

[228] Germon, C., 1986.

[229] Brunsson, N. and Jacobsson, B., eds., 2000, p. 10.

nate, social life. Traditional economic theory contrasts two prime ways of ordering society. The coercive way of ordering society belongs to the realm of formal organizations, of which the State is a prime example. Characteristic of the coercive way of ordering is that rules are imposed upon its subjects or members. In contrast, the second type of ordering is established by the self-interested voluntary choices of individual actors in the market economy. Viewed collectively, these voluntary individual choices establish the common good of the community as a whole, famously captured by Adam Smiths 'invisible hand' metaphor.[230] Brunsson adds another category to this classic distinction. In his view, standards provide a third way of ordering or coordinating human conduct by facilitating contract, cooperation and trade.[231]

In his analytical framework, Brunsson assesses these categories in the light of legitimacy and responsibility. Characteristic of the formal organization is the membership relation, which legitimizes the coordinating role of the hierarchical organization. Within corporations, this role is derived from ownership and property relations. Within States, legitimacy is established by democratic representation.[232] In contrast, the coordinating roles of standards and markets are legitimate because they leave the individual actor free to pursue their private interests. Markets allow individuals to pursue their interests by using their buying power. The adaptation of standards, according to Brunsson, is also a voluntary decision.

In terms of responsibility, there are also differences. Formal organizations, tend to be hierarchical, the prime responsibility for coordinating behavior lies with its leaders. Within markets, there is a shared responsibility between producers and consumers, although ultimately, the consumers bear the prime responsibility for allocating the means of production by using their purchasing power. In the case of standardization, Brunsson holds that all standards are adapted voluntarily, which ultimately makes the users responsible for the coordination of human conduct

Brunsson's model is a general model for standardization designed to discuss standardization as a form of rulemaking. As such, the model is not tailor made for technical standardization. The main reason why the model is not suitable for all types of technical standards is that within the area of technology, standards are not always voluntarily adapted. In his classic work on standardization, Cargill acknowledges this by distinguishing between two types of standards, regulatory and voluntary.[233] Regulatory standards, according to Cargill, are traditionally State imposed and are generally considered useful if only one single acceptable solution to a given problem is required. Regulatory standards traditionally regulate specific types of activities such as speed limits, but also food safety requirements for example, fall into this category. Voluntary standards on the other hand, presume a freedom of choice and, according to Cargill, are generally considered more useful in a world

---

[230] Smith, A., 1776.

[231] Brunsson, N., 2000.

[232] Civil society groups, within this model could be categorized as hierarchical membership organizations. For the purposes of this section however civil society groups are not relevant as such.

[233] Cargill, C.F., 1989, p. 23.

characterized by competing solutions and applications. Voluntary standards require more user input in order to obtain the necessary public support than regulatory standards. An example of a typically voluntary standard is the QWERTY standard for computer keyboards. Designed as the most effective way to write English on a mechanical typewriter without having the type hammers collide and jam together, it eventually became the keyboard standard for nearly all English speaking users to date, despite competition from other arrangements.[234] Many technical standards however, are regulatory in nature in that they often tend to provide a single solution to a given problem. An illustrative example is the voltage of the electricity net. Interestingly, despite the fact that Internet standards have regulatory characteristics, they are, contrary to what Cargill suggests, generally not imposed by States.

5.2.1 The Code is law thesis

Although Brunsson's model is not in all respects suitable for describing technical environments, the major assumption underlying his model is very interesting in the context of this inquiry. His major assumption is that by coordinating social life, standards are instruments of control.[235] In his book Code and Other Laws of Cyberspace,[236] Lessig takes on this theme in the context of the Internet. In order to show how technical architectures affect behavior, Lessig distinguishes four types or modalities of constraints, laws, norms, markets and architectures. All four modalities of constraints put constraints on behavior. In other words, they influence or 'regulate' our actions to use Lessig's terms.

Architectures regulate much in the same way that laws do. Similar to laws, they put constraints upon behavior and contain values because they determine the degree of individual freedom that can be exercised. Moreover, since architectures, again similar to laws, are designed entities, they are expressions of values and hence can be designed in various ways according to the values they express. The Internet architecture consists primarily of software (Lessig uses the term 'code') and this software or code determines the Internet users' behavior to a significant degree. The similarity between law and software or code in terms of regulating human conduct is captured by his well-known thesis 'code is law'.

Lessig's major point is that once architectural constraints are in place, they continue to constrain our behavior until stopped. The reason is that once implemented, a variety of vested interests is prone to prevent the development of better standards. This is also the reason why the decisions we make today are likely to determine the liberties we enjoy in using these architectures for some time to come. Consequently,

---

[234] Though initially introduced as a voluntary standard by Remmington it remains to be questioned to what extent the current use of the QWERTY design for computer keyboards is voluntary in the classic sense. An interesting historical analysis suggesting a historical path-dependence of the continuation of standards can be found in; David, P.A., 1985.

[235] Brunsson, N. and Jacobsson, B., eds., 2000, p. 1.

[236] Lessig, L., 1999.

Lessig stresses the need to think twice before implementing decisions that affect the Internet's architecture. Since code imposes normative constraints upon its users similar to law, and since code similar to law is a man-made artifact, code, similar to law, can become an instrument of social and political control.[237]

The strength of Lessig's approach in contrast to Brunsson's is that although he initially presents the four modalities of regulation (law, norms, markets and architectures) as analytically distinct ways of coordinating human conduct, he suggests that the four modalities of constraints influence one another. In his 'CODE 2.0', Lessig sketches a world of control exercised by commercial technologies backed by the rule of law. Commerce will provide the tools that eventually lead to more control. Government will back the market in developing and using those tools. This picture describing a particular configuration between government on the one hand and commerce designing architectures on the other hand, poses difficulties for modern society according to Lessig if we want to preserve certain liberties in using our architectures. The reason is, according to Lessig, that commerce will provide the tools of control much outside the scope of the constitutional review process. Whereas laws, norms and markets are checked by judgment, architectures are self-executive. Once the decision is made, the architecture of control is simply in place and it is not easy to redesign and rebuild faulty architectures.[238]

In order to stop this development, Lessig urges individual States, notably the US, to play a more active role in shaping the Internet based on fundamental values. Lessig's dream is that governments (preferably united) will take control of the Internet in order to develop an Internet based on fundamental constitutional liberties. Without an existing global pact of governments governing the global Internet at hand, it is not clear how Lessig's dream should be realized.

Lessig's exposition is useful in the context of this inquiry in that it highlights the role of artifacts in our society and the ability of architectures to constrain behavior. Whereas the thrust of his argument is well captured by the equation 'code is law', this equation is less useful when trying to analyze standard setting processes in terms of the influence of individual States on the process. Particularly since laws are generally associated with States and in the context of the Internet, code is primarily provided by the private sector.

The approach taken in this chapter uses Brunsson's distinction based on responsibility in order to distinguish between sources of coordinating social life. With

---

[237] Within the context of a computer game Lessig's thesis is immediately clear. Within the well-known computer world Second Life (<http://secondlife.com/whatis/>) for example, the technical architecture of the game allows its characters to fly from one part of the world to another. The same architecture can also be used in a similar game for pedestrians only to walk on the pavement and for cyclists only to cycle on pre-defined cycle lanes. Viewed in this way, indeed, architecture becomes an instrument of control, even absolutely. All artifacts impose constraints on behavior. Try reading a book when driving a car or entering your house without opening a door. Of course artifacts, whether physical objects or software constrain our behavior. Sometimes limits imposed by artifacts control our behavior to a significant extent.

[238] Lessig, L., 2006, p. 343.

Lessig, the approach followed in this chapter acknowledges the impact of the technical architecture of the Internet on behavior. It differs from both approaches in that it does not take the various means of coordinating conduct primarily as autonomous actors. It rather looks at the means by which an individual State (the US) attempts to shape the development of the Internet by trying to influence the development of Internet standards. In addition to making laws, it also looks at other ways for States to deploy their powers to influence standard setting, for example, through diplomatic maneuvering or by using its buying power.

5.2.2 Internet standards

The international and technical aspects of the Internet suggest that the definition of ISO/IEC[239] sufficiently applies to Internet standards. However, the definition poses two problems. First, it suffers from a bias towards institutional/formal recognition of standards. Limiting the ability to set standards to formally recognized institutions raises questions as to what the criteria for such organization are. By what law or procedure do they need to be established? Do such organizations require formal recognition by States? On the Internet, its most important SSO, the Internet Engineering Task Force (IETF), is essentially an informal organization. What criteria establish the IETF as a recognized SSO? In addition, many standards are set without being recognized by a formal organization at all: the strength of standards is primarily in their use, not in their recognition by some formal institution. A second problem with the ISO/IEC definition is that it does not acknowledge that opinions concerning the optimum community benefits of technical standards tend to vary between persons and States. In order to accommodate these and other problems that are specific to Internet standardizations, De Vries has developed the following definition of a standard. It is a,

> 'specification of a limited set of solutions to actual or potential matching problems, prepared for the benefits of the party of parties involved, balancing their needs, and intended and expected to be used repeatedly or continuously, during a certain period, by a substantial number of the parties for whom they are meant.'[240]

Essentially, then, similar to the OECD definition mentioned in the beginning of this chapter, standards are solutions to particular kinds of problems, viz. matching problems. They harmonize interrelated entities or relations between entities (things and persons).[241] The matching problem central to the standards used on the Internet is

---

[239] See Section 5.2: 'A standard (...) is a document, established by consensus and approved by a recognized body that provides, for common and repeated use rules, guidelines or characteristics for activities or their results aimed at the achievement of the optimum degree of order in a given context .... Standards should be based on the consolidated results of science, technology and experience and aimed at the promotion of optimum community benefits.'
[240] De Vries, H.J., 1999, p. 15.
[241] De Vries, H.J., 2006, p. 5.

the way in which to guarantee interconnection and communication of different hosts and applications. The typology developed by De Vries allows for a more detailed specification into three main and two sub-categories.[242]

Basic standards provide structured descriptions of (aspects of) interrelated entities to facilitate human communication about these entities and to facilitate use in other standards. Terminology standards and the metric system of measurement for example, fall into this category. *Requiring* standards set requirements for entities or relations between entities. When they set margins of deviation from the basic standards, they are called performance standards. Grade requirements for oil used in particular engines are performance standards.[243] When requiring standards are solutions for matching problems they are called design-based standards. A good example of a design-based standard is the gauge width as a requirement for connecting two railway systems. The third main category consists of *measurement* standards providing methods for checking whether the criteria of the requirement standards are met.

It is clear from the exposition given on the Internet in Chapter 3 that the requirements establishing communication (or interoperability) and interconnectivity on the Internet are essentially design-based requirement standards. Following Simons and De Vries, they are a particular kind design-based requirement standard, namely *compatibility* standards. The reason is that they concern the fitting of interrelated entities to one another in order to enable them to function together.[244] In sum, Internet standards are regulatory compatibility standards offering design-based (architecture) solutions to matching problems (interconnectivity and interoperability).

5.2.3   Standard setting on the Internet

Many standard setting processes are formally organized in SSOs. The world's largest international standardization body, the ISO, publishes a large variety of technical standards ranging from implants for surgery and soil fertilizers to the application of statistical measures and the quality of paper. Electric and electro-technological standardization is in the hands of the IEC, the world's second largest international standard setting organization. Both the ISO and the IEC are voluntary organizations that operate internationally and leave plenty of room for member States to participate in the development of standards.[245] In general, they act independently

---

[242] Ibid., p. 6.

[243] Tassay, G., 2000, p. 591.

[244] Simons, C.A.J., 1995.

[245] An organization is voluntary or unincorporated when two or more persons are bound together for one or more common purposes by mutual undertakings, each having mutual duties and obligations, in an organization which has rules identifying in whom control of the organization and its funds is vested, and which can be joined or left at will. *Conservative and Unionist Central Office* v. *Burrell (Inspector of Taxes)* [1982] 1 WLR 522. The definition was for tax purposes, but was expressed to be of general application.

but also join their expertise in many fields. In information technology, for example, they have formed a joint technical committee (JTC1), which includes a subcommittee on interoperability (SC25). The JTC1 focuses primarily on end-user equipment rather than actual networking standards.[246]

In addition to the field of electrical and electro-technological standardization, there is yet another field in which the ISO does not have standard authority. The standards required for telecommunications are authorized by the International Telecommunications Union (ITU) and particularly by its standardization branch the ITU-T (Standardization Telecommunications Sector). The ISO, IEC and ITU form, in Cargill's words, the senior standard bodies that affect the field of information technology.[247] Unlike ISO and the IEC, the ITU-T is not a voluntary standard setting organization but a formal treaty organization running under the auspices the United Nations. The ITU-T has the formal right and duty to set international regulatory standards, which are administered by governments rather than industries.

The voluntary character of the ISO and IEC and the fact that they are not intergovernmental in a classic treaty-based sense, does not mean that they are free from national considerations. In fact, despite the incorporation of non-stately organizations in their decision-making procedures, all three organizations focus on the nation-State as their primary unit of judgment.[248] The ISO consists of membership bodies that are 'most representative of standardization within its country' and over seventy percent of its membership organizations are governmental institutions or organizations incorporated under public law.[249] The IEC's structure is largely similar. It also consists of national members representing the interests of countries and other stakeholders like individual users, manufacturers and trade associations. The ITU-T, as pointed out, also establishes consensus based on national input. As a result, the members of these organizations, including the members of the aforementioned JCT1, first take a national viewpoint on standards, followed by a viewpoint from a standard profession and only then take the interests of the sponsors an the industry into account in order to arrive an international perspective.[250] The most important Internet SSO, the IETF, as we shall see, diverges considerably from this approach since it is a largely informal organization thriving on the input from volunteers.

Before exploring the IETF and its role in Internet standard setting, it serves to have a closer look at the historical role of the State in the development of communication standards. The following examination of US in this regard, suggests that States are unlikely to promote the liberal values that are the focal point of Lessig's plea for more government involvement in Internet standardization.

---

[246] The scope of subcommittee SC25, Interconnection of Information Technology Equipment, is illustrative to this end, details of which are available at <http://sc25.iec.ch/txt/sc25/presentation/sc25structur.htm>.

[247] Cargill, C.F., 1989, p. 125.

[248] Ibid., p. 147.

[249] Ibid., p. 127.

[250] Ibid., p. 138.

5.3   US COMMUNICATION POLICY

The previous sections defined Internet standards as regulatory compatibility standards offering design-based (architecture) solutions to matching problems (interconnection and interoperability). The two aspects of Internet standards that are of
particular interest in the light of this section, and already touched upon in the short
exposition of Lessig's work, are the regulatory (or normative) and design-based
nature of standards. The normative character of standards has traditionally been
very helpful in achieving State objectives. The most important objective perhaps, is
that standards facilitate commerce by defining the quality of products and services.
They also facilitate production and supply processes enabling a division of labor.

Standard setting is a well-established national practice and already in the early
constitutions, the role of the State in standard setting was established. Both the US
Articles of Confederation and the later US Constitution, for example, granted the
State the power to set the standards for weights and measures. In addition, the coin-
age and valuation of money (as a standard for exchange) were also explicit State
responsibilities.[251] In France, the need for standards was also considered crucial in
building the New France. The National Assembly called upon the French Academy
of Sciences already in the midst of the revolution (1790) to determine an invariable
standard for all the measures and weights.[252]

The standard setting power of the State extends to more than basic standards.
The State sets standards regarding safety and healthcare issues and it sets standards
for critical infrastructures, as the development of the railway system for example
shows[253] The communication infrastructure is also a critical infrastructure, and,
similar to the railway system, individual States have also played important roles in
setting standards in this field.

Standards are not only suited to facilitate commerce. As stated above, they can
also be very useful government tools for exerting control. A uniform system of
measures and weights, for example, facilitates the State's ability to levy taxes. The
same holds for other valuation standards, like those used in accounting. The standards used in critical communication infrastructures are particularly interesting from
a State perspective since they determine the amount of control States can exercise
over communications. Consequently, communications standards have long been
recognized as valuable targets for State manipulation. Lessig's work outlined above
touched upon the relation between State policies and standards.[254] It is particularly
this aspect of the relationship between technology and law, which makes technical
standardization such an interesting area for States to exert their influence. As the
Internet Governance report puts it: there is often a close relationship between tech-

---

[251] Articles of Confederation and Perpetual Unity, Arts. III, XI; Constitution of the United States of
America, Art. 1, Section 8.
[252] O'Connor, J.J. and Robertson, J.F., 2003.
[253] Puffert, D.J., 2002.
[254] Dommering, E.J., 2006.

nical factors and policy.[255] Certain policy choices may be constrained by technical architectures or concerns about technical feasibility. On the other hand, States pressure standards developers to embed or reflect policy decisions in their standards development, for example, to facilitate the enforcement of policy choices. The interdependency between policy choices on the one hand and technical standards on the other hand makes global standardization processes a fascinating battlefield for pursuing one's interest as a State.

Lessig's argument is that State involvement is necessary in order to develop an architecture based on fundamental freedoms. The US attempts to influence the development and employment of communication standards, however, suggest a rather different picture. The most important governmental US pressure groups pushing communications standard setting have not shown much concern with the privacy and other individual freedoms enjoyed by the users of national communications systems. On the contrary, the pressure on standard setting originates primarily from law enforcement agencies trying to use standard setting in order to gain more control. The following US attempts to influence the use of technical communication standards reflect the US attitude in this regard. They also show that influencing Internet standards unilaterally, poses some significant difficulties due to the Internet architecture.

5.3.1 Digitalization and encryption

Originally, wiretapping meant to monitor telephone calls with a concealed listening device connected to the circuit. Today, it includes, for example, also wireless communications, fax and other data transmission. Wiretapping in the US legal system is legal but constitutionally restricted. Wiretapping is considered a kind of search that is protected under the fourth amendment.[256] Consequently, it requires a court order before execution.[257] Although the wiretapping for criminal investigations was codified under Title III of the Omnibus Crime Control and Safe Streets Act (OCCSA) (1968), it took another ten years before the Foreign Intelligence Surveillance Act (FISA) (1978) established a court order requirement on wiretapping practices for national security reasons.[258] The late date of this codification says something about the great store the US set to wiretapping practices in the national interest. One of the key government agencies employing wiretap facilities is the Federal Bureau of Investigation (FBI). Its mission is to protect and defend the US against terrorist and foreign intelligence threats, to uphold and enforce the criminal laws of the United States, and to provide leadership and criminal justice services to federal, state, munici-

---

[255] Mathiason, J. et al., 2004, p. 10.

[256] The Fourth Amendment to the US Constitution asserts 'the rights, of the people to be secure in their persons, houses, papers and effects against unreasonable searches and seizures'.

[257] See *Berger* v. *New York,* 388 US 41 (1967), and *Katz* v. *United States*, 389 US 347 (1967).

[258] Omnibus Crime Control and Safe Streets Act (1968), 42 USC § 3711; Foreign Intelligence Surveillance Act (1978), 50 USC §§ 1801-1811, 1821-1829, 1841-1846, and 1861-1862.

pal, and international agencies and partners.[259] In practice, the FBI is the US' prime federal law enforcement agency responsible for federal criminal investigations. In addition it also serves as the US' domestic intelligence agency. Although the OCCSA and the FISA bound the use of wiretaps to certain conditions, it remained an important tool for the FBI for investigation purposes.

The digitization of society[260] had an enormous impact on the way in which governments handle communications. It has improved the quality and storage possibilities of communications, but has also provided new tools for enhancing the privacy of its users. One such example is the invention of encryption techniques designed to conceal information from third parties.

When at the end of the 1980s the digitization of the US telecommunications was completed, the FBI started to worry about their ability to intercept phone calls. The break up of AT&T in 1984 had increased the number of companies and many of them were experimenting with new technologies in order to satisfy their customers. In addition, the statutes of neither the OCCSA nor the FISA imposed direct obligations on providers to design their systems so as not to impede the lawful interceptions. This posed problems for the FBI for two reasons: first, because they lacked the technical expertise in order to deal with the changing technologies, and secondly, because unlike its analogue predecessor the digitized telecommunications system provided opportunities for information to be encrypted before being sent to the receiver. Encryption is the process of transforming information using an algorithm to make it unreadable to anyone except those possessing special knowledge (or 'a key' in cryptology terms). It provides a security technique to messages transmitted over channels that are entirely out of the control of either the sender or receiver. Since encryption would hamper the FBI's investigation techniques significantly, they set forth to lobby for additional legislation in order to make digital telephony wiretap ready.

The first FBI attempt to do so was by its 1992 Digital Telephony Proposal,[261] which mandated the inclusion of provisions for authorized wiretapping in the design of telephone switching equipment. This proposal was fiercely objected to both by the telecommunications industry and civil society groups. Telecommunications and related businesses objected on the grounds that it would stifle innovation. The reason was that the implementation of the techniques would impose additional costs on them. Civil society groups objected because of privacy concerns. The result was a complete lack of congressional support for the FBI's proposal.[262] A second at-

---

[259] The FBI's mission is available at <www.fbi.gov/quickfacts.htm>.

[260] Digitization is the process of transforming or replacing traditional types of information, like for example the analogue telephone signal, books, photographs etc., into digital format. Within the digital format information is organized into discrete units of data (called bits) that can be separately addressed. Digitizing information makes it easier to preserve, access and share information. For telecommunications the advantage of digital signals is that they can be compressed and hence use less bandwidth when sent over the network.

[261] The Digital Telephony Proposal (1992).

[262] See, Congressional Record, 1992.

tempt limited wiretapping to common carriers and allocated USD 500 million to cover their costs. Accommodating the concerns of both business and civil society, this attempt resulted in the Communications Assistance for Law Enforcement Act (CALEA) in 1994. Section 103 explicitly states that:

> '... a telecommunications carrier shall ensure that its equipment, facilities, or services ... isolating and enabling the government.(1) to intercept ..., (2) access call-identifying information ..., (3) delivering intercepted communications and call-identifying information to the government, and (4) facilitating authorized communications interceptions and access to call-identifying information unobtrusively.'

The FBI had won the first part of the battle. At base, the CALEA did not stretch the FBI's powers significantly. The type of wiretapping at stake in the CALEA was used within the traditional analogue telephone network before 1994. Despite the FBI's initial desire to apply the existing analogue telecommunications to all new techniques,[263] congress struck a balance between law enforcement needs, privacy considerations and technological innovation.[264] As a result, the CALEA only required that new features of the already regulated telecommunications carriers were not to interfere with traditional government wiretapping techniques and activities.[265] It explicitly did not stretch the CALEA requirements to information services and other Internet applications and maintained that the application of the law's definition of a 'telecommunications carrier' to new technologies would require a public interest finding and substantial market penetration as a replacement for local telephone exchange services.[266] Moreover, the new law maintained that,

> '... a telecommunications carrier shall not be responsible for decrypting or ensuring the government's ability to decrypt ... unless the encryption was provided by the carrier and the carrier has the information necessary to decrypt the communication.'[267]

This latter provision largely freed the telecommunications carrier from decryption responsibilities. The next strategy for the US law enforcement lobby was to route around the encryption exemption.

Attempt 1: The Clipper Chip

One of the ways in which the FBI tried to work its way around the encryption exemption was by developing encryption techniques that would allow for relatively light encryption techniques while allowing a backdoor for government to access the information. The solution was found in key escrowed encryption. It used the

---

[263] Freeh, L.H., 1994.
[264] Dempsey, J.X., 1997.
[265] Communications Assistance for Law Enforcement Act (CALEA), HR 4922 (1994).
[266] Hancock, E., 2007, p. 187.
[267] Communications Assistance for Law Enforcement Act (CALEA), HR 4922, Section 103(b3).

federal standard setting power to develop a federal information-processing standard intended to improve the security and privacy of telephone communications. This Escrowed Encryption Standard (EES) used an algorithm (called Skipjack) that could be incorporated into communications devices including voice, fax, and computer data. EES provides all the features that make encryption so attractive, except for the ability of law-enforcement officials to intercept the communications given a court order allowing them to do so. This interception is made possible by means of a Law-Enforcement Access Field (LEAF), along with two decryption keys, one held by the National Institute of Standards and Technology (NIST) and the other held by Automated Systems Division of the Treasury Department. Each key would be worthless without the other. Only when properly authorized the keys would be distributed to law enforcement agencies.

The EES technique was implemented in a chip designed for use in personal and business communications systems (including computers). The telephone model containing a Clipper Chip, specifically designed by AT&T to secure telecommunications traffic only sold 17.000 models, including the 9000 models bought by the FBI to seed the market. Despite the possible interests of secure communication devices in the private sector (banking, healthcare institutions and knowledge based industries), the very idea that through key escrow government would be able to intercept messages created privacy concerns. Even if the escrowed keys were never accessed at all, the very possibility that government could be listening limited one's conversation freedom considerably.[268] Despite the advantages of providing secure communication for businesses (financial, information and health institutions for example), the chip was not very successful in other commercial products either. Possibly the fear for becoming mandatory devices in all electronic communications devices and the concern about governmental abuse, prevented the Clipper Chip from becoming a success. In effect, the Clinton administration's attempt to influence the civilian use of cryptology by using its federal standard setting and buying power to push for key escrowed encryption techniques failed miserably.

Attempt 2: Export control

Export controls on encryption techniques have also been an important instrument for the US to prevent the use of standards. The export of strong encryption[269] techniques runs counter to the US interests because it would disable the US to intercept strategically relevant information. More important, however, in the US strategy was the prevention of a widespread use of encryption techniques that would be

---

[268] Diffie, W. and Landau, S.E., 2007, p. 236ff.

[269] Encryption techniques transform data into something unrecognizable by a mathematical algorithm. The basis for the algorithm is a key consisting of a number. The strength of the encryption depends on the length of this number. Whereas 16-bit key systems yield just over 65.000 keys, a 128-bit key system has more than $3.4*10^{38}$ possible keys and hence is difficult to crack even by the most advanced computers.

strong enough to withstand real-time decoding. A widespread use of this type of encryption would prevent the US to distinguish between types of information, with the effect of hampering the US's ability to select traffic relevant to law enforcement and military purposes. In line with this strategy is the prevention of the adoption of standardized cryptographic systems. A common standard would spread the use of encryption to almost any user and would hamper the US' monitor abilities. A last reason for export limitations on encryption techniques is the government objective of maintaining an ongoing assessment of the quality, availability and functioning of commercially supplied cryptographic equipment.[270]

US exports fall under two categories. Under the Arms Export Control Act,[271] the department of State has the power to regulate the export of everything it considers weapons of war (or munitions). Munitions require individual export licenses designating the customer, application and the conditions for handling or redeployment of the items under consideration. All encryption techniques suitable for military governmental use fell under this act. Export items that are not munitions but can have military applications are called dual-use items, and fall under the Export Administration Act.[272] Dual-use items also require licenses. Under the Export Administration Act, only exports that are likely to prevent foreign customers from using the product can be restricted. If the customer can acquire similar products easily somewhere else, there is no reason for withholding an export license under this act. Under the Export Administration Act, for example, particular encryption techniques were exported for use by foreign banks in order to secure bank-to-bank wire transactions but not for most other applications. In 1996 the US allowed the export of key escrowed encryption techniques of a limited length (64 bits) on the condition that (1) it prevented interoperability with non-escrowed versions of the same system and (2) used US escrow agents or agents in countries having bilateral agreements as to grant the US access to the keys. The technological developments left the US eventually to drop the key-length restriction and the interoperability requirements.

After the clipper controversy, Congress called for a National Research Council Report on encryption. The report published in 1996[273] urged a loosening of the export regulations on the basis that the US would be better off with a more widespread use of encryption techniques rather than the current limitations. In addition, it explicitly held that the current export requirements significantly hampered the use of encryption techniques domestically, which in turn threatened the security interest of individuals, businesses, government agencies and the nation as a whole. In addition, the international lobby for the use of key escrowed encryption at the OECD was not successful either. Due to a widespread difference in opinion be-

---

[270] Diffie, W. and Landau, S.E., 2007, p. 121ff.
[271] Arms Export Control Act, 22 USC 2571-2794.
[272] Export Administration Act, 50 USC App. 2401-2420.
[273] NRC, 1996.

tween the individual OECD members and despite the intense lobbying of the US government, the OECD's guidelines issued in 1997 did not contain any recommendations regarding escrowed encryption. In fact, the guidelines explicitly stated that 'the development and provision of encryption methods should be determined by the market in an open and competitive environment'. They also contended that the development of international technical standards, criteria and protocols for cryptographic methods should be market driven instead of being the result intergovernmental agreements.[274]

The export restrictions posed problems for the US' internal market. First, the export restrictions forced businesses to use different encryption software for the internal and export market. The costs involved led many businesses to omit security features altogether. Secondly, the export controls decreased the incentive for businesses to develop strong encryption devices sufficiently secure for governmental use; the expected return on investments was simply too small for commercial software suppliers. Consequently, this posed enormous costs on the US government, which needed to rely on tailor made solutions.

The final blow to the export program was the exposure of the intercept network ECHELON, an association among the US, the UK, Canada, Australia and New Zealand designed to filter commercial intelligence using keyword search.[275] When it became apparent that the European information exchange was targeted in the program, the EU responded by relaxing the use, manufacture, sales and export of cryptography. As a result, in January 2000, the US export constraints based on the strength of cryptography were also abandoned.[276]

5.3.2   CALEA and Voice over IP (VoIP)

The US decision to liberate its export laws regarding encryption did not stop the FBI from pursuing their interests to be able to control communications. Already in 1992, the FBI had tried to incorporate all new techniques in its Digital Telephony Bill. Eventually the law enforcement pressure for wiretapping resulted in the CALEA that applied only to the telecommunications carriers, a defeat that lead to the fierce lobby for the use of key escrowed encryption techniques backed by federal buying power (Clipper Chip) and export controls. When the economic reality forced the US to loosen its export controls the Internet had developed into a global medium with many unforeseen applications. The next inevitable FBI target was VoIP, the Internet's answer to traditional telephone communication.

In 2004 the FBI in conjunction with the Department of Justice and the Drug Enforcement Administration petitioned the Federal Communications Commission (FCC) in order for the CALEA also to cover VoIP, the Internet telephony system

---

[274] OECD Guidelines for Cryptography Policy (1997).
[275] See, Woolsey, J., 2000a; 2000b.
[276] Revised U.S. Encryption Export Control Regulations (2000).

that uses packet switching techniques instead of circuit-switching technology (see also Chapter 3). The reason they gave was that the Internet was already undermining the FBI's surveillance capacities.[277] In august 2005, the FCC announced that broadband providers of VoIP must comply with CALEA,[278] making it illegal for US citizens to use VoIP services unless the software complies with CALEA requirements.

VoIP is a general term for a variety of competing Internet applications. VoIP services use a variety of techniques, many of them still being under continuous reconstruction. Currently, CALEA applies to two particular types of VoIP services: (1) services using their own lines between end user and the Internet, and (2) interconnected providers offering services between end users on the telephone network and VoIP services.[279] These VoIP services show a striking resemblance to traditional carriers in their connection with controllable lines or links. Still it is a victory for the FBI in that the US has extended its reach to applications that traditionally were considered information services. This development raises the question to what extent these interception services will be expanded to other information services on the Internet. Particularly in the light of the USA PATRIOT[280] Act, brought to Congress within two weeks after 9/11 and lowering the FISA requirements for legal wiretapping, it only seems one step from trying to gain control over other Internet communications. This however, requires something stronger than national legislation.

In addition to the two aforementioned types of VoIP services, there are types of VoIP providers that use software to be downloaded by the user to establish the connection and transfer the data, independently from the ISPs. These types of VoIP services resemble the archetypical Internet application in terms of control. These services are extremely decentralized in nature and hardly allow to be controlled centrally. Skype is perhaps the most well known exponent of this type of VoIP providers.

The problem of intercepting VoIP services running over the Internet network poses the problems from an interception point of view because the Internet's global nature prevents a central control of the handling and processing of information, and its packet-switching technique significantly complicates interception because different packets can take different paths over the Internet as Chapter 3 has pointed out. Since VoIP uses different sets of protocols for call-signaling information (necessary for setting up the connection in a telephone network), and for the actual exchange of information over the network, possible interception activities are complicated even further because both data clusters can be handled differently over different network paths.[281] The effect is that one might intercept information with-

---

[277] OpenNet Initiative 2005, Para. 19.
[278] FCC, 2005a.
[279] FCC, 2005d.
[280] USA Patriot Act (2001).
[281] Hancock, E., 2007, p. 192.

out knowing where it is coming from or intercept the connection without intercepting the information. The effect is incomplete information and at most retrieval of IP address n exchanging VoIP signaling information to IP address m. The mobility of Internet users and the use of fake identities again increase the problem. In addition, when, as Skype, the supplier of the service, does not fall within the jurisdiction of the country that wants to regulate the services[282] it will become factually impossible to control the communications flows transmitted in this way.

US residents can easily use Skype and related VoIP services that fall outside US's jurisdiction and do not have to comply with CALEA requirements. Consequently, the CALEA requirements would significantly hamper the ability of US competitors to compete, simply because, first, making VoIP services CALEA-ready is costly and these costs will have to be passed on to the consumers. In addition, it will affect the innovative power of US companies because CALEA requirements might hamper them in the creation of new products. Interestingly, for the Skype type of VoIP to be compatible with the CALEA legislation, the protocols used at the core of the Internet have to be adjusted to a significant extent.[283] In effect, this would violate Internet's end-to-end design principle and hence threaten the innovation that has contributed so much to the Internet's development and success.[284]

In conclusion, then, the examples showed in Section 5.3 show that Lessig's plea for more governmental direction in the development of standards is based on an overly optimistic belief in the power of the constitution to preserve information and communication liberties against executive branch pressures. Within public governance there is always a tension between security and protection objectives, and individual liberties like privacy concerns. The US attempts to influence communications standard setting suggest that States are prone to favor control over individual liberties in balancing out the interests of their citizens, particularly when information and communication freedoms are concerned. The reactions to the 9/11 attacks also show how fragile this balance is. The first conclusion of this section, then, is that the State is not necessarily the best candidate for guaranteeing individual liberties on the Internet. The second conclusion of this section is that the VoIP example confirms the thesis outlined in Chapter 3 that the interdependence imposing nature of the Internet architecture prevents individual States from controlling information flows and the handling and processing of information unilaterally. The last conclusion that can be drawn from this section is that the pressure for control over individual liberties is still significant on the side of the US government. It is likely to include the interception of Internet traffic in due course if the US gets its way. This last observation again confirms the first conclusion that States are unlikely to be the right vehicles for guaranteeing individual liberties on the Internet.

---

[282] Skype Technologies S.A. is registered in Luxembourg, source <http://about.skype.com/>.
[283] Landau, S.E., 2006, p. 428ff.
[284] Ibid., p. 428.

5.4 STATE INTERESTS AND INTERNET STANDARDS

Internet standards have extensive implications for public policy as we have seen, but the technical architecture of the global Internet poses problems for national control. In the case of Skype-type VoIP services, the lack of persistent links with traditional means of control (lines) would even require adjustments to the core protocols of the Internet. Since the Internet is essentially a collection of standards, the natural locus for States to influence the development of these standards is, of course, where currently the standards are set for the future to come: within the Internet SSOs. The most important SSO on the Internet in this regard is the Internet Engineering Task Force (IETF).

The background paper to the WSIS (2005), a summit largely financed by the United Nations, identifies two major players in technical Internet standardization,[285] the International Telecommunications Union standards-setting branch, ITU-T and the IETF. The ITU-T has a broad perspective but cost-efficient accessibility to the Internet and the interoperability of next generation networks are currently high on the agenda. Another typical ITU-T area is the interoperability of the Internet and the telephone system, an operation concerned with matching the telephone number based PSTN (Public Switched Telephone Network) to the IP-based Internet. Despite the variety of issues that the ITU-T is concerned with, its Internet related standards primarily concern operations that are conceptually located at the edges of the network, focusing on accessibility and interoperability of novel or (as yet) incompatible networks and the existing Internet.

The IETF is considered to be the more important one of the two since it has defined most technical standards used by the Internet itself, establishing interconnectivity and interoperability between nodes and hosts.[286] Because the IETF sets standards for the core of the Internet and these standards determine the amount of freedom and control that can be established on the Internet, the standards that are set by the IETF appear the most interesting targets for States to push their interests. Its mission is defined as follows.

> 'The mission of the IETF is to produce high-quality, relevant technical and engineering documents that influence the way people design, use, and manage the Internet in such a way as to make the Internet work better. These documents include protocol standards, best current practices, and informational documents of various kinds.'[287]

Its standard setting activities can roughly be divided into three major fields. (1) Routing: ensuring the fast and effective transmission of information over the Internet, (2) International Domain Names (IDN): ensuring the use of non-western letters and signs next to the existing DNS based on the English language. (3) Secu-

---

[285] Mathiason, J. et al., 2004, p. 15.
[286] Ibid., p. 12.
[287] IETF RFC 3935.

rity: ensuring a safe transmission of information over the Internet, including identification and authentication tools ensuring adequate lookup mechanisms in order to
identify domain names and network numbers, and people. This section identifies
the State's interests at stake and shows that the interests of individual States vary.

5.4.1   Routing

Routing standards are designed to transmit data over different nodes of the Internet,
unchanged and preferably by the shortest route. The State interest governing routing standardization is rather general in nature, the overall aim being to establish an
effective information transmission. There are, however, particular issues in which
States may have diverging interests as the following examples illustrate. The first
example concerns quality of service (QoS) of real-time applications. A second sub-
area is the transition a new Internet protocol. As Chapter 3 has explained, the Internet
can be characterized by the end-to-end architecture and the packet switching transmission technique. One of the features of this technique is that every node in the
network systems waits until the complete packet has arrived before sending it to the
following node. Another feature is that different packets might be sent over different routes to their destination (as in certain VoIP applications). Unlike the telephone
system, the advantage of this technique is that one does not have to maintain an
open connection in order to communicate. The downside of the system is that real-
time applications, like telephony, video conferencing or on-line gaming require
rather much from a system in order to operate adequately.

The IETF develops standards establishing the QoS needed for real-time applications. States have different attitudes towards these standards. China, for example,
still has State-owned fixed-line telecom providers. Improving QoS standards for
real-time applications is not an important point on their agenda since on-line telephone services for example would decrease their income from the State-run network.[288] For the US on the other hand, QoS is of pivotal economic importance
since videoconferencing over the Internet, for example, can reduce travelling costs
for both politicians and businessman alike. Due to its private telecom industry, the
US, are not reluctant to participate actively in the development of increased QoS
standards. Of course, this example only shows the divergent interests of two different countries with the ultimate effect of one country inclined to support the development of a particular standard while another more inclined to delay its development.
Still, there is a difference in State interests regarding the development of new standards.

A second issue relevant to individual States is the introduction and transition to
a new IP system called Internet Protocol version 6 (IPv6).[289] The IP system, as

---

[288] The fact that China has actively blocked Internet users from using Skype's VoIP services seems
to confirm China's lack of interest in increased real-time QoS initiatives. See: Kewney, G., 2005.

[289] The specification for the IPv6 standard can be found in; IETF RFC 2464.

stated in Chapter 3, assigned one unique number to each unique host. The current IP system is based on the Internet Protocol version 4 (IPv4) standard.[290] When IPv4 was designed in 1981, the current success of the Internet systems could not possibly be envisioned. The IPv4 standard only allows for a limited number of IP addresses to be assigned and particularly the recent rise in Internet connections in Russia and China has increased the demand for IP addresses to such an extent as to exhaust the IPv4 addresses in due course. IPv6 is supposed to solve this problem since it allows for more IP addresses to be distributed. For countries like Russia and China, the development of secure IPv6 addresses is currently an important issue since the vast amount of those addresses will be assigned to those countries. The US on the other hand is less interested in this development because its domestic market is well equipped with (a vast amount of) IPv4 addresses. Whereas due to network effects of an expanding Internet, the US will of course benefit from additional hosts on the Internet, the US incentive to contribute to the development of IPv6 is significantly less than the incentives of Russia and China in order to develop this standard.

5.4.2   International Domain Names

The second area of State concern is in the field of International Domain Names. Due to its American heritage, the DNS was designed to consist only of ASCII (American Standard Code for Information Interchange) codes, consisting of strings of letters and signs based on the English alphabet. The global use of the Internet has called for a wider variety of domain names containing accents, like the one's frequently used in French and German and new signs like for example the ones used in Chinese and Arabic languages. The IETF has developed the IDNA (Internationalized Domain Names in Applications)[291] in order to solve this problem. Whereas strictly speaking this task belongs to the application layer of the Internet, it is, in effect a necessity in order to overcome a 'digital divide' of sorts between the 'haves' and 'have-nots' of an easy and natural way to navigate on the Internet. The State's interests are again obvious in this case. Users that prefer non-ASCII code are inclined to stimulate the development of robust standards in this area. Users employing languages that are ASCII code expressible have a diminished incentive to stimulate this development. The network effects that were applicable in the adaptation of IPv6 mentioned above apply less to the field of non-ASCII domain names since this would effectively erect a linguistic barrier between users of Internet. On top of this, the introduction of IDNs might even decrease traffic over ASCII code domains due to an increased competition and subsequently generate a decrease in revenue (either through advertisement & sales for private corporations and as a consequence decrease tax revenues for States) for the ASCII domain name holders.

---

[290] The current IP standard, IPv4, is defined in IETF RFC 791.
[291] IETF RFC 3490.

5.4.3   Security, authentication and identification

Also regarding security issues, the IETF plays an important role in developing standards that secure a safe transition of information. The development of the Security Extensions standard to the DNS (DNSSEC) is particularly interesting in this respect. DNSSEC aims to add security to most of the threats involving the DNS, like packet interception by third parties and name chaining, a form of cache poisoning which causes the right name to refer to the wrong host on the following query.[292] Security interests, and particularly interests related to authentication, are particularly important for on-line commerce. Whereas transactions in on-line environments can generally be traced back to particular computer equipment and software, the responsibility for the transactions must be attributable to individuals and organizations in the material world. In order to hold these latter parties legally accountable, an authentication system needs to be in place in order to identify the computer users. To date, there has not been a uniform authentication system in place in order to secure electronic commerce. The result is the spread of internationally operating criminal organizations evading national law enforcement efforts.[293] Here we immediately encounter one of the major State imperatives for developing authentication systems: to fight crime and to secure trust in order to maintain a stable information infrastructure (law and order).

For commercial purposes, it is important to know the identity of the other party involved in the transaction. One of the key problems here is the link from the computer to the user.[294] In order to prevent unwanted activities like phishing, pharming and spyware attacks[295] the IETF is developing the DNSSEC standard based on public key encryption (PKE) in order to obtain security. In order for DNSSEC to work properly, all domain names need authentication. Since the DNS is a hierarchical system (see Chapter 4), the parent server effectively operates as a trusted third party facilitating the exchange of information between the resolver looking up a particular domain name and the child zone. The hierarchy in the DNS authentication process means that ultimately the root also needs to be encrypted and authenticated.[296] Consequently the following questions arise, (1) who maintains the private

---

[292] A more detailed list of the problems that the DNSSEC standards are trying to solve can be found in: IETF RFC 3833.

[293] Cameron, K., 2005.

[294] Ibid., p. 10.

[295] *Phishing* is the is an attempt to criminally and fraudulently acquire sensitive information, such as usernames, passwords and credit card details, by masquerading as a trustworthy entity in an electronic communication. *Pharming* is an attack aimed to redirect one website's traffic to another, bogus website. This latter form of attack can be conducted either by changing the hosts file on a victim's computer or by exploitation of a vulnerability in DNS server software. *Spyware* concern the installation of computer software behind one's back on a personal computer to intercept or take partial control over the user's interaction with the computer, without the user's informed consent. Often it is used to send surfing behavior to an interested third party.

[296] Kuerbis, B. and Mueller, M., 2007, Appendix A: How Does DNSSEC Work?

key and signs the root zone file, and (2), perhaps more importantly, who is to decide whether the root will or will not be signed? Already the (State-based) battle for the private key has begun with the Department of Homeland Security (founded as an overall coordinator of homeland security after 9/11) expressing the wish to have the private key to sign the DNS root zone file put safely in the hands of the US.[297] This, in effect would enable the US authorities to track the DNSSEC all the way back to the servers that represent the name system's root zone on the Internet. In short, they would be able to identify every user generating traffic on the Internet. So from this perspective, there is a definite interest from States and these interests are competing, non-US residents are more prone to grant the key to a more neutral party.[298]

In addition to the controversy regarding key signing of the root zone file, there are other interesting issues affecting States. If the DNSSEC indeed makes it virtually impossible to intercept messages, change the content of the message or returning a 'denial of service' reply, countries like China would have problems monitoring the Internet content (the topic of Chapter 6 'Interdependence and Search Operator Censorship'). Other countries on the other hand, may find the authentication deployed in the DNSSEC the solution to many problems concerning the rise of Internet crime, and will use the information that is potentially available in the DNSSEC system in order to device laws to obtain this information in the national interest. Other States may be cautious towards this type of standards altogether since it runs the chance of being used to infringe privacy concerns. Again, different States have different interests regarding security standards.

To sum up, Section 5.4 identified the IETF as the Internet's most important SSO in terms of interconnectivity and interoperability (communication). In addition, Section 5.4 distinguished three major areas in IETF standard setting: routing, internationalization of domain names and security. In each of these areas, States (can) have different stakes, which makes global standard setting processes strategic targets for pursuing State specific interests.

5.5   STATE PARTICIPATION IN INTERNET STANDARD SETTING

The examples in the previous sections show that Internet standards raise public policy concerns that are likely to be addressed differently by different States.[299]

---

[297] Ermert, M. and Morris, C., 2007.

[298] Note that this debate, albeit similar in many respects is not identical to that of the case study handled in chapter four regarding ICANN and the US power over the root zone file. The availability of alternative root zone servers does solve the problem of ICANN against a possible deletion from the root zone file. The problem with the DNSSEC is more complicated since everyone needs to participate in order for it to work. In addition, the alternative of a parallel universe (DNS-wise), would divide the world into a secure network and an insecure 'shadow' network, causing problems of its own in addition to possible compatibility complications.

[299] For more information on this theme, see also: Morris, J. and Davidson, A., 2003. For developments related to privacy and standardization, see also: Diffie W. and Landau, S.E., 2007.

Since unilateral attempts to influence standard-setting processes are not very successful nationally due to the Internet's interdependency imposing nature, one would expect the individual States to pursue their interests within the room allowed by the institutional structure of the SSOs themselves. This section investigates this conjecture by looking at the institutional structure of the cluster of SSOs associated with the IETF and the way in which States participate in the standardization process itself.

5.5.1   Institutional setting

The IETF's root lies in the Internet Activities Board (IAB, 1983), the successor to the Internet Control and Configuration Board (ICCB, 1979), which was established to oversee the design and deployment of protocols within the connected network of computers that existed at the time. Soon after its foundation, the IAB managed to evolve into a full-fledged *de facto* standards organization dedicated to collect and ratify standards used within the Internet.[300] At this point, the network had just become 'de-militarized' and the National Science Foundation had just assumed funding the Internet project. The IAB was to coordinate the activities of various task forces, each of which focused on a specific architectural or protocol issue. In 1986, the IETF held its first meeting and a reorganization of the IAB simplified its structure with only two organizations left. The first organization, the Internet Research Task Force (IRTF) was an oversight organization devoted to research activities related to the TCP/IP protocol suite and the architecture of the Internet. The second organization, the IETF was to concentrate on short to medium-term engineering issues related to the Internet. Still the IETF was a US-government sponsored enterprise despite its informal organization. It was mainly a community of interested academics and technical researchers.

The Internet's commercialization and the subsequent demand for internationalization stimulated the National Science Foundation (NSF) to form the Internet Society (ISOC, 1992) since it realized the US would eventually withdraw its financial support. The ISOC was supposed to provide an international institutional home for the IETF and the Internet standard setting process, but more importantly, it was to provide a source for financial support.[301] The ISOC set out to obtain funding for the activities of the IAB and its sub organizations internationally. In order to reflect its new role as part of the ISOC, the Internet Activities Boards was renamed the Internet Architecture Board. The ISOC provides a legal and financial home for the IETF and IRTF, as they have historically been a part of the IAB.[302] Figure 10 depicts the IETF as embedded within ISOC and the IAB schematically.

---

[300] SSOs can be distinguished in *de facto* and *de jure* SSOs. *De jure* SSOs are legally/formally established by law. *De facto* SSOs are not formally established by law. Nevertheless they do provide standards in point of fact.

[301] Cerf, V., 1995.

[302] IETF RFC 3160.

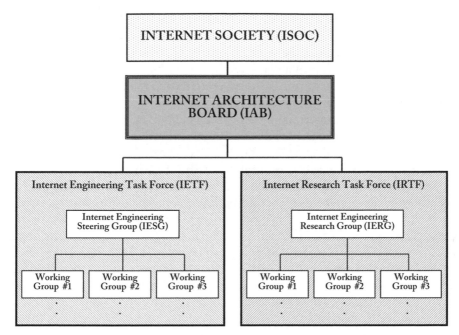

Figure 10. Internet Standards Organizations[303]

The IETF

At the bottom of Figure 10, depicting the cluster of IETF related organizations, we encounter two organizations, the IETF and its sister organization the IRTF. The IRTF is a rather small research oriented organization that overlooks the long-term aspects of the Internet and TCP/IP technologies. As such, its power is rather small and not appealing for States to pursue their interests. The IETF, on the other hand, is rather more influential and interesting from a State perspective. The IETF is divided into a number of working groups (WGs) responsible for developing standards and technologies in a particular area, such as routing, internationalized domain names, and security. Area directors serve on the Internet Engineering Steering Group (IESG) and manage each area in the Internet standards development process. From its inception, the IETF's structure has been rather informal and although it has become embedded in a more formal structure, the standard setting process has retained its informal nature.

The IETF is what the Internet Governance Project[304] characterizes as non-State (a term that speaks for itself), and informal. This latter term means that the organization is not incorporated in law. The process of standard setting within the IETF consists of a division of labor in working groups administrating the standardization

---

[303] Source: The TCP/IP Guide – version 3.0, available at <www.TCPIPGuide.com> (retrieved on December 31, 2009).

[304] Mathiason, J. et al., 2004, p. 15.

processes that are largely based on the input of volunteers. The standardization process is open to individuals independent of possible ISOC membership. Since the individual participants in the standard-setting processes are only judged on the technical merit and instrumental value in solving problems and not as representatives of corporations or governments there is hardly any room for individual States to pursue their idiosyncratic interests.

Also in cooperative undertakings States can hardly influence the process. The IETF cooperates with a variety of other SSOs of which the ITU is the most important one. As already explained the ITU is a State-based SSO working under the supervision of the UN. The ITU is a traditional SSO, which manages and maintains standards related to telecommunications. The reason for cooperation is, amongst others, that the developments in the telecommunications industry call for a conversion of the telephone number identification system towards a number identification system based on IP addressing. As a result, the ITU-T has been granted the opportunity by the IETF to work on the conversion of telephone to IP numbers (the ENUM project) and quality of service over IP networks. Similar to the influence States can exert though the IETF itself, the influence for individual States by means of the ITU-T is rather limited. Due to its Stately character, the ITU-T only approves recommendations if all member States agree, which hardly leaves any room for one State to pursue its interests unilaterally, particularly not in a cooperation with the IETF.

The IAB

The IAB manages the overall development of Internet standards. As ISOCs technical advisory group, it makes 'big picture' policy decisions related to how Internet technologies and structures should work. It ensures that various standardization efforts are coordinated and that they are consistent with overall development of the Internet. It is responsible for publishing Internet standards (also known as Requests for Comments or RFCs). It advises the ISOC, and oversees the IETF and IRTF; it also acts as an appeals body for complaints about the standardization activities performed by the IETF.[305] The IAB is responsible for approving appointments to the IESG from among the nominees submitted by the IETF nominating committee.[306] It sponsors the IRTF and it judges the IETF working groups on consistency within the architectural framework. The nature of its primary task, consistency of the architectural framework, does not make the IAB suitable for active State lobbying or active participation by stakeholders.

The ISOC

Although the ISOC, as Figure 10 illustrates, serves as a mother organization for the IETF and related bodies, it hardly influences the technical decisions that guide the

---

[305] IETF RFC 2850.
[306] IETF RFC 1602.

Internet standard setting processes. The ISOC basically has two tasks: first, relieving the people involved in the standard setting process from personal liability claims, and secondly, it provides the financial means for the SSOs to perform their tasks; amongst others, it sponsors the IETF's board consisting of 13 technical advisors.[307]

States can influence ISOC in two ways: through participation and funding. Participating in the ISOC is not an often-used route for States. The list of eighty organizational members mentions only four Stately organizations explicitly; the (US) Defense Information and Systems Agency, the UN based ITU, the Egyptian Ministry for Communications and Information Technology and the Swiss Federal Office for Communications.[308] The funding component is another option in order to stimulate the development of particular standards. The financial reports however show that only 2 percent of ISOCs revenues have imposed restrictions on the use of the donations in order to stimulate particular types of standardization development.[309] This figure confirms IETF RFC3160 that describes the ISOC as a hands-off organization that only provides the much needed funding and legal insurance of the people involved in the standard setting process.[310] From this is can be concluded that the ISOC is not useful to individual States to advance their particular interests.

5.5.2 Procedures and principles

If there is one characteristic feature of the IETF in comparison to the classic international SSOs it is its informal character, a feature that contrasts sharply with the organizational structure of the traditional SSOs like the ISO, IEC and ITU-T.[311] Where these latter organizations primarily develop their standards on the input of their most influential members, usually related to nations and governments, the IETF thrives on individual participation in its standardization process. Its informal make up already characteristic to the early standard setting processes in the sixties remained largely the same after the establishment of ISOC. In fact, establishment of ISOC can be seen as a successful attempt of self-privatization in order to preserve the informal features of the IETF's standard setting process.[312]

Proposals for Internet standards begin the process as a draft by participants, edited according IETF specifications. By submitting a proposal as an Internet Draft,[313] the drafter of the proposal effectively puts the proposals faith in the hands of the Internet community. The IETF publishes the proposal in order to ask the interested users for feedback (RFC procedure), and if considered useful enough,

---

[307] A list of the names of the members is available at <www.iab.org/about/members.html>.

[308] The full list of ISOC's organizational members is available at <www.isoc.org/orgs/members.php>.

[309] Within 2007 the restricted revenue was under USD 9000 on USD 13,847,000 total revenue; ISOC, 2007.

[310] IETF RFC 3160.

[311] See also: Section 5.2.3 'Standard setting on the Internet'.

[312] Mueller, M., 2002, p. 95.

[313] IETF RFC 2026.

the Draft is presented to the IESG for consideration. After having given its stamp of approval, the IESG will hand it back to the IETF for another round of comments after which it gets published as a Proposed Standard. After six months, the Proposed Standard is published as a Draft Standard if there are minimally two implementations of the standard available and there are no significant objections. After two years and additional review by the IESG it can become an Internet Standard.

The strength of the procedure is its open structure in which anyone can propose and improve drafts. This makes the procedure highly decentralized and hence difficult to influence. The proposals are subsequently judged on their technical merit independently from the drafter's background. The non-proprietary nature of the Internet Drafts makes that proposals are subject to change that can be rather substantial during the standardization process. This poses risks for States proposing controversial standards in terms of success and reputation. The lack of formal membership relations, voting procedures and the fact that the Internet, rather than frequent gatherings, is the prime means for exchanging ideas, makes lobbying by corporate, State or other types of organizations effectively impossible. Illustrative in this regard is the discussion that was aroused at the end of 1999 when the IETF addressed the question whether it should take action to allow wiretapping capabilities onto the Internet. Despite the efforts of public policy organizations such as the Center for Democracy and Technology and the American Civil Liberties Union, the main discussion on the topic took place between members of the IETF community.[314] Based on technical principles the outcome of the discussion was negative. In addition to hampering lobbying activities, its decentralized informal structure is advantageous in that it allows for quick decision making, sometimes necessary in order to respond to the fast changing Internet environment.

The internationalization of the Internet and the subsequent privatization of the standard-setting procedures did improve the transparency of the standard setting process as ISOCs statement of principles stressing the use of open standards in an open environment shows.[315] Open standards are standards that can be used by everyone and an open environment indicates a large degree of transparency, a commitment also the IAB has picked up.[316] The IETF embraces openness and technical competence as participation criteria[317] and is only open to participants acting as individuals, not as formal representatives of corporations, governments or organizations. The lack of formal membership relations, voting procedures and scarce physical meetings also hampers the State's active lobbying possibilities considerably.[318]

---

[314] The discussion on wiretapping can be found in the IETF's archives at <www.ietf.org/mail-archive/web/raven/current/maillist.html>, the final conclusion is available as; IETF RFC 2804.

[315] The ISOCs mission and principles at their website available at <www.isoc.org/isoc/mission/principles/> (retrieved on December 31, 2009).

[316] IETF RFC 2850.

[317] IETF RFC 3925.

[318] In contrast, the ITU is increasingly being criticized by the lack of transparency and openness in their standard setting processes, particularly excluding non-State interest groups as independent scholars increasingly point out. See for example, Ermert M., 2008.

5.5.3   Standard setting in action: IPv6 and privacy

Although the previous sections showed that it is hard to influence the standard setting process as individual States, this is not to say, that there are no possibilities to influence the setting of global standards. Illustrative in this regard is the development of IPv6. Designed to overcome the shortage in IPv4 addresses, IPv6 has a much larger address space. It also differs in other respects from the IPv4 standard. For the purposes of this inquiry, the link created by IPv6 between the IP address on the one hand and the communication hardware is particularly interesting.

Under IPv4, the IP address was typically not associated with a particular machine or user. Hence, the standard allows for a reasonable amount of anonymity and privacy. Under the IPv6 standard, however, it is in many cases possible to establish a user's address through the unique Medium Access Control (MAC) address[319] embedded in the user's Ethernet network card. The Ethernet network cards are part of a computer's hardware and are not easily changeable. Whereas the IPv6's use of the MAC address as a unique identifier was presented as a clever device for guaranteeing IP address uniqueness in RFC 2464,[320] it does have some severe privacy implications. By tying an IP address to a unique identifier it is much easier to monitor the users' on-line behavior, particularly since it allows to determine the location of a computer independent from the connection point at which the user accesses the Internet. This poses significant consequences for the privacy and anonymity of the Internet user. Whereas it is not clear whether the privacy implications were deliberately designed or even widely understood by its designers, it is striking that RFC2464 describing the standard, was proposed by a government employee working for Fermi National Accelerator Laboratory (Fermilab), a US Department of Energy national laboratory specializing in high-energy particle physics.[321] The publication of the proposal triggered a heated discussion by technical experts and civil society groups. The issue was finally resolved with the publication of an optional addressing scheme for IPv6 adding privacy protecting alternatives while using MAC addresses (IETF RFC 3041). As expected, this solution was not the work of State representatives or civil servants. Its drafters had corporate backgrounds working for IBM and Microsoft.[322]

5.6   CONCLUSION

This chapter set out to identify the effects of global standard setting on constitutional governance by exploring the changing role of the State in the light of its

---

[319] More information on MAC hardware address can be found at <www.erg.abdn.ac.uk/users/gorry/course/lan-pages/mac-vendor-codes.html>.

[320] IETF RFC 2464.

[321] Ibid.

[322] See, IETF RFC 3041.

traditional standard setting powers and responsibilities. Several conclusions can be drawn from this case study.

(1) It confirms the thesis developed in Chapter 3 that the Internet poses significant problems for traditional means of national control.

The Internet architecture hinders the central regulation of the processing and handling of information to a significant extent because it allows for a development of applications independent from networks and network owners. The discussion about the VoIP architectures showed that as soon as VoIP services are linked to traditional line services, by ownership of the network or by linking to traditional services, they do not significantly differ from traditional telephone networks. As soon however as the resemblance breaks down the story becomes considerably more complicated in terms of control. When internet applications are based on downloadable software that runs on the end user's computers in an environment that allows for relatively great mobility (like the VoIP services that Skype provides), it is virtually impossible to control the information to the degree traditional wiretapping is designed to do.

(2) The Internet as transnational interdependence imposing communication infrastructure stimulates private initiative and functional organization as alternative to territorially organized governance.

Similar to DNS governance outlined in Chapter 4, the most important Internet SSO dealing with interoperability and interconnection, the IETF, is also private in nature. It has evolved from a largely government run organization dealing with the collection and publication of standards that were already used to form computer networks, to a private organization involved with the development of global Internet standards. The self-privatization by establishing ISOC effectuated the internationalization of the global standard setting process, independent from the US, whilst maintaining its informal structure. Thus, similar to the ICANN example discussed in the previous chapter, the Internet's interdependency imposing nature combined with its global reach stimulates the development of private initiative on the Internet. The difference between the DNS and global Internet standard setting is that ICANN's privatization was a US government decision. The internationalization of the Internet standard setting process was achieved by self-privatization of the IETF 'Dons'. Both cases show that the internationalization and privatization worked very well for the operations in question (DNS management and Internet standardization) which have become more open and transparent in the process.

(3) Unlike Lessig's dream, the State is not necessarily the best candidate for promoting freedom in terms of innovation and individual liberty in global communications infrastructures.

Lessig's 'code is law' thesis is a very instructive metaphor for clarifying the way in which technical architectures (and governmental policies) determine social life. With the technical architecture being largely developed outside the scope of the Constitution, Lessig is concerned about the future Internet, particularly in terms of liberty. The exposition of the way in which US law enforcement agencies have been shaping public policy by influencing the standards used in the communications infrastructure, shows a clear bias towards more control at the cost of the individual liberties the digitization of society promised in terms of privacy and innovation. This continued bias disqualifies the State, despite its constitutional commitments, as the great advocate of individual liberties for global standard setting purposes on the Internet.

(4) The private, informal and decentralized nature of the IETF and associated SSOs make them better equipped than States to guard individual liberties in an interdependent context.

The decentralized standard setting process, using the Internet rather than physical meetings, encourages the global deliberative process more than State-based summits and intergovernmental organizations ever could. These characteristics enhances the a-political nature of the process because the standards proposed are introduced by individuals, and are solely being judged on their functional merit. They are not negotiable on the grounds of territorial or other interests. The elimination of States as representatives of groups of people purifies the process conducted in the public interest. Since States are more inclined to favor control over individual liberties than individuals do, the de-politicization of the standard-setting processes strengthens the maintenance of individual liberties. It also prevents States or powerful corporations from blocking the development of particular innovations.

The Internet's decentralized nature and absence of physical power centre also prevents active lobbying groups from gaining too much power or for politics to interfere in the standard setting process. In addition, the informal way of organization allows for flexibility and easy access for interested parties. Following the DNS case study, this inquiry shows that the transnational interdependence created by the Internet, empowers the individual. In the IPv6 case, private initiative allowed the creation of privacy enhancing standards related to the IPv6 implementation. It is unlikely that traditional State-centered SSOs would have encouraged the development of this type of standard in this way.

(5) In general, this case study shows that the Internet's transnational interdependence-imposing architecture has given rise to private initiatives taking over traditional State responsibilities based on functional rather than territorial grounds.

As in the former case study, these findings largely disqualify the State as the sole protector of traditional constitutional responsibilities. In addition, the interdependence-imposing nature of the Internet stimulates the development of (State-)neutral and open policy standards. Both sets of principles incorporated by the IEFT and ISOC confirm this conclusion. The specific wishes of organizations like the FBI are specifically countered referring to technical principles. In addition, the Internet has also encouraged the development of standardization processes open to all interested parties and with an unprecedented level of transparency regarding the standardization processes and decision making.

Chapter 6
INTERDEPENDENCE AND SEARCH OPERATOR CENSORSHIP

Although the nature of the Internet forecloses national control to a degree, it also provides opportunities for pursuing national interests abroad. In fact, the Internet has gradually become a battleground for competing ideologies. One problem from a US point of view is China's censorship regime. Whereas China's economic reform program demands a free flow of information,[323] its commitment to the Communist Party China (CPC) seems to require the opposite.[324] China's information policies also affect foreign parties. Whereas its liberal economic policy has opened up the Chinese market to foreign businesses, its political commitment to the CPC has induced foreign businesses, including US corporations, to engage in Internet censorship. Since these latter activities run counter to fundamental US values, they are a thorn in the flesh of the US government.

The Global Online Freedom Act (GOFA),[325] a US bill specifically designed to fight foreign censorship activities on the Internet, addresses the conduct of US corporations under censorship regimes. Since search operators are pivotal players in the dissemination of Internet content, this exposition takes Google's censorship activities in China as a case in point and shows why the GOFA, designed to fight this conduct, does more harm than good in this respect.

Due to the intimate connection between information access and barriers to trade, economic and political objectives largely coincide on the Internet. This chapter shows the disadvantages of a rights-based approach, as proposed in the GOFA, and explores the possibilities of an economic approach based on antitrust law. It concludes that although this route could offer a promising and more effective way to fight censorship activities abroad, it requires a shift in economic policy the US is not yet ready to endorse.

6.1   INTRODUCTION

The previous two chapters focused on the influence of individual States on processes that are privately coordinated by global organizations. Whereas these chap-

---

[323] Cabral, L.M.B., 2000.

[324] Opennet Initiative, 2005.

[325] Global Online Freedom Act 2009 (2009) HR 2271, previously introduced as HR 275 (2007).

R.W. Rijgersberg, The State of Interdependence
© *2010, T·M·C·ASSER PRESS, The Hague, and the author*

ters did touch upon the way in which the US attempts to influence these processes by implementing laws aimed at regulating individual conduct, their main emphasis was institutional in nature. Both Chapters 4 and 5 focused on the extent in which individual States, lacking national means to influence these processes, are able to promote their citizen's interests within the institutional make-up of the global organizations in question. In contrast, this chapter investigates the way in which States attempt to promote their values globally by regulating private actors. The case study under investigation focuses on the way in which States attempt to use information services providers to actively promote their values. Google's[326] operations in China form the starting point of the investigation because, first, Google's situation in China is a good illustration of the thesis that States increasingly view the Internet as a new realm for promoting national values. Secondly, it is a timely topic since Google's censorship practices have recently generated fierce debates, in US Congress, in academic circles and in the media.

States have a tradition of using information services to promote their values both domestically and abroad. The Internet opens up new avenues for doing so. Search operators are particularly interesting in this respect since they have become indispensable tools for making Internet content available. The use of search engines has become so important to the average user that existence on the Internet has become virtually synonymous to search operator indexation. Without search engines most Internet content would be effectively unavailable. Hence, the first reason this chapter focuses on search operator censorship is that search operators are indispensable tools for finding one's way on the Internet. They have become the prime windows through which to view Internet content. Consequently, this has made them important tools for advancing information policies, both nationally and abroad. The second reason why search operator censorship is interesting in the light of this inquiry is because a free flow of information touches the heart of the modern State in at least two respects. First, a free flow of information forms a prerequisite for a well-functioning liberal democracy in terms of democratic deliberation, and secondly, it forms a critical factor in adequately allocating the means of production in market economies as will be explained in the next sections.

6.2   The Significance and Workings of Search Operators

In order to understand the relationship between the State, censorship practices and search operators, it is useful to get to grips with the operations and role of search operators on the Internet. In the early days of the Internet, navigation consisted primarily in guessing the name of the webpage or a related webpage followed by one of the TLDs like *.edu, .org,* or *.com* or by clicking on the hyperlinks embedded in web pages of the World Wide Web. The increased availability of information,

---

[326] Google is the most successful Search Operator on the Internet, see <www.google.com>.

however, soon led to a call for more sophisticated alternatives to the DNS for finding information and resources on the Internet. Traditional library techniques were
of no avail here since the art of finding and accessing content on the Internet differs
from the traditional non-digital, non-networked environments in important ways.[327]
First, the information and resources vary significantly in kind[328] and purpose[329]
creating additional challenges to intermediaries labeling and indexing the information in order to create searchable databases. Secondly, the lack of persistence of
information on the Internet requires regular checks on the availability of information and resources. These features, added to the sheer quantity of content, effectively disqualify human intermediaries as reliable assistants in finding specific
information on the Internet. General-purpose search operators conducting automated
Internet navigation are specifically designed to address these types of challenges by
systematically giving prominence to some sites at the expense of others.[330]

6.2.1   Basic tasks

The operations of a search operator consist of three basic tasks; collecting web
content, indexing the content found and matching user queries to the indexed content. Software robots called spiders or crawlers conduct the first search operator
task: collecting web content. These search programs traverse the Internet systematically using preset criteria defined by the search operator. The collected information is subsequently dumped in a central depository, which, in combination with the
predefined search strategy of the spider, forms the basis for allocating the results of
the end-user queries. The predefined search strategy of the spiders is one of the
search operator's distinguishing features since it determines the coverage and depth
of the content collection process. In addition, the frequency by which a spider re-
visits a webpage can contribute to a search operator's success. The freshness of the
indexation decreases the risk of users receiving search results referring to outdated
or empty pages.

The second task is the indexation of content. The search operator creates indices
from the depository in which the spider drops the retrieved content. It simply lists
the addresses of all collected web pages for a given word or a combination of words.
In addition, search operators can also record additional information like the size of
the document of the location of the word (in the header or body of the text). The
degree in which the search operator creates indices of the collected content contrib-

---

[327] The technical exposition of the following paragraphs is largely based on the following exposition; NRC, 2005, p. 295ff.

[328] The kind of information displayed on the Internet varies from text documents, podcasts, pictures and video, etc. In addition, these different types of information are in turn divided into a wider
variety of formats, i.e., html, pdf, jpeg, etc.

[329] The purpose of the information displayed on the Internet ranges from public to commercial and
from informative to entertainment and advertisements, all in all a vast expansion of what is generally
held in a traditional library environment.

[330] Introna, L.D. and Nissenbaum, H., 2000.

utes to the performance of the search operators in that it forms the raw material for matching the collected content with the user's query.

The basis for performing the third function of the search operator, matching the query with the indexed results, seems to be relatively straightforward. By typing, for example, 'prime' and 'numbers' in the toolbar, the search operator will simply retrieve all indexed web pages containing (or labeled in the case of video performances, for example) both strings. Search operator Google for example turns out over 49 million results and search operator Yahoo! turns out even over 76 million results.[331] Since the results obtained from general-purpose search operators are too extensive for inspecting each result individually in order to find the required information, it is clear that the art of finding and accessing specific information does not lie in the quantity of the displayed results. The key to the art of finding information on the Internet then lies in the ordering of the results.

The quality of the response largely depends on the references displayed on the first page displaying the results. There are several ways of doing this.[332] One of the key features of Google's celebrated PageRank™ algorithm is its use of the link structure of the web in order to determine the relevance of the indexed content.[333] The crux to the matter is that every link or reference from page A to page B counts as a 'vote' by A for B and hence says something about the quality of the content since apparently A wants to associate itself with web page B. In this sense, a link is a quality 'vote' for, in this case, B. The algorithm also distinguishes between votes. A vote from page X is given higher weight if the web site of page X itself is also frequently referred to. In sum, PageRank™ combines the intrinsic value of the indexed web page, based on the indexing of words and labels, with the popular 'vote' of links or references. The unique way in which Google has managed to do this has contributed much to its success.[334]

6.2.2   Gateway function

Search operators are pivotal players on the Internet. The exposition above mainly emphasized the search operator in its role as platform for end users wanting to obtain information. Search operators, however, also play another vital role on the Internet, that of platform for content suppliers. Similar to organizations handling the allocations of domain names, search operators serve as intermediaries between two worlds, a role Van Eijk adequately described as a two-directional gateway.[335]

---

[331] This experience was conducted on December 31st, 2009 by the author.

[332] An overview of ranking determinants can, for example, be found in: Van Eijk, N., 2006. Whereas Van Eijk's objective is to focus in the various ways in which search results can be manipulated, the aim of the exposition here is simply to sketch the main features of Google's ranking system in order to show the fairly simple ways in which these techniques can be employed to conduct censorship.

[333] For the original and more elaborated exposition of the PageRank™ algorithm, see, Brin, S. and Page, L., 1998.

[334] Heft, M., 2007.

[335] Van Eijk, N., 2006.

Search operators both determine what information the consumer *can* find and what information the consumer ultimately *will* find. The ability to determine the supply side of information dissemination (to index or not to index information) and simultaneously being able to control the demand side of information provision (by ranking the results) makes search operators rather powerful players on the Internet. This position increases when the search operator has obtained a significant market share. Within China, Google is currently the second largest search operator with just under 30 percent market share.[336] A 2007 report showed Google to be the second-choice search operator for 75 percent of all Chinese users using more than one search operator.[337]

The search operator's ability to control the demand and supply of Internet content has made them into powerful actors on the Internet. For business they have become increasingly interesting for advertisement and marketing purposes, for states they form valuable tools for pursuing their information policies. For example, since France prohibits the publication of Nazi propaganda on the Internet, Google filters this type of content from the search results.[338] In Germany, where the publication of holocaust denials is prohibited, Google also deletes results in order to comply with German law.[339]

6.3   CHINA'S INFORMATION POLICIES

Although search operators are rather cooperative in blocking content in order to comply with local regulations, the Chinese attempts to influence search operators in censoring web content however, take on rather different proportions. China is not only the largest country in terms of Internet connections,[340] but is also considered the most sophisticated regime in terms of Internet filtering.[341]

An estimated force of 30.000 State officials monitors and controls the dissemination and display of Internet content. The estimated ratio of one controller for

---

[336] China Technews Staff, 2009. This figure has been relatively stable, see for example, Lu, P., 2008.

[337] CNNIC, 2007.

[338] *LOI Gayssot*, 1990.

[339] German Criminal Code (1998), Section 130(3), (4).

[340] Bardoza, D., 2008.

[341] See for example, OpenNet Initiative, 2005. The OpenNet Initiative is a collaborative partnership of four leading academic institutions. Its aim is to investigate, expose and analyze Internet filtering and surveillance practices in a credible and non-partisan fashion. As their website shows, the initiative intends to uncover the potential pitfalls and unintended consequences of these practices, and thus help to inform better public policy and advocacy work in this area. See also: Human Rights Watch, 2006. There is an abundance of information available on China's Internet censorship practices on the Internet. For a more extended list of references see the web site of Amnesty International devoted to Censorship in China, available at <www.amnestyusa.org/business-and-human-rights/internet-censorship/page.do?id=1101572&n1=3&n2=26&n3=1035>.

every 37.000 users is unmatched by any other regime in the world.[342] China's Internet network is connected to the global (foreign) Internet by only three large pipelines. Since the Chinese government heavily monitors and censors the information passing through these pipelines, it causes delays in the international Internet traffic and unreliable access to foreign content. Within the literature, this information barrier is known as 'China's great firewall'.[343] In addition to this barrier, the Chinese government also employs other devices to control Internet content. It maintains an extensive patchwork of national laws directed at Internet Service Providers (ISPs), Internet Content Providers (ICPs), Internet Café's and individual Internet users in order to monitor and control the transmission and access to certain types of information.[344]

China's information policies and censorship practices affect foreign business in a variety of ways. The Great Firewall is a prime censorship tool for the Chinese government in order to keep foreign content from reaching the Chinese citizen. It limits access to information and services in two ways. First, keyword filtering at the borders disables access to particular foreign information on the Internet.[345] Secondly, the keyword inspection of content at the borders significantly slows down the information exchange between China and the rest of the world. Consequently, this practice discourages international Internet traffic.[346] China's patchwork of laws and regulations forces corporations to comply with censorship requirements *within* China.

For Google, the delays in obtaining foreign Internet content caused by the Great Firewall led to the establishment of its Chinese business (Google.cn) within China, which included placing its servers, containing the indexed material and its ordering algorithm, on Chinese soil.[347] In the context of Google's operations in China, the patchwork of laws and regulations results in an amended set of search results that, because Google itself composes these results, makes Google an active accomplice to the Chinese censorship practices. In order to promote fundamental US values and fight censorship activities by US corporations operating abroad the Global Online Freedom Act was introduced to Congress.

6.4   THE GLOBAL ONLINE FREEDOM ACT

The Global Online Freedom Act, first introduced to Congress in 2006 by Senator Smith, is supposed to be the US answer to the censorship related activities con-

---

[342] French, H., 2005. French quotes as much as 50.000 public officials involved with the Internet censorship program though the number is widely contested. See for example, Villeneuve, N., 2005.

[343] See for example, Clayton, R., et al., 2006.

[344] OpenNet Initiative, 2006; Villenueve, N., 2006.

[345] See again; Clayton, R. et al., 2006. Note that despite the fact that the firewall might be circumvented in several ways, like for instance by proxy servers, at the end of the day, the last station to pass before the information reaches the end user is the ISP. This ISP is legally obliged to monitor content and is liable for the content it passes on. Hence, circumventing the Great Firewall itself is not enough to exchange sensitive information safely.

[346] See, OpenNet Initiative, 2006.

[347] See, Schage, E., 2006.

ducted by US corporations cooperating with or operating under foreign censorship regimes. The bill is particularly interesting since it sets out to use US corporations to actively promote the US ideals abroad. Although the bill has not yet been approved by congress and is fiercely opposed by the industry, the Bush administration has already implemented key parts of the bill. The Department of State has launched an Internet Freedom Task Force[348] and the US human rights country reports already include specific sections on the level of Internet freedom enjoyed.[349] In Europe, the idea of actively promoting Western values has also caught on. The Dutch EU politician Jules Maaten is currently preparing a EU version of the bill.[350] The GOFA is a good example of one of the likely consequences of globalization; an increased tendency for States to extend their legislative frameworks to export values abroad using private actors. The GOFA tries to achieve this by incorporating foreign policy objectives into the national legal frameworks designed to regulating private conduct.

6.4.1   General outline and effects

The GOFA aims (1) to deter US corporations from cooperating with repressive censorship regimes, and (2) to institutionalize the active promotion of US values abroad. It expresses the US commitment to use all appropriate instruments of US influence to promote the freedom of information for all people,[351] particularly in battling political censorship by US corporations in Internet restricting States. The bill furthermore expresses the sense of Congress that the President should actively promote Internet freedom internationally. It also explicitly states that US-business conduct restricting on-line access to US sponsored content like *Voice of America* and *Radio Free Asia*, etc., counters US foreign policy interests and undercuts the efforts to promote freedom of information for all people.

The bill's substantial provisions establish an Office of Global Internet Freedom to take specified actions to strengthen global freedom of electronic information. It directs the US President to designate Internet-restricting countries and provides minimum standards for US corporations with respect to the protection of on-line freedom in foreign countries. In addition, the bill authorizes the establishment of export controls against Internet-restricting foreign countries and seeks to amend

---

[348] An outline of the Global Internet Freedom Taskforce is available at <www.america.gov/st/ freepress-english/2008/July/20080715094516xjsnommis0.3989832.html>.

[349] See, Department of State, 2008.

[350] Directive concerning the EU Global Online Freedom Act.

[351] This latter phrase, 'freedom of information' is also expressed by Article 19 Universal Declaration of Human Rights; Everyone has the right to freedom of opinion and expression: this right includes freedom to hold opinions without interference and to seek, receive and impart information and ideas through any media and regardless of frontiers. Note that both Section 101(2) and Section 102(1) allude to the possibilities within the legal framework. Section 101(2) GOFA emphasizes the promotion of the free flow of information by all appropriate means, but only mentions 'diplomacy, trade policy and export control' as examples. Global Online Freedom Act, (2009), Section 102(1), expresses the presidential role in obtaining bilateral and multilateral support for protecting Internet freedom.

the Foreign Assistance Act[352] to include, in reports relating to foreign economic and security assistance, assessments of the freedom of electronic information in each foreign country.

Whereas the bill proposes several countries to be labeled 'Internet-restricting' by the President, the congressional hearing on the Internet in China,[353] held the day before the introduction of the bill, clearly indicates that the bill is specifically designed to fight censorship involvement of US corporations in China. At the hearing, four corporations testified about their involvement in Chinese censorship activities. Cisco Systems testified regarding the delivery of routers used for Internet filtering. Microsoft testified regarding its closing down of a blog on MSN spaces at the request of the Chinese government and Yahoo! testified about their transfer of e-mail account data to the Chinese government leading to the imprisonment of a journalist. The fourth corporation to testify was Google. Whereas they all called upon the US government to help them dealing with censorship activities, Google's statement[354] is particularly interesting since it allows us to focus on its specific role in Internet censorship as a search operator. At the hearing, Google testified about its decision to explore the business opportunities in the Chinese market by means of Google.cn, and its accompanying decision to place its servers on Chinese soil. Google explained its deliberate choice to engage in censorship activities, blocking what it calls 'politically sensitive' content from its search results. For Google and other search operators, particularly the proposed 'minimum corporate standards' (Title II GOFA) are relevant. They have the following consequences for search operators.

Direct effects

The GOFA would significantly hamper Google's activities in China and would harm Chinese-US relations.

(1) The bar on content providers to locate personally identifiable information in 'Internet restricting countries' would force Google to locate its servers.[355] Currently Google's servers, containing IP addresses and possible other personally identifiable information, are located on Chinese soil. A forced relocation of these servers, outside China, would prevent Google for delivering a quality of service necessary to operate in China's competitive search operator market.

---

[352] Foreign Assistance Act (FAA), 22 USC 32 (1966). The FAA reorganized the US foreign assistance programs and separated military and non-military aid. It mandated the creation for an agency to administer economic assistance programs (US agency for International Development). The agency unified the economic and technical assistance operations of the International Cooperation Agency, the loan activities of the Development Loan Fund, the local currency functions of the Export-Import Bank, and the agricultural surplus distribution activities of the Food for Peace program of the US Department of Agriculture. In 2004 the Act was amended to incorporate the treatment of orphans and other vulnerable children.

[353] Congressional Hearing (2006) (retrieved on December 31, 2009).

[354] Schage, E., 2006, p. 65ff.

[355] Global Online Freedom Act (2009), Section 201.

(2) The bar on filtering US-supported content in its search results makes search operators effectively US government tools for propaganda, hampering US content providers to operate in foreign markets where these values are not shared.

(3) It's requirement to provide the Office for Global Internet Freedom with all the terms, parameters and lists provided by the Internet-restricting governments, as well as copies of data and content that content providers have removed, blocked or restricted on their behalf, turns content providers into US government instruments.

(4) The bar on US corporations to provide personally identifying user information to the officials of the host country except for 'legitimate law enforcement purposes',[356] creates an unworkable situation as in the context of the GOFA, the control, suppression, or punishment of peaceful expression of political or religious opinion, which is protected by Article 19 of the International Covenant on Civil and Political Rights, does not constitute a legitimate foreign law enforcement purpose.[357] What this effectively means is that the US is to decide what counts as legitimate in the case of Chinese laws.

In sum: Effect (1) would foreclose Google's Chinese activities flat out due the need to locate Google's servers on Chinese soil in order to remain its competitive edge. Conditions (2) and (3) would make Google effectively a US government tool rather than a private and free profit maximizing enterprise. Combined with the previous measures, effect (4) would significantly harm China-US relations because it would leave the US to decide about the legitimacy of national Chinese decisions.

Indirect effects

GOFA's most significant aspect, its extraterritorial application of national US law compelling US corporations to advance US values abroad[358] also has far ranging indirect effects increasing legal insecurity, challenging both China's sovereignty and UN authority to some degree.

(1) The yearly evaluation and presidential designation of 'Internet restricting' countries with the attached legal consequences discourages corporations to establish foreign subsidiaries. The bill, if enacted, reinforces legal uncertainty. Because the applicability of the law depends on annual reports, the applicable law for foreign search operators can vary each year, which hampers the exploration of new markets.

---

[356] The phrase 'Legitimate law enforcement purposes' means 'for purposes of enforcement, investigation, or prosecution by a foreign official based on a publicly promulgated law of reasonable specificity that proximately relates to the protection or promotion of the health, safety, or morals of the citizens of that jurisdiction'.

[357] Global Online Freedom Act (2009), 1 (b), Section 3.

[358] Ibid., Sections 102(2) and 205.

(2)   The extraterritorial application of human rights based legislation challenges the sovereignty of States. In the case of Google's activities in China, the bill challenges China's sovereign power to run its own internal affairs. The bill's primary aim is to deter US corporations like Google from affecting political censorship of US sponsored Internet content.[359] The bill justifies this by referring to both Article 19 of the Universal Declaration of Human Rights (UDHR) and Article 19 of the International Covenant for Civil and Political Rights (ICCPR).[360] Since the UDHR is not a binding document and the ICCPR is not ratified by China, a decision to control US search operators on this basis will inevitably be considered a direct infringement on China's sovereign power to conduct its internal affairs.[361]

(3)   The bill also challenges the authority of the UN to some extent. The (US-based) Office for Global Internet freedom is to develop global programs to combat State-initiated censorship, traditionally an important UN objective.[362] Whereas the UN might support the GOFA initiative to develop a voluntary business code of conduct for US businesses, the fact that it attempts to take the UN Global Compact Initiative's (GCI) into its own hands, challenges the authority of the UN to some extent.[363]

6.4.2   GOFA's inconsistency

At a more fundamental level, the GOFA violates the very values that it seeks to promote. A free flow of information touches the very heart of the constitutional democracy. From a political point of view, a free flow of information is necessary to provoke debate and hence forms a prerequisite to democratic decision making.

---

[359] Ibid., Section 3(12-14).

[360] Ibid. Section 2 'findings' (1), and Section 3(8) sub B. Art. 19 UNDHR: 'Everyone has the right to freedom of opinion and expression; this right includes freedom to hold opinions without interference and to seek, receive and impart information and ideas through any media and regardless of frontiers.' Art. 19 ICCPR: 'everyone shall have the right to hold opinions without interference. Everyone shall have the right to freedom of expression; this right shall include freedom to seek, receive and impart information and ideas of all kinds, regardless of frontiers, either orally, in writing or in print, in the form of art, or through any other media of his choice.' The exercise of these rights carry special duties and responsibilities which can be infringed by law and are necessary (a) for respect of the rights of reputations of others; (b) for the protection for national security or of public order (*ordre public*), or of public health or morals.

[361] See, United Nations Charter (1948), Art. 2(4). Moreover within US law, the Act of State Doctrine has been developed as a Common Law principle that prevents US courts from questioning the validity of a foreign country's sovereign acts within its own territory. US law however also recognizes a human rights exception. For an exposition see, Bazyler, M.J., 1986.

[362] For an exposition of the United Nation's mission see <www.un.org>.

[363] More information about the Global Compact Initiative (GCI) is available at <www.unglobal compact.org/AboutTheGC/index.html>. The Global Compact Initiative's principles aim to (1) support businesses and respect for internationally proclaimed human rights; and (2) to ensure business not to be complicit in human rights abuses, see <www.unglobalcompact.org/AboutTheGC/TheTenPrinciples/index.html>.

From an economic point of view, a free flow of information is a necessary tool for establishing an effective allocation of the means of production in a market economy, a second building block of the constitutional democracy. The GOFA, designed to export fundamental US values, challenges both commitments. First, the bill's focus on political rights seems to preclude serious considerations of economic interests resulting in the infringement of a free exchange of services and goods. Secondly, the bill diminishes the deliberative process in Congress by transferring the decisions regarding the applicability of the law to the executive, hence undermining the foundations of a well-functioning constitutional democracy based on a balance between the three branches of government. Thus, by trying to promote US values extraterritorially, the GOFA simultaneously violates these very interests from a domestic point of view. Promoting fundamental values abroad on the one hand, and violating fundamental values domestically on the other hand, is neither convincing nor effective as will be shown shortly.

Economic values

Although the bill acknowledges that information services have become a major US export industry, it undervalues the commercial role of search operators for the US economy and ignores the economic consequences of Internet censorship. The dissemination of information is of pivotal importance for businesses trying to enter the Chinese market. Not only is the provision of information regarding markets indispensable for new corporations, also the availability of foreign information services through search operator indexation and ordering serves an important role for Western businesses that try to establish or develop market share in China.

Preventing information providers like Google from setting up a business in China is a direct infringement of the free choice of private actors to conduct business abroad. More fundamentally, it is a violation of the private allocation of the means of production central to the market economic principles that form one of the cornerstones of the constitutional democracy outlined in Chapter 2. The long-term economic consequences of the GOFA can be far-reaching, because turning US technology and Internet companies into State tools for disseminating its political ideology is unlikely to advance US commerce in societies with other ideological backgrounds. In addition to effectively establishing a boycott of many US corporations operating in China, applied to search operators it deprives the Chinese consumers from a Western window to navigate over the Internet. This would deprive the Chinese consumer from a (relatively) reliable and effective tool for obtaining information. In addition, viewed from a US perspective, it would deprive US corporations from a low-barrier steppingstone for US corporations to enter the Chinese market. Particularly Google's strong position in the US market has earned them enough credit to serve as an effective and reliable platform for the promotion of US products and services in China.

With over 338 million Internet connections,[364] China is the largest Internet market in the world followed by the US with nearly 228 million connections.[365] However, whereas the Chinese percentage only covers approximately 25 percent of its population, the US figure represents 74 percent of its population. Consequently, the Chinese market for Internet related products offers abundant potential considering that 75 percent of its population is still not connected to the Internet. Furthermore, China's annual economic growth average is 9 percent per year and in 2008 its online sales increased by 128 percent compared to the year reaching 120 billion Yuan (USD 127.56 billion).[366] The Chinese market potential consisting of one-fifth of the world's population in addition to the relevance of the growing information services industry in the US, makes the Chinese market of the utmost importance to the US.

As the statistics of the US Bureau of East Asian and Pacific Affairs show,[367] China has become one of the most important markets for US exports: in 2008, US exports to China totaled USD 69 billion, more than triple the USD 19 billion when China joined the WTO in 2001. The United States is China's second-largest trading partner (after Canada).[368] US exports to China have been growing more rapidly than to any other market and the US imports from China grew from 11 percent (2008) to 16.8 percent in 2008, bringing the US trade deficit with China to more than USD 268 billion.[369]

With a US trade deficit with China of over USD 268 billion in 2008, a figure that has steadily been rising since 2000, the US simply cannot afford to ignore China as an emerging market. Google's current presence in China in this regard is an example for other US companies to enter a market of 1.3 billion potential customers. Moreover, as a search operator, Google also provides opportunities for US businesses to reach the Chinese customer through their availability in Google's search results and by providing a platform for advertising their products. Hence, Google can play a pioneering role for the US industry in promoting US business. As such, Google can serve as an important catalyst in the Chinese economic reform process helping China to open up to foreign business.

Democratic values

The second fundamental weakness in the GOFA is the way in which it uses the domestic legal framework to actively push national values abroad. As stated above, the GOFA aims to establish an Office for Global Internet Freedom.[370] This Office is designed to advice the President on the level of Internet freedom enjoyed in

---

[364] CNNIC, 2009.
[365] Nielsen/Netratings, 2009.
[366] See China Daily Staff, 2009.
[367] US Census Bureau, 2008.
[368] US Census Bureau, 2007.
[369] USDoS, 2009.
[370] General Online Freedom Act (2009), Section 104(a).

various countries. Based on the Office's advice, the President makes a decision to label or de-label a country as 'Internet restricting'.[371] If a country is labeled 'Internet restricting', the GOFA applies with all its consequences. Putting the bill into effect thus establishes a power transfer from the legislator to the hands of the executive since the President is to decide over the applicability of the law. The establishment of an Office for Global Internet Freedom is not improving the deliberative process since as an administrative unit it is part of the Department of State, the President's prime advisor on foreign affairs.

One of the few writers on globalization that have taken the internal workings of the State as a starting point for an investigation into the globalization process, is Saskia Sassen. Sassen[372] shows that the effects of globalization cannot solely be attributed to the factors of a changing environment independent from the State itself. Within the State, certain prerequisites have to be in place in order to incorporate the effects of an interdependent world into its decision-making processes. Sassen specifically points out that the democratic deficit due to the emergence of non-state actors involved in standard setting, public policy making and rule creation, is not the sole reason for a decrease in democratic deliberation. She shows that since the eighties the power of the executive has increased at the expense of the legislative branch in government, i.e., Congress, and distinguishes a continuous trend of increasing executive power since the Reagan administration, particularly after the 9/11 attacks. Whereas the GOFA as a piece of extraterritorial legislation combining national legislation with foreign policy objectives does not use this particular strategy, it certainly confirms the general development of an increased power of the executive at the expense of the deliberative process conducted in Congress. As Sassen puts it;

'Passing new laws in Congress is a far more visible event than are the executive's decisions. When these amount to "lawmaking", we can begin to speak of a serious democratic deficit at the heart of the liberal state but one resulting from the accumulation of the powers of the executive. The public deliberations and public oversight typical of congressional debates are absent in executive decision-making. Such public deliberations would have helped make evident to the average citizen and politician the depth of the changes that were being instituted.'[373]

The reliance on the President for executing extraterritorial legislation decreases the democratic accountability of the applicability of regulation. Without the deliberative process by representatives characteristic for Congress and constitutive of a well-functioning democracy, the shift in power to the executive at the expense of Congress undermines the very values that form the heart of the constitutional democracy.

---

[371] Ibid., Section 104(b).
[372] Sassen, S., 2006.
[373] Ibid., p. 184.

To sum up Section 6.5, the GOFA violates market economic commitments in limiting access to emerging markets while its design, shifting its power to the executive branch, paradoxically violates the very fundamental values it aims to promote by decreasing the deliberative process in Congress. Enforcing the promotion of US-supported content and political values on the Internet is unlikely to weigh up to the harm the bill can do, particularly in economic terms. The compulsory promotion of US values effectively limits the dissemination of US values to States that already adhere to these values, that is, free countries with democratically chosen governments that do not have to fear the freedom of information on political grounds. In order to advance a free flow of information in China therefore, it might be useful to explore an alternative route, avoiding the problems mentioned above.

6.5   China's Road to Reform

Information freedom, i.e., freedom to receive and impart information, form the basis of a free society since they form a prerequisite for both market economic and democratic ideals. Consequently, censorship practices erode both fundamental pillars of the modern State. This observation, combined with the realization that the GOFA would mean the end of its Chinese adventure, has led Google to suggest to the US government to treat censorship practices as barriers to trade.[374] In order to understand why a trade-based solution could offer an attractive coherent alternative for advancing fundamental Western values abroad and particularly in China, it is useful to have a closer look at the Chinese reform program which is characterized by a two-sponged approach. The first and most pressing prong is the economic reform program designed to make the transition from a planned economy to a market economy. The second prong, a corollary of the economic reform program is its political reform program, which endorses a democratization of society. The combination of these programs establishes China's slow conversion towards the Western archetype of organized political life: the constitutional democracy.

6.5.1   China's economic reform program

In the mid-1950s, China introduced a Soviet-style centrally planned economy. The essence of a planned economy is to organize society as one big factory and to allocate resources, i.e. land, capital, labor and enterprise, by the administrative means of the central planning organ. In a planned economy, the State or government completely controls the production factors and the distribution of income. In order for the system to work effectively, there are two prerequisites. First, the central planning committee needs *complete information* concerning all the economic activities of the country, and secondly, the committee needs to be able to integrate all interest

---

[374] Schage, E., 2006.

in society into one *single interest*. Both assumptions are very hard to realize in real life. The costs of obtaining adequate and timely information, in addition to the costs involved in designing and implementing the detailed plans makes the system inherently inefficient.[375] In addition, the lack of appropriate feedback mechanisms informing producers about consumer needs makes it impossible for the central planning committee to react adequately to changing circumstances.

The alternative to a planned economy, a (free) market economy, is an economic system in which individuals rather than government make the majority of decisions regarding economic activities and transactions. Private property rights form the foundation of the market economy since these rights provide citizens with a basis for exchanging goods and setting prices by mutual consent free from government interference. Since the prices of products are set by mutual consent between buyers and sellers, the price of a product indicates its scarcity. Hence, the market economy provides a transparent and reliable feedback mechanism for producers to determine the allocation of the means of production. As a result, the system is considerably less expensive to run and forms an efficient basis for allocating the means of production,[376] and therefore a more successful route towards stable economic growth based on increasing efficiency rather than on creating more output.[377]

Currently, China is in a transitional phase, both politically and economically. Whereas much needs to be done, the reform program has already made significant progress. One major breakthrough in the Chinese transformation from a centrally planned economy to a free market system was its accession to the World Trade Organization (WTO) in 2002. A second major breakthrough, China's recent decision on the annual meeting of the National People's Congress in Beijing (March 2007) to constitutionally protect private property rights,[378] definitively shows that China has reached an important stage in its economic reform program.

6.5.2 China's political reform program

The Chinese reform program did not start at the dawn of the 21st century. Transforming a country of 1.3 billion people from a planned to a free market economy cannot be done overnight and requires both economic and political changes. The start of the Chinese reforms dates back to 1958 when the first steps were taken to implement a decentralization of China's administration in order to make the system more flexible.[379] This decentralization process marked the beginning of the eco-

---

[375] Wu. J., 2005, pp. 18-20.

[376] This phenomenon is called 'the calculation problem'. An exposition of this debate can be found in; Screpanti, E. et al., 2005, p. 296ff.

[377] Both economic models outlined here are pure forms of resource allocation. Whereas the Chinese economic model of the mid-1950s can safely be characterized as a centrally planned economy, most economies have elements of the other model as well. Notwithstanding this, all Western economies are primarily market economies.

[378] BBC Staff, 2007.

[379] Wu, J., 2005, p. 39.

nomic reform in that profit sharing with local authorities and the ability to raise taxes at a local level provides the system with a feedback mechanism of sorts that brings the production process closer to the consumer and enables the central government to react more adequately on consumer needs. At the same time, it also formed the first step in bringing governmental control closer to the people. Similarly, the recent commitment to free trade and the constitutional protection of private property rights cannot be seen independently from a democratization process, putting people more in control of their own faith.

Since the early 1980s, the Chinese government has gradually introduced direct democratic elections at grassroots level. The 16th National Congress particularly emphasized the promotion of democratic politics and a democratization policy.[380] In 2002 for example 40 percent of the towns in the province Sichuan (about 2000 in total), had implemented a system of direct competitive elections for town heads and vice town heads.[381] Whereas the political reform program primarily takes a bottom up approach, starting at a local level, also at the national level, China seems to have opened up to non Communist Party members to join government as the (2007) appointments of Wan Gang as Minister of Science and Technology and Chen Zhu as Health Minister show.[382] Hence, also from a democratic point of view, the Chinese reform program is slowly making progress.

6.5.3   Censorship and Chinese reform

According to Sen,[383] political freedoms serve three important roles. First, value for human life and wellbeing. Preventing participation in the political life of the community is a major deprivation. Secondly, they have *instrumental* value in enhancing the hearing people get in expressing and supporting their claims to political attention (including economic needs). Thirdly, they are *constructive* in that it gives citizens an opportunity to learn from one another and help society to form its values and priorities.

Consequently, political rights, including freedoms of expression and information, are not only pivotal in inducing social responses to economic needs; they are also central to the conceptualization of economic needs themselves. In other words, in addition to the pricing mechanism of a free market economy, the information freedom central to a constitutional democracy serves as an important additional feedback mechanism in order to determine the allocation of resources. In optimizing the market economy therefore, democracy and political freedoms, like the freedom of speech, constitute essential elements in perfecting the free market economy.

The economic and political commitments of a modern constitutional democracy intimately connect at various levels. For example, private property, the basis of a

---

[380] Ibid., p. 437.
[381] Ibid., p. 426.
[382] Embassy of the People's Republic of China in the USA, 2007.
[383] Sen, A.K., 1999.

free market economy, provides a basis for individuals to act independently from the State in such a way that the security obtained by private housing and the income generated from privately owned resources, form the basis for citizens to challenge the State and hold it accountable for its decisions.[384] In a more direct fashion, private property rights and freedom of contract form the basis for a variety of other rights including information freedoms. The very meaning of private property is that the property is at the disposal of the owner in question, protected from public appropriation over which the owner has exclusive and absolute rights.[385] This means that the owner of land can build meeting halls, invite people and use the various means for communication at his disposal to make his voice heard (by using pens, paper, sound systems, websites etc). People who do not own property can rent the facilities based on the freedom of contract that is a corollary of private property rights.[386] Vice versa, the political commitments to a limited government facilitates the development of a market economy based on private property rights as for example the exposition about the French revolution in Chapter 2 has already pointed out. It provides the stability needed to accumulate capital and hence sustain welfare.

In view of China's current situation, economic reform inevitably entails more than implementing a few laws. It also requires a degree of legal certainty. For example, in order to be able to enforce property rights a State has to commit itself to acting in accordance with the rule of law.[387] Transparent legislation and publicly publicized jurisprudence are also preconditions in order to guarantee a State free zone for citizens and similarly is an independent judiciary. In short, the very commitment to guaranteeing private property rights is a commitment to a cluster of elements essential to a constitutional democracy including a limited government.[388] Put in perspective, China's reform process, driven by economic needs, inevitably pushes China towards the governance model of the constitutional democracy.

Social change creates uncertainty. The main precondition to a successful transformation process is political stability. Currently, the increased awareness of the gap between the rich urban population and the poor farmers in China is a risk to its political stability and hence a threat to the reform program. If China is to make genuine progress and if it is to remain a political unity (which is one of the natural objectives of any type of State), it is paramount that the government carefully monitors the economic reform process and ensures a slow and steady transformation of society. Objectionable as this may be from a Western perspective, China's informa-

---

[384] Fletcher, G.P. and Sheppard, S., 2005.

[385] Black, H.C. and Garner, B.A., 1999, entry 'private property', p. 1233.

[386] For a more general exposition on the relation between property rights and other rights within the context of a market economy, see, Reiss, G., 1996, p. 23.

[387] China has committed itself to the rule of law at the 15th National Congress of the PCP in 1997.

[388] The work of De Soto is particularly interesting in this regard since he shows the complexities involved in developing a well-functioning system of property rights. He also shows that particularly for the poor, a well-functioning system of property rights forms an essential basis to capitalize on property as to ensure productive investments; De Soto, H., 2000.

tion policy, including its current Internet policy, is rational implementation of this strategy. As Amartya Sen[389] has pointed out, a minimum degree of welfare is a prerequisite in order to enable people to make choices and actualize their freedom. At the same time, a developed middle class is also elementary in the maintenance of a stable legal system.[390] With 1.3 billion people, of which, 21.5 million of its rural population live below the official 'absolute poverty' line (approximately USD 90 per year), and an additional 35.5 million rural population above that but below the official 'low income' line (approximately USD 125 per year),[391] economic growth is China's primary objective. Its Internet censorship policy ties in with this aim.

6.6   THE USE OF LEGAL FRAMEWORKS

The previous sections sketched the relevance of search operators in the information society and their contribution to China's censorship practices. Section 6.4 pointed out that the GOFA, designed to fight US censorship compliance and to promote a free flow of information seems unable to further the US interests successfully. In addition to forcing US businesses like Google to stop their operations in China, it violates both democratic and market economic foundations that lie at the heart of the US constitution forming the basis of a free and open society. This section locates the origin of the GOFA's inconsistency in its use of legal frameworks. Furthermore, it explains how a trade-based route could be an attractive way to fight censorship abroad whilst overcoming the negative consequences of the GOFA.

6.6.1   The fragmentation of legal frameworks

The GOFA as a piece of extraterritorial legislation is not a legal freak. Many laws have relied for their application on the discretion of the executive branch. Within the context of export restrictions, for example, this is common practice. The compulsory active dissemination of US propaganda however exceeds export restrictions in terms of government intervention and seems to mark a new step in US foreign policy. The negative consequences of this type of legislation stem from a single source, its attempt to reconcile traditionally fragmented legal frameworks.

In order to see what is at stake it is useful to distinguish between traditional legal frameworks. Maintaining a foundational role for the constitution, Figure 11 schematically depicts a division of traditional legal frameworks based on the *scope* of the framework (horizontally) and a division based upon the *reach* of the legal frame-

---

[389] Sen, A.K., 1985; 1973; 2009.

[390] In a two-classed society (rich v. poor), nobody is interested in a well-functioning legal system. The rich are prone to do as they please because they have the money to influence decisions and the poor have nothing to lose. Hence, neither class has an important incentive to create a well-functioning legal system.

[391] CIA, 2009.

work (vertically). The scope or purpose of the legal divides into two distinct frameworks, one advancing *political* ideals on the one hand and one advancing *economic* ideals on the other hand. In addition, the figure shows a vertical division of legal frameworks into those that advance the aforementioned ideals *nationally* and those that advance these ideals *internationally*.

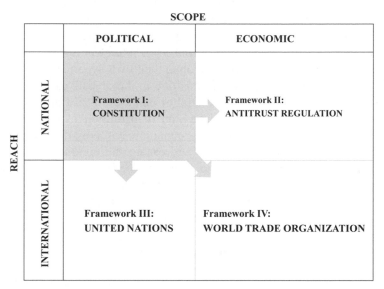

Figure 11. Traditional legal frameworks

At a national level, the prime legal framework advancing political values, and the basis for the other legal frameworks, are constitutions (framework I). They form society's attempt to limit the exercise of government by protecting the values it cherishes most, hence the constitutional codification of individual rights. At an international level, the dominant platform for advancing political ideals is provided by the UN through the UNDHR (framework III). The UN was set up for this purpose just after WWII with the aim to prevent war, to protect human rights, to provide a mechanism for international law and to promote social progress and fight poverty.[392] As its website puts it, The UN 'affords the opportunity for countries to balance global interdependent and national interests when addressing international problems.'[393] In sum, constitutions are society's attempts to protect itself from oneself.[394] Neither the UN, nor the constitution is designed to guarantee a free market as such. Nevertheless, they do guarantee a protection of private property rights that forms the basis for a free market economy.

---

[392] See the Preamble to the United Nations Charter (1948).
[393] See the UN website <www.un.org/Pubs/CyberSchoolBus>.
[394] Chemerinsky, E., 2002, p. 6ff.

At a national level, the prime legal framework for guarding the smooth operations of a market economy is the antitrust framework (framework II). The purpose of the antitrust framework is to ensure fair competition between private (corporate) actors. The WTO[395] provides the framework for advancing economic ideals at an international level and is designed to liberalize international trade between States by lowering barriers to trade (framework IV). As such, it provides a platform for governments to negotiate trade agreements and settle disputes. Neither the WTO framework nor the antitrust framework is designed to promote political freedoms.

In the words of Shaw, since the different legal frameworks were designed for their particular purposes, they have developed their own dynamics and operate independently in that they are largely insensitive to the objectives of other frameworks.[396] Consequently, where the national or domestic legal frameworks define the relation between the individual and the State (constitutions), or address the conduct of private actors (as is the case in the economic realm by the antitrust framework), international legal frameworks addressing the conduct of States Also horizontally, the legal frameworks tend to be fragmented. The WTO framework designed to promote free market values, is neither designed nor used to establish political reform. Frameworks designed to address political values, like the UDHR, do not leave room for (market) economic considerations.[397]

6.6.2   Limitations to a human rights framework

Despite the fact that a free flow of information is generally associated with political rights, and hence with political content, the GOFA's objective to promote US values by addressing the conduct of private actors operating abroad, does not fit in well with either of the human rights based frameworks. The UN framework is primarily designed to govern State behavior and is therefore not a suitable framework for addressing the conduct of individual private corporations.[398] The political rights-components in the Constitution seek to protect US citizens from the abusive of powers of the US government. As such, neither the UN framework nor the Constitution is well equipped to address Google's censorship activities in China.

The GOFA's incorporation of foreign policy objectives is effectuated by using principles developed under the UN framework to condemn foreign censorship regimes (State-to-State)[399] with national statutory law designed to address the behav-

---

[395] The WTO's website can be found at <www.wto.org>.

[396] Shaw, M.N., 2003, pp. 2-3; Cottier, T. et al., 2005, 'Introduction' and 'Freedom of Expression'.

[397] The UN department of economic and social affairs does stimulate cooperation in the use of technical developments and stimulates small third world businesses to export their goods. Whereas it supports the free trade objectives of the WTO, it is primarily designed to coordinate development programs and projects.

[398] The UN framework only allows the prosecution of individuals in the exceptional cases of war crimes, crimes against humanities and genocide. For more information, see the Rome Statute of the International Criminal Court. For the purpose of this inquiry this exception is not relevant, particularly not since neither China nor the US is a party to this treaty.

[399] GOFA, Section 3(8b) specifically refers to Art. 19 UNDHR.

ior of private actors. Although this construction to address private actors based on international principles is part of the GOFA's appeal and strength, particularly in terms of effectiveness,[400] it also turns out to be its weakness. The incorporation of *particular* foreign policy objectives, fighting foreign censorship practices by particular regimes is responsible for the decrease in deliberative process in Congress because labeling particular foreign countries is a subject matter of the executive branch (foreign affairs). The second problem with the human rights frameworks is that despite the incorporations of the rights that form the foundations of a market economy,[401] they tend to focus on political rights as *intrinsic* values for human life and wellbeing.[402] A strict adherence to political rights as intrinsic values blinds the GOFA for other, notably economic interests. In sum, the harm done by Internet exceeds the harm done by failing to promote US values disseminated by US-sponsored content. The GOFA's use of human rights based frameworks narrows its scope to the political consequences of censorship causing both the democratic deficit and the neglect of economic objectives.

Overcoming the democratic deficit resulting from the increase in executive power would require the elimination of the need to resort to foreign policy analysis for the applicability of the bill. This is complicated because the human rights-based framework used as a basis for the GOFA tends to addresses the behavior of States, not individuals. Since assessing the activities of foreign States is not a congressional activity but an activity belonging to the executive branch, the legal framework does not leave room for an obvious alternative that would restore the deliberative process in congress. Restoring this deliberative process would require a *universal* rule applicable to all relevant companies in every country at all times. Since nearly every country in the world restricts its citizens in obtaining and distributing information, fighting censorship activities based on political ideals invariably requires some mechanism of assessing the legitimacy of the restrictions in question. Since these judgments concern foreign States, it is hard to eliminate the executive branch from the procedure. Despite the fact that the executive branch is accountable to both congress and the judiciary, amending the GOFA to overcome its two most fundamental effects (lack of incorporating economic interests and the democratic deficit resulting in legal uncertainty) nevertheless must include restoring the deliberative process in congress.

Compared to the democratic deficit, the economic consequences of implementing the GOFA are even more pressing since this effectively prevents corporations like Google from operating in China. The effects of which, both practically and ideologically, runs counter to the general US economic interests. Amending the GOFA as to include economic considerations into the assessment of the legislation

---

[400] The GOFA's strength is that in addressing private conduct, it is generally likely to generate results easier, more effective and faster than attempts to address foreign-State conduct tend to do.

[401] See for example the private property provisions in Art. 17 UDHR.

[402] See Section 6.5.3 above for Sen's distinction in three roles of political values: *intrinsic, instrumental* and *constructive*.

proposed to fight censorship activities of US corporations abroad, is not straightforward because the human rights-based framework which has shaped the GOFA does not leave room for analysis that includes economic considerations. Human rights, within these legal frameworks, are generally considered non-negotiable, intrinsic values. Including economic considerations while assessing censorship issues would effectively mean abandoning the human rights-based frameworks altogether. Overcoming the problems associated with the GOFA within the context of a human rights framework then, is unlikely to succeed.

Since a free flow of information is a political as well as an economic prerequisite to a well functioning constitutional democracy, it largely dissolves the traditional distinction between political and economic ideals. On the Internet, the two objectives coincide, particularly since current censorship techniques used on the Internet do not distinguish between commercial and political content. The result of which is that inevitably more information is being blocked than strictly necessary from a political point of view. For example, blocking the complete youtube.com channel because of one foreign film offending local officials (despite the agreement to IP block illegal videos by the foreign country) can be considered a barrier to trade because it prevents *YouTube* advertisers to reach the Chinese market. Information industries (Internet companies, news channels etc.) depend upon a free flow of information in order to sell, deliver and promote their services abroad. In preventing services like Google to operate effectively on the Chinese market, the GOFA does nothing to protect the US corporations that are not engaged in censorship activities and are nevertheless limited in their ability to enter the Chinese market due to the censorship practices of US search operators. If censorship limits access to the Chinese market, also US corporations, particularly those in the information industry, potentially miss access to a market consisting of 20 percent of the world's population. In designing a policy to fight Internet censorship abroad, therefore, it is not only realistic to include economic considerations, it is paramount to do so.

6.6.3   Search operator censorship revisited

Because the human rights-based frameworks do not leave room for economic considerations and in view of the link between a free flow of information and the ideological and practical connections between political and economic ideals, this section explores the possibilities of a route based on economic legal frameworks for fighting censorship abroad. Such an approach is tempting at the outset because it incorporates economic considerations by default and furthers political ideals by advancing economic ideals. A starting point for an alternative US policy is the strategic role of search operators on the Internet and the way in which they are engaged in censorship activities.

Censorship is typically thought of as a government activity. Indeed, many countries try to prevent their citizens from accessing material they consider harmful or politically sensitive. This is partly why the publication of child pornography is illegal in the US[403] and the Internet publication of holocaust denials is illegal in Germany[404] and France.[405] Whereas in most Western countries the law tends to be quite specific about the definition of harmful and sensitive content, the situation in China is considerably less transparent. Information creating social uncertainty, spreading rumors, damaging State security and destroying the country's reputations are but a few justifications in Beijing's so called '11 commandments'[406] designed to hold the Internet liable for the content they display or distribute. Other laws do not specify these regulations and the Chinese government does not issue an itemized list of forbidden words requesting them to be blocked[407] and in addition, case law on these matters is not publicly available. Consequently, Internet Content Providers like Google are left to fill in the gaps by interpreting the laws and regulations single-handedly. The result is a type of self-regulation transcending the boundaries of a mere complicity with the Chinese regulations. In effect, Google is proactively censoring content by blocking information it deems necessary in order to comply with the regulations.

In addition to Google's guesswork, the current blocking techniques have not reached the sophistication that would enable censors to filter only the exact web pages containing the sensitive information. Censorship inevitably prevents access to pages with unrelated content and domain names or URLs that resemble the malicious page but contain harmless information. This phenomenon is called *overblocking*. Since the Chinese regulations leave the interpretation of 'sensitive political content' and other 'harmful content' up to the ISPs and ICPs, it effectively stimulates over-blocking by these corporations inclined to take stringent precautions in order to avoid possible repercussions. In Google's situation, this policy stimulates over-blocking content in two ways. First, the self-composed blacklist is likely to put an extra layer of privately blocked content over and above the minimum level of censorship actually required by the censorship regime. Secondly, since automated keyword blocking does not distinguish between commercial and political content it is inevitably blocking more content than intended by the censors.

6.6.4   Trade-centered solutions

At a recent congressional hearing on the Internet in China,[408] Google's Elliot Schrage, Google's VP Global Communications and Public Affairs, made exactly this point when he stated that,

'The US government should seek to bolster the global reach and impact for our Internet information industry by placing obstacles to its growth at the top of our trade

---

[403] Sexual Expoitation of Children, 18 USC § 2251.
[404] German Criminal Code (1998).
[405] LOI Gayssot (1990).
[406] Reporters without Borders, 2005.
[407] See also: Open Initiative, 2006.
[408] Congressional Hearing, 2006.

agenda. At the risk of oversimplification, the US should treat censorship as a barrier to trade and raise that issue in the appropriate fora.'[409]

Judged by Western standards, the Chinese economic reform program is more advanced than their political reform program. Particularly since China's WTO membership has increased China's sensitivity towards trade related arguments, fighting censorship as a trade barrier is likely to have more effect than the human rights based route.[410] The WTO is to promote free trade by lowing barriers to trade. Hence, by considering censorship practices as barriers to trade, it could also be used as a platform for addressing the barriers that the Chinese Internet policy causes, for example in delaying international Internet traffic caused by the Chinese firewall.[411] This approach, put forward by Google, suggests that the US government should address the censorship restrictions that China puts upon Internet businesses in the bilateral WTO agreements and in the multilateral trade agenda's.[412]

However, the WTO framework is essentially the international trade-based counterpart to the UN human rights-based framework and, as such, suffers from similar handicaps in terms of enforceability and effectiveness. Nevertheless, it does offer a theoretical possibility in trying to get States to comply with conditions that are not necessarily directly associated with free trade. The US could incorporate anti-censorship conditions into the bilateral trade agreements that are established under the WTO framework. The US could also use its lobbying power to include anticensorship provisions in the overall framework of the WTO. The recent discussions regarding labor standards suggest that the economic framework at least leaves some room for the incorporation of extra-economic considerations and best practices into its overall framework.[413]

Still, the WTO framework does not allow for an effective remedy for individual censorship activities of US corporations operating abroad. Pre-WTO attempts to create a comprehensive normative framework for international economic relations[414] did consider antitrust provisions designed to regulate private conduct to form an important element in the framework, but the attempts failed in both cases. Within the context of the WTO, the issue of developing an international antitrust regime has not even made it to the agenda. The lack of community sense within the WTO disqualifies it as a suitable framework for doing so and even if there were such a community sense, there would be disagreement over competing antitrust regimes.[415] Consequently, the WTO is a framework for addressing State conduct and is likely to remain just this for some time to come.

---

[409] Schage, E., 2006.

[410] Especially since China has not ratified the ICCPR.

[411] See WTO at <www.wto.org/english/thewto_e/whatis_e/tif_e/fact1_e.htm>.

[412] See, Google, 2007.

[413] Fore more on this topic see, WTO, 1999.

[414] The first attempt to create a normative framework was made during the Geneva International Economic Conference in 1927 and a second attempt was made after WWII when trying to establish the International Trade Organization (Havana Round, 1947).

[415] Gerber, D.J., 2007.

The GOFA's aim to address censorship activities by addressing private actors is one of its most attractive features. The regulation of private actors is easier, more effective and faster than attempts to influence State actors because of the effectively enforcement mechanisms available to States. Moreover, due to their powerful role, search operators form attractive targets for disseminating US values by compelling them to include pro-US content into their search results. In addition, the Chinese situation makes proceedings against private actors particularly interesting, specifically in the light of (1) China's vague legislative environment, which blurs the distinction between private and State responsibilities regarding censorship and (2) the current censorship techniques that are prone to over-block Internet content over and above the censor's requirements.

As Figure 11 showed, the dominant domestic legal framework addressing a smooth operation of the market economy is the US antitrust framework. Because the framework, like the GOFA, is designed to address the operations of private actors, and Internet censorship affects both commercial and politically relevant content, the following sections explore the possibilities of using the antitrust framework in order to fight private censorship activities.

6.7   An Antitrust Solution

According to former Federal Trade Commissioner, Professor Calvani, the US antitrust legislation is intended to yield the most efficient allocation of economic resources, producing both the lowest possible prices and the highest quality for the greatest number.[416] The Supreme Court has even gone as far as to state that, in addition, the antitrust legislation simultaneously provides an environment conducive to the preservation or our democratic, political, and social institutions.[417] Whereas not necessarily every scholar would subscribe to this latter claim, the Supreme Court's claim that antitrust legislation forms a charter for economic liberty aimed at preserving free and unfettered competition as a rule of trade[418] is more widely accepted. At base, the antitrust legislation then is the domestic counterpart of the WTO framework in that it is designed to remove barriers to trade. The WTO framework provides the framework to address restraints on trade by States. The antitrust framework, in turn, does this by addressing private actors.

In addition to the ability to address private conduct, the antitrust framework has additional features that are interesting in the light of fighting censorship activities. First, it has an established extraterritorial reach. Second, it allows for both consumer and US export protection and third it has incorporated a doctrine of foreign compulsion allowing the US to respect the foreign country's sovereign ability to determine its own affairs. This section sets out to (1) explain the relevant features of

---

[416] Calvani, T., 1988.
[417] *Northern Pacific Railway Company* v. *United States*, 365 US 1, 6 (1958) at 4.
[418] Ibid.

the antitrust framework, (2) identify to what extent this framework is potentially able to address censorship practices by US corporations abroad as barriers to trade. The subsequent section (3) suggests possible amendments to the system and (4) assesses the feasibility of those changes.

6.7.1   General features of the antitrust framework

The antitrust framework consists of three basic pillars. The Sherman Act (1890) prohibits cartelization and monopolization (including attempts). The Clayton Act (1914) deals with four specified types of monopolistic practice, i.e., price discrimination, exclusive dealings and tying contracts, acquisitions of competing companies and interlocking directorates, conduct that becomes unlawful when its 'effect may be to substantially lessen competition or tends to create a monopoly'.[419] The third pillar of US antitrust legislation is the Federal Trade Commission Act (FTC) (1914). This third act is mainly concerned with the establishment and the operation of the FTC, but its substantive provisions declare unlawful 'unfair methods of competition in or affecting commerce, and unfair or deceptive acts or practices in or affecting commerce'. Its authority includes but is not limited to violations of the Sherman and Clayton Act. In terms of execution, the Sherman and Clayton Acts can be enforced both by the US Department of Justice (DoJ) (criminally and for injunctive relief) and by private parties filing suit (treble damages, injunctive relief and attorney fees).[420] In contrast, the FTC Act can only be enforced by the FTC who can issue an order to cease and desist the activity, which in turn is subject to review by the federal courts of appeal.[421]

Extraterritorial reach

One of the great advantages of using the antitrust framework in order to battle US business Internet censorship abroad is that the extraterritorial application of US law is well established.[422] In comparison to the legal frameworks that have been developed in order to advance human rights, the antitrust framework already applies well beyond national (US) borders. Although initially the antitrust law dealt with the power of large interstate companies like railroad and oil businesses on American soil, the development of case law gradually came to apply the framework extraterritorially. In the landmark case *Alcoa* (1945) Judge Learned Hand introduced the 'objective territoriality' principle in antitrust law, meaning that when there is a substantial and foreseeable effect on US commerce, the US antitrust legislation applies.[423] Subsequent rulings qualified this approach by introducing balancing tests

---

[419] Joelson, M.R., 2006, p. 3.

[420] 15 USC §§ 3, 4, 12, 15, 25-26.

[421] 15 USC § 25.

[422] See also Figure 12 'Extending Traditional Legal Frameworks' in this respect.

[423] *United State* v. *Aluminum Company of America*, 148 F.2d 416 (2nd Circ. 1945) stating that national jurisdiction exists with respect to conduct with an intentional or at least reasonably foreseeable and not insubstantial effect to the nation's commerce.

in order to include foreign interests in the equation. The *Timberlane*[424] and *Mannington Mills*[425] precedents developed a comity analysis against which the interest of the US and foreign nations were balanced. The Third Restatement of Foreign Relation Law[426] adapted a similar 'reasonableness test' as an affirmative element of jurisdiction permitting jurisdiction over conduct that was intended to produce significant effects or in fact produced such effects in the US.[427] Nevertheless, the Supreme Court neither ever adopted a 'balancing of interests' approach nor was this approach ever followed by the federal appellate courts. In *Hartford Fire*,[428] the Supreme Court abandoned the balancing approach and reaffirmed the extraterritorial applicability of the Sherman Act, remaining the policy to date. The case established that the scope of antitrust law includes conduct outside US borders if such conduct has significant and direct anticompetitive effects within the US.

Consumer and export protection

In addition to its geographic application, also the objective of antitrust legislation has widened gradually. An important breakthrough made in order to incorporate US business interests into the equation, was the Bush administration's repeal of 'footnote 159' of the 1988 Guidelines on International trade. The footnote stated that,

> '[A]lthough the Foreign Trade Antitrust Improvement Act extends jurisdiction under the Sherman Act to conduct that has direct, substantial and reasonably foreseeable effect on the export trade or export commerce of a person engaged in such commerce in the United States, the Department is concerned only with the adverse effects on competition that would harm U.S. consumers by reducing output or raising prices.'[429]

The repeal of the footnote, confirmed by the Department of Justice,[430] effectively means that the Antitrust Division could now act both against foreign conduct directly harming US consumers, and against conduct that foreclosed foreign markets to US export trade.[431] Both the 1995 guidelines[432] and subse-

---

[424] The *Timberlane* cases; *Timberlane Lumber Co.* v. *Bank of America,* 549 F.2d 1378 (9th. Circ. 1976), and *Timberlane Lumber Co.* v. *Bank of America* , 749 F.2d 1378 (9th Circ. 1984) adopted a seven-factor analysis to be applied in deciding whether international comity dictates that a court decline to exercise jurisdiction.

[425] *Mannington Mills Inc.* v. *Congoleum Corp.,* 595 F.2 1287, 202 USPQ 321, 1979-1 Trade Cas. (CHH) P 62547 (3rd Circ. 1979) adapted ten factors to be considered.

[426] Para. 402, Restatement of the (Third) Foreign Relations Law (1987).

[427] Kessler, J.L., 2006, p. 242ff.

[428] Hartford Fire Ins. Co. v. California, 509 US 764 (1993).

[429] USDoJ (1988).

[430] USDoJ (1992).

[431] Ordover, J., 1995.

[432] USDoJ (1995), Section 3.1 confirms that 'the anticompetitive conduct that affects US domestic or foreign commerce may violate the US antitrust laws regardless of where such conduct occurs or the nationality of the parties involved'.

quent jurisprudence[433] confirm the application of antitrust laws to protect US export commerce.

The doctrine of foreign compulsion

Although extraterritorial reach of the antitrust framework is well established, there are still limitations to the applicability of the antitrust legislation abroad. For our purposes the doctrine of foreign compulsion developed in the *InterAmerican Refining Corp.* v. *Texaco Maracaibo Inc.*[434] is particularly relevant. Based on the principle of equity, this doctrine relieves a party from choosing between two evils. It allows the private party to act anti competitively without incurring liability under US law only if it is able to prove that foreign compulsion requires the specific conduct. It can do so by proving that it was specifically ordered to do so by a government official[435] or by proving it was compelled by foreign legislation.[436] The courts however have been reluctant to accept this type of defense. A mere knowledge, approval, participation or even encouragement of the unlawful restraint by a foreign government has proved insufficient to provide immunity for a private firm violating antitrust laws.[437]

6.7.2   Implications for battling censorship

If censorship activities by US corporations operating in foreign States could be subsumed under the antitrust framework, it would overcome the first problem associated with the GOFA. Since the extraterritorial applicability of the antitrust framework does not depend on a foreign affairs analysis of political or business situation or anything else, an antitrust approach would prevent a power shift from the legislative to the executive. In other words, it would not pose a threat to the deliberative process in congress. This is not to say that the foreign situation would not affect the applicability of the antitrust laws on the conduct in question. On the contrary, the *doctrine of foreign compulsion* would compel the alleged violator of the law to prove that he was forced to operate in line with the existing regulations in the respective State. Within the context of Google's censorship activities, the court's reluctance to accept this type of defense makes it very difficult for Google to convince the judge of the compulsory nature of their censorship activities if China's legisla-

---

[433] In the *Hoffmann-LaRoche Ltc.* v. *Empagran S.A.,* 542 US 155, 161 (2004) the court held that the Foreign Trade Antitrust Improvements Act does not apply to '(1) export activities and (2) other commercial activities taking place abroad, *unless* those activities adversely affect domestic commerce, imports to the US, or exporting activities of one engaged in such activities within the US.'

[434] InterAmerican Refining Corp. v. Texaco Maracaibo Inc., 307 F. Supp 1291 (D. Del 1970).

[435] Ibid.

[436] *Continental Ore Co.* v. *Union Carbide & Carbon Corp.* 370 US 690, 706 (1962). In *United States Watchmakers of Switzerland Info. Ctr. Inc.,* (SDNY, 1965) the court specifically states the 'if, of course, the defendants' activities had been required by Swiss law, this court could indeed do nothing'.

[437] Kessler, J.L., 2006, p. 457.

tion on the subject is too vague. With the lack of an explicit governmentally provided blacklist of keywords and websites to be filtered, Google's conduct in China is unlikely to qualify as compulsion.

It has to be noted that fighting censorship by means of the antitrust framework can only constitute a partial approach. Since it only addresses the conduct of private actors and refrains from assessing the legitimacy or level of censorship involved in the respective foreign country, a more complete anti-censorship policy would naturally include a complementary use of international frameworks in order to address the conduct of States. Still, an antitrust route would be able to establish something very valuable, it would hold the private actor to account for his particular censorship activity that is not directly imposed by the foreign State. This would have two important consequences. First, it would be an important tool for fighting over-blocking. If a US search operator were to block entire news websites because of one particular news item they considered 'politically sensitive' in the context of Chinese law, a private suit filed under the 'new' antitrust regime would force the search operator to prove his blocking was directly compelled by the Chinese government. Consequently, search operators would be less prone to block information and would be stimulated to develop more sophisticated blocking tools. In addition, it would provide the US government with the exact information about what is *actually* censored by the respective governments, which in turn could serve as concrete leads for addressing foreign States on the censorship activities and for developing specifically targeted foreign anticensorship policies. The second consequence of an antitrust approach is that it would refrain from blurring the distinction between private actors as free profit maximizing actors on the one hand, and the public policy objectives developed by the State on the other hand. The compulsory use of private actors as government tools (compelled to disseminate State-sponsored content) runs counter to the US ideal of a market economy. Using an antitrust approach, in contrast to the GOFA, would maintain a more strict division between the public and the private realm.

6.8   AMENDMENTS TO A FRAMEWORK

The previous section explained the relevant features of the antitrust framework that makes it a potentially attractive framework for addressing censorship activities and identified the extent to which this framework is potentially able to address censorship practices by US corporations abroad as barriers to trade. Despite its promising basis, however, the current framework is not yet suited for the purposes of fighting private censorship activities abroad. This section sets out to identify the necessary amendments to the system in order to be able to address private censorship activities and assesses the feasibility of those changes. In order to identify the shortcomings of the current antitrust framework a return to an amended version of the figure depicting the traditional legal frameworks is illustrative.

Figure 12, 'Extending Traditional Legal frameworks' depicts the location of the GOFA within the context of human rights frameworks on the one hand and 'extended' antitrust approach in the context of the existing traditional economic frameworks based on Figure 11, 'Traditional Legal Frameworks'. When considering the GOFA's extraterritorial reach and the fact that it addresses private conduct, it becomes immediately clear that the GOFA is an extraordinary construct within the context of a human rights framework. Unlike the constitution and the UN framework, it is designed to address private conduct, and as such, it does not fit in well within the human rights framework. The economic frameworks however show a different picture. Whereas the antitrust framework is essentially a domestic framework as depicted in Figure 11, it has become clear from the exposition in the previous sections that it already has an established extraterritorial applicability, an extension of the framework that is incorporated in Figure 12.

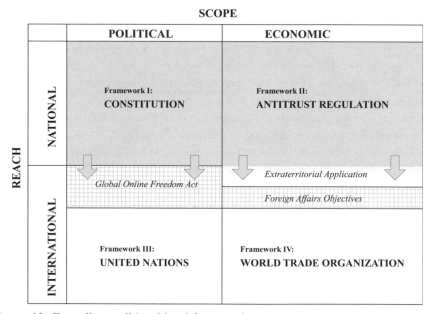

Figure 12. Extending traditional legal frameworks

Despite the well-established extraterritorial application of this framework however, there remains a gap between the WTO and the antitrust framework because in addition to the difference in addressee, also the objectives of the two frameworks, designed to encourage trade, do not seamlessly flow over into one another. The crux of the matter lies in the scope of the framework. The WTO framework encourages free trade by providing a platform designed to liberalize trade, for example, to establish lower tariffs, import taxes and other barriers. The antitrust framework encourages trade by stimulating competition, that is, fighting anti-competitive behavior within the context of a given market. The Sherman Act (Section II), for example, aims to detect and remedy 'unilateral conduct that threatens consumers and economic efficiency'.[438] Clearly, search-operator censorship in China does exactly this. It potentially limits US exports by limiting access to information within China. This is not enough to qualify as a violation of the Sherman Act, however, since the additional requirement is to do this as an attempt to monopolize. In Google's case, blocking a particular content provider is not done for the sake of excluding rivals from market entrance.[439] After all, Google as a search operator does not compete with content providers like news sites or television and radio services. The reason why Google blocks content is simply out of fear for (Chinese) government repercussions. In other words, limiting access to any type of business other than (possibly competing) US search operators would not fall under the provisions of the Sherman Act.

Within the confinements of the FTC there is hardly any more room for addressing the issue despite its aim and authority to promote export trade and prevent unfair methods of competition and unfair or deceptive acts or practices in or affecting commerce.[440] The 'Unfair Methods of Competition Clause' mentioned in the FTC Act, again runs into the relevant market problem.[441] Fighting censorship activities by forcing US search operators (like Google) to include other US search operators (say Yahoo!) in their search results is not an effective way of addressing Internet censorship. The open-ended Unfairness Regarding Acts or Practices in or Affecting Commerce clause[442] and the Deceptive Acts and Practices clause,[443] also part of the FTC Act, neither offer a great chance for success because they both aim at protecting the US consumer. The possible harm done to the US consumers by preventing content providers of social networks to gain access to the Chinese market because of Google's filtering activities is (if at all) indirect and very hard to prove. It seems that the consumers who would benefit the most are the Chinese consumers, a group of people US antitrust law does not seek to protect.

6.8.1   Advantages

Extending the antitrust framework as to include general trade objectives would close the gap between national antitrust legislation and the international WTO framework. Whereas Figure 12 confirms this, it also suggests that an incorporation of economic foreign affairs objectives, that is, general trade objectives that are already

---

[438] Antitrust Modernization Committee, 2005.

[439] Antitrust Modernization Committee, 2006.

[440] 15 USC 2(1), Para. 45.

[441] The classic *Cellophane* case (*United States* v. *E.I. du Point de Nemours & Co.* 351 US 377 (1956)) shows that even Cellophane is not defined as a unique product market but rather as a market for 'packaging materials' shows that it is unlikely that the wider category of ICP is to apply to describe Internet search operators.

[442] FTC (1980), see also: *FTC* v. *Sperry & Hutchinson Co.*, 405 US 233 (1972) which provided three factors to be weighed (1) is the practice (substantially) injuring customers, (2) does it violate established public policy, and (3) is the practice unethical or unscrupulous.

[443] FTC (1983).

present in the WTO framework, would make the antitrust network sufficiently strong for fighting censorship practices abroad. What it suggests is that this extension can be construed as a natural extension of the existing antitrust framework.

The advantages of an economic approach are plentiful. First, an economic approach would advance economic ideals and interests of the US because as an economic approach it would incorporate the economic interests of the US by default. Hence, the economic problems associated with the GOFA would be overcome. Second, it would avoid the hostility raised by a human rights-based approach because there is more overall consensus regarding the benefits of free trade[444] than regarding the universal applicability of human rights.[445] Third, the approach would ensure legal certainty because it would create a private liability for all blocked content not specifically demanded by the host country. Hence there would be one universal rule, applicable to all corporations in every country at all times.[446] Four, it would require minimal changes to the existing framework and it would be cost effective. By enabling private actors (instead of only the DoJ) to sue search operators or other information providers for not incorporating relevant information into their search results on free trade grounds, neither the traditional provision regarding the 'relevant market' nor the provisions confining the antitrust framework to the 'US customer' would limit the applicability of the antitrust laws. Since the extraterritorial application of the US antitrust legislation is well established, the only novelty would be the use of international principles in order to justify a wider reach of the legislation. The strategy developed in the GOFA poses clues as to how to go about this. Leaving it up to the wronged parties to take legal action when other actors violate the legislation would relieves the State from the need to actively enforce the law in question.

6.8.2   Practical implications

There are several ways to incorporate general free trade interests in the antitrust framework. Within the context of the Sherman Act, the courts have long distinguished between 'per se' violations of antitrust law and a 'rule of reason' analysis in order to distinguish between those cases that deserve a full investigation and those in which a shorter analysis can be used.[447] One way is to consider 'exclusionary conduct by means of restricting access to Internet content' as a *per se* antitrust violation. This would neither require the plaintiff to prove intent to eliminate rivals

---

[444] A list of WTO members is available at <www.wto.org/english/thewto_e/whatis_e/tif_e/org6_e.htm>.

[445] The Universal Declaration of Human Rights (UDHR) (1948) is not a binding document by international law, but a 'common standard of achievement for all peoples and nations', see its preamble and Shaw, M.N., 2003, p. 259ff. The International Covenant for Civil and Political Rights (ICCPR), a document that is also mentioned in the GOFA is, for example, not ratified by China.

[446] See also Section 6.6.

[447] Areeda, P.E. and Hovenkamp, A., 2006.

nor an investigation into its reasonableness of the alleged violation. The incorporation of a *per se* violation into the current antitrust framework would require an
amendment in the form of a law.

Another lead for a possible incorporation of the broader free trade principles
into the framework can be found in *Socony-Vacuum*.[448] Parallel to the conduct in
question in this case, censorship practices by a US business could be banned because of 'its actual or potential threat to the central nervous system of the economy'.
The crux to the incorporation of international trade concerns into the antitrust framework is to consider *competition* to be a general abstract economic principle rather
than a notion applying only within the boundaries of a certain geographical product
market. The *per se* approach would consider censorship practice by US businesses
inherently anticompetitive and injurious to the public since it would exclude parties
to enter the market. With a wide interpretation of competition (or relevant market),
one would even be able to protect companies such as the Voice of America and
other US sponsored Internet based companies to promote competition of ideas over
the Internet. This solution would establish a reinterpretation of the current laws that
is unlikely to be established in the courts. This road, if possible at all, would either
require a new law (*per se violation*) or it would require a policy change by the
respective administration, which in turn would be subject to judicial scrutiny.

6.8.3 Feasibility

The anti-censorship approach based on an antitrust framework, however, is controversial. A first reason is that the US antitrust framework is primarily aimed to fight
cooperation between companies that aim to raise prices, maintain market share or
exclude rivals in their respective market. There are relatively few provisions prohibiting certain types of unilateral conduct. Still, there is theoretically room for an
extension of the framework along the lines sketched above. A more fundamental
reason why the approach is controversial is due to the nature of the framework.
International trade is an ideological extension of the market economy. The antitrust
framework like the WTO framework is designed to allow for a smoother operation
of the market economy. The US antitrust framework however is also designed to
protect *American* consumers, *American* markets and *American* exporters. At base,
by advocating a national approach, the US antitrust legislation is not designed to
further the general market economic ideal at all. In fact, the framework is inherently anti-free market in that it effectively serves and was designed as a barrier to
free trade: as a limitation in the free choice of entrepreneurs.

---

[448] *United States* v. *Socony-Vacuum Oil Co.,* 310 US 150 (1940) concerned the *per se* regulation of
price fixing such an approach is in principle also feasible regarding censorship practices. Unfortunately, there seems to be a trend towards dismantling this distinction because it is very hard to draw the
line between the different types of cases. In *California Dental Ass'n* v. *FTC*, 536 US 756 (1999) the
Supreme Court even called for a 'sliding scale of analysis in which the extent of the analysis should
depend on the particular agreement and the circumstances surrounding it.

Whereas its initial goal was to 'protect' the US consumer, later this extended to the ideal of protecting the US market by for example protecting national export. Incorporating free trade objectives into the antitrust framework does not necessarily advance the US objectives of protecting their own markets. One interesting example in this respect is the application of the Foreign Trade Antitrust Improvements Act (FTAIA) (Section 7 Sherman Act), which exempts the formation of export cartels from the application of the antitrust framework. In the context of the FTAIA one can even distinguish a transition in the overall aim of the antitrust framework from an emphasis on stimulating *competition*, that is protecting the consumer from the powers of business by fighting monopolistic behavior, to stimulating *competitiveness,* that is, recognizing a potential national vulnerability in the face of concentrated foreign economic power.[449] At base, one could conclude that it is exactly the national character of the antitrust legislation, a feature that enables it to address private conduct abroad, that prevents an incorporation of general, international legal principles into the antitrust framework.

6.9   CONCLUSION

Whereas, the transnational interdependence imposed by the Internet has led to an increased confrontation of diverging State-views regarding fundamental values, its global reach also opens up opportunities for States to advance their values extraterritorially. One of the ways in which States are inclined to do so is by regulating private actors in order to fulfill their foreign policy strategies. This chapter set out to identify the effects hereof in the light of the modern State's constitutional commitments and responsibilities by exploring the way in which the US attempts to address the censorship activities of US corporations operating abroad. The case study in question assessed the effects of the Global Online Freedom Act on Google's operations in China and resulted in the general conclusion that the fragmentation of legal frameworks limits the export of fundamental values by regulating the conduct of private parties. Whereas the theoretical and practical considerations disqualify GOFA's human rights approach as an effective way of exporting US values and ideals, the theoretically superior economic approach developed in this chapter, requires an incorporation of international values into national legal frameworks, a shift in economic policy the US does not seem ready to endorse just yet.

The basis for the evaluation of the GOFA and the development of the alternative economically oriented approach, form two distinct but interrelated constitutional ideals. Politically, the constitution forms the basis for the democratic ideal of a limited government. Economically, the constitutional democracy provides the basis for the ideal of a market economy. Despite the fact that these two ideals are intrinsically connected both ideologically and practically, the legal frameworks designed

---

[449] Harvard Law Review Note, 2001, p. 2145.

to promote these ideals are fragmented to the extent that they hardly allow for an integrated approach weighing both economic and political ideals and interests simultaneously.

Part I. The political (human) rights-based approach

The first part of the inquiry focused on the GOFA's inconsistent nature and the reasons for its failure. The conclusion of which are outlined below.

(1) The human rights framework is not an adequate framework for exporting US values and ideals through the extraterritorial regulation of private actors.

The further States in transition are removed from the constitutional democratic ideal, the less sensitive they tend to be for human rights-based arguments. For States in transition, economic reform is paramount. Political reform tends to be seen as a subservient prerequisite for economic change. China's reform program is a case in point as the exposition above shows. The insensitivity of States in transition to human rights-based arguments and the inability for rights-based legislation to incorporate economic considerations, are the prime reasons why the GOFA fails to deliver what it sets out to do and causes the GOFA to become an inconsistent piece of legislation. By using a human rights framework to regulate US corporations abroad, the GOFA violates both the political and economic ideals underlying the constitutional democracy.

(1.1) The GOFA's conflation of foreign policy goals with statutory law regulating domestic corporations causes a shift in power to the executive branch of government at the expense of the deliberative process in congress.

The GOFA's incorporation of explicit foreign policy goals, makes the applicability of the bill dependent on executive branch country assessments. Since assessments of foreign States is not typical of the GOFA but likely to be part of most regulatory actions taken by nations attempting to promote their values extraterritorially in the context of human rights, it is safe to say that the human rights focus of this type of regulation eludes the deliberative process in congress.

(1.2) The GOFA's human rights focus violates US economic ideals and interests because it limits the freedom of corporations and effectively creates a boycott of US products and services.

Forcing US corporation to refrain from filtering US sponsored content violates the free choice underlying the market economic ideal. It even effectively deprives US corporations from conducting their activities in the respective designated country. In addition to creating a degree of legal uncertainty for business by making the designation 'internet restricting' dependent on annual review and executive decision making, the GOFA violates the direct economic interests of the US by depriving US companies from operating in certain countries.

In sum, the human rights framework is not adequately equipped to address the censorship conduct of US corporations operating abroad. At the minimum it is an ineffective measure. Preventing US corporations to operate in the designated Internet restricting countries is neither going to establish information freedoms, nor other US ideals and values like a free market and a democratically chosen limited government in the designated country.

Part II. An economic approach

The second part of the inquiry focused on an alternative solution to the censorship problem, one that would both overcome (a) the democratic deficit, and (b) the violation of economic ideals and interests. Economic and political ideals go hand in hand. Since both ideals require a free flow of information in order to flourish, a natural candidate to turn to in the light of this inquiry was the economic framework. In this regard, censorship practices and particularly those conducted on the Internet are not only problematic from a political point of view they also can form barriers to trade. Moreover, a free flow of information stimulates trade because information itself is a product.

Filtering and blocking information can limit access to markets, particularly when the corporation in question has a relatively large market share or (like Google) forms one of the few convenient 'windows of opportunity' for US corporations to enter the foreign market. Since the values associated with a market economy tend to be more widely accepted than those of the human rights frameworks by States in transition:

(2) Theoretically the economic framework offers a promising framework for exporting national values extraterritorially through the regulation of private actors.

The prime international economic framework, the WTO, provides a platform for States to lower barriers to trade. Because it is primarily equipped to address the conduct of States, the framework is not suitable for fighting censorship activities by private actors abroad. The antitrust framework, because it is designed to address private conduct, offers more opportunities: (1) It is designed to address private behavior and (2) it already possesses an extraterritorial reach. (3) It is designed to protect both national consumers and exports, and (4) contains a clause acknowledging the international legal concept of State sovereignty (the doctrine of foreign compulsion). Consequently, the antitrust framework already provided a promising basis for the purposes that the GOFA set out to address. Because an antitrust solution would not allow for an assessment by the executive branch it would, in contrast to the GOFA, maintain legal certainty (solving problem 1.1). Similarly, since the economic framework is designed to take economic ideals and interests into account, it would most likely overcome the second problem afflicting the GOFA (problem 1.2), its ignorance of economic ideals and interests. The 'Doctrine of Foreign Compulsion' turned out to be particularly interesting in the light of this inquiry. By putting the burden of proof of censorship activities on individual corporations subject to antitrust legislation, it limits over-blocking by individual corporations and helps to clarify the exact parameters of foreign censorship. These parameters in turn can be used to address censorship practices in an intergovernmental setting.

The prime advantage of this approach is that it would be able to maintain the presence of US corporations in Internet restricting countries, which in turn would stimulate international trade and create opportunities for US corporations (information and information service providers) to US Google as a steppingstone for entering the Chinese market. In addition, increased trade with foreign (US) corporations is likely to stimulate both economic and political reform.

One of the conclusions in this chapter was that the GOFA inability to achieve its aims is due to a fragmentation of legal frameworks. Also within the context of frameworks advocating market economic ideals there remains a gap between the domestic and international framework that is not easily overcome. The crux of the matter is that the body of antitrust legislation is designed to fight barriers to trade within *particular* markets while the WTO framework advocates a liberalization of markets in general. Although the definition of markets can be interpreted rather broad, in order for the antitrust legislation to serve as a useful tool for fighting censorship activities and promoting US values, the notion of the relevant market needs to be extended in such a way as to incorporate *general* trade objectives into the framework. Ultimately however, the antitrust legislation is primarily designed to protect national (US) consumers and national (US) markets. In a way, the antitrust framework counters the free market ideal by protecting national markets in view of competing foreign markets. Since this remains the US policy and it remains explicitly part of US foreign policy to promote similar legislation within foreign States.[450] Thus, despite the theoretical possibilities, in *practice* the economic framework does not offer an effective framework for regulating foreign conduct by private actors in order to fight censorship and actively promote national values abroad.

Although the increased interdependency has created new opportunities for States to advance their values extraterritorially, unilateral attempts using private corporations to directly export national values abroad are not very fruitful. The fragmentation of legal frameworks prevents economic ideals and objectives to be incorporated into the human rights frameworks and prevents a smooth incorporation of international values into the domestic legal frameworks. And although the economic approach developed in this chapter provides a promising approach in terms of theoretical consistency and practical feasibility, the fragmentation of international and domestic frameworks to advance economic ideals and interests also prevents an immediate implementation of the antitrust approach.

---

[450] HR Rep. No. 97-686 at 13-14 (1982) 'The clarified reach of our own laws could encourage our trading partners to take more effective steps to protect competition in their own markets.'

Chapter 7
INTERDEPENDENCE AND NETWORK NEUTRALITY

The recent integration of communications services has revived the debate in US Congress whether regulation is required to prevent broadband operators from favoring signals running over their networks in terms of origin, nature or content. This chapter evaluates this debate, regarding the possible need for non-discriminatory or 'net neutrality' regulation, in the context of global interdependency and shows that (1) one of the most persistent preconceptions informing the debate, that the Internet is information neutral due to its very architecture, is ill founded. At base, network neutrality is not about preserving technical principles, but about how to stimulate the development of the Internet in terms of open communications (stimulating equal access) and innovation (stimulating freedom of choice). It shows that, contrary to a widespread belief, (2) the current regulatory regime is well equipped to deal with the most harmful form of discrimination on the Internet: the outright blocking of content. In addition, this chapter shows that (3) the scope of the current debate is too limited to come to a balanced judgment because it leads both sides in the debate to overvalue the US' ability to shape the (global) Internet of the future. Its focus on broadband networks ignores the potential of alternative technologies and its distinctive national focus ignores the transnational aspects of broadband regulation in a global context.

The technical nature of the Internet requires a global implementation of policies in order to be effective. The interdependent nature of the Internet prevents States from shaping the global network at large unilaterally. This bears important strategic implications for national policy setting. Since in an interdependent context domestic policies immediately affect foreign actors and vice versa, national communication policies demand an evaluation in transnational terms. For the US, this translates into the economic question how to maintain technological and commercial leadership on the Internet. Simultaneously, it poses the political question how to overcome the democratic deficit caused by the lack of representation of affected foreign parties in national decision making.

7.1 INTRODUCTION

The net neutrality debate can be termed in different ways depending on which aspects of the debate one is prone to emphasize. In economic terms, the debate is

R.W. Rijgersberg, The State of Interdependence
© 2010, T·M·C·ASSER PRESS, The Hague, and the author

about stimulating competition and promoting innovation. In terms of rights, the debate centers on access rights to the Internet. At base, the question is whether regulation is required to prevent broadband operators from favoring signals running over their networks in terms of origin, nature or content.[451] The debate is particularly timely, first because currently network operators are spending millions of dollars to upgrade their networks. Under a net neutrality regime, they could only incur their costs by expanding their customer base. Without such regulation, they could incur the costs by offering different levels of services at different prices. A second reason why the debate is timely is that currently US Congress is at a crossroads on the matter. Although most of the net neutrality bills put before Congress were killed at an early stage, the 2008 presidential elections have caused a shift in Congress through which democrats, who tend to favor net neutrality regulation, have acquired a solid majority. Consequently, there is a fair chance that net neutrality regulations may be imposed on broadband operators and Internet service providers.

The net neutrality debate is relevant in the light of the general context of this inquiry in a variety of ways. First, it affects the heart of the Internet since the means by which both end users and content providers access the Internet form important potential bottlenecks for Internet connectivity and hence Internet communication. The availability of reliable connections to access the Internet is crucial for a well-functioning information infrastructure. Hence, the connections that link end users to the Internet network form a critical element in facilitating national, but also global interaction over the Internet.

The net neutrality debate is also relevant to this inquiry in terms of interdependency. Since the Internet architecture creates a type of transnational interdependency that is acute (immediate) and outright (complete), national network regulation inevitably has an effect beyond the national State borders. In this respect, the outcome of the debate is directly relevant to the central question this chapter sets out to answer concerning the effects and consequences of national regulation on the development and accessibility of a global critical infrastructure.

The last relevant aspect of the net neutrality debate on the inquiry's general topic is its connection with the changing role of the State. The investigation into the effects of national legislation on the development of the Internet as an interdependency-imposing global medium not only provides insight into the extraterritorial effects of national regulation, it also provides insight into the effects of globalization on US policy making in an interdependent context.

7.2   NET NEUTRALITY, PHRASING THE QUESTION

Net neutrality is not a neutral concept. Different writers have proposed different definitions of the concept depending on the interests of the parties involved. The

---

[451] See <www.savetheinternet.org>. Net Neutrality prevents Internet providers from blocking, speeding up or slowing down Web content based on its source, ownership or destination.

concept however is not as vague as many proponents suggest it to be although various parties have defined net neutrality according to their specific interests. The interests at stake roughly divide the stakeholders into three groups (1) the end users, (2) content providers, including application and services providers[452] and (3) network owners/operators. The end users or consumers requiring the services of network operators to connect to the Internet are divided on the issue. According to the proponents, consumers should favor net neutrality regulation since it would guarantee consumer choice to access content, services and applications at a uniform rate.[453] However, some applications, particularly those requiring real-time processing of information, benefit considerably from increased quality of service arrangements. Hence, end users for example using video-conferencing techniques or engaged in on-line gaming are likely to object to net neutrality requirements. The second group of network users consists of content, application and services providers. The large players in this group like Google and Yahoo! also tend to favor net neutrality regulation since it would prevent the network operators from implementing tiered services, that is, varied service level arrangements at varied prices. Tiered service agreements could potentially raise prices for companies like Google and Yahoo!, or could downgrade their services in favor of other applications and content providers. Again, tiered service agreements could also create opportunities for novel applications and companies. The last interest group, the network operators generally agree that net neutrality regulation is against their interests since it would deprive them from a lucrative source of income enabling them to retract the costs made in order to build, maintain and improve the their networks.

Depending on the interests then, the keywords associated with the net neutrality debate also vary. From a consumer point of view, the right to access legal content at a uniform price tends to be emphasized by the one group, while consumer-choice tends to be emphasized by the opponents of the regulation. Content providers might focus on the need for competition on the network in order to stimulate the development of novel applications. On the other hand, some established players favor the net neutrality proposals in fear of the potential additional charges a tiered access system would generate. The network operators in turn, have a clear interest in an unfettered exploitation of the network in order to ensure future investments and improve, maintain and stimulate innovation in building the networks of the future.

---

[452] Note that there is a difference between Internet Services Providers and Internet Service Providers. The Services providers provide services using the Internet which can vary from providing information storage facilities to online advice. Internet Service Providers generally only provide one particular service, that is, access to the Internet over a physical or wireless connection. Within the context of this inquiry the service of connecting end users to the Internet is generally provided by broadband operators.

[453] See, Transatlantic Consumer Dialogue (TACD), 2008. The TACD is a forum of US and EU consumer organizations. This consumer view will be put into perspective later on since many end users favoring real-time applications used in for example, video-conferencing techniques, real-time voice applications and online gaming, generally would benefit considerably from an increased quality of service.

A variety of writers have emphasized that the notion of net neutrality is hard to capture because various interests groups tend to define the matter according to their needs and ideologies.[454] Reconciling the different views and definitions is considerably less problematic when taking a more neutral route in assessing the need for net neutrality regulation. The question that concerns us here is to what extent the proposed net neutrality regulation, preventing broadband operators from favoring signals running over their networks in terms of origin, nature or content, is required from a state point of view in the light of its traditional constitutional responsibilities and commitments. A constitutional perspective naturally requires a balanced view on the topic, including the interests of the parties involved. At base, the issue is about conflicting views on the purpose and effects of regulation. Before however engaging in the exercise of assessing the pros and cons of net neutrality regulation, it is useful to unravel one persistent myth that has dominated the net neutrality debate since its inception: the myth that somehow non-discrimination or net neutrality is related to an architectural Internet-design principle.

7.3   THE ARGUMENT FROM DESIGN

As Chapter 3 has already explained to some extent, the Internet's architecture can be explained by referring to three architectural principles: (1) The packet switching transmission technique ensures a network structure capable of enduring conventional military attacks. (2) The layered design model enables a design based on different levels of functionality (connectivity and communication). (3) The end-to-end (e2e) design principle in turn,[455] depicts a communication-network design as a simple or 'dumb' network core with more complicated or 'intelligent' design features at its outer ends. Whereas all three principles intertwine, particularly the e2e design principle has gained almost mythical proportions in the net neutrality debate.[456] The reason is that because the e2e design creates a 'dumb' network core, it does not discriminate between source, type or content of the data sent over the network.

The Internet has in common with the traditional telephone services that it is primarily a communications platform. Since the Internet has taken the notion of communications at a significantly higher level than the traditional telecommunications system ever did, the telecommunications platform is frequently contrasted

---

[454] See for example Hahn, R.W. and Wallsten, S.J., 2006; and Singer, H.J., 2007; Chong, R., 2007, suggesting that net neutrality is a very complex phenomenon. See also: Gilroy, A.A., 2008, claiming that the concept 'net neutrality does not have a single definition.

[455] Saltzer, J.H., et al., 1984.

[456] The myth has particularly been promoted in: Lemley, M. and Lessig, L., 2000; Also Columbia professor Wu has done a lot in order to increase the popularity of this myth, see for example his website <http://timwu.org/network_neutrality.html>, in which he stresses the point that 'network neutrality can best be understood as a network design principle'.

with the Internet. There are good reasons for doing so. As Chapter 3 has pointed out, the telecommunications system used a circuit switched wire-line system in order to establish connections between its users. The characteristic of this traditional system is that the network at the centre of the system provides the specific know-how needed to transmit the information adequately. The telephones connected at the edges of the web are simple or 'dumb' devices only designed to send and receive the information travelling over the intelligent network. Consequently, the telephone system was network-specific, that is, completely reliant on the network that was specifically designed for its purposes. As a result, it hampered the development of non-voice applications on the network because the development of the network was completely in the hands of the network operators.

The general textbook story on the Internet shows a different picture. It stresses that the Internet's e2e design principle was a breakthrough in that it established a network structure logically independent from its underlying physical structure and indifferent to the type of both information and application used in the network. The 'dumb' network structure enabled the development of myriad devices and types of information to be transmitted, whether plain text, voice or video, because in an e2e network, operators are not in a position to discriminate between types of content or applications. The e2e design has contributed much to the Internet's success because it creates an environment encouraging innovation at the edges due to the minimal amount of constraints posed on the applications by the core network structure. In addition, it created an environment in which competition at the edges of the network allowed equal opportunities for application designers to compete for the public's favor.

For many writers on net neutrality, the secret to the Internet's success is a function of this e2e design principle and hence serves important social and commercial goals. In Lemley and Lessig's words:

> 'It [e2e] maximizes the number of entities that can compete for the use and applications of the network. As there is no single strategic actor who can tilt the competitive environment (the network) in favor of itself, or no hierarchical entity that can favor some applications over others, an e2e network creates a maximally competitive environment for innovation, which by design assures competitors that they will not confront strategic network behavior.'[457]

Thus, the e2e design principle is said to have laid the foundations for a competitive environment enabling the development of applications independent of the network itself. Due to the strict division between the core of the network and the applications, both amateurs and professionals could develop new ways of exploiting the use of the network independent of the network owners. According to the textbook story, the 'dumbness' or 'application and information neutrality' of the Internet architecture was responsible for an immense amount of creativity and competition,

---

[457] Ibid., p. 8.

a competition between players operating at the edges of the network, the 'winners' of which are still with us today.

The 'argument from design' now holds the following: (1) The e2e principle has certain benefits in terms of innovation and access because it ensures non-discriminatory exchange of data. (2) Currently these architectural benefits are under threat because of recent commercial and regulatory developments. (3) The only way to retain or restore the original e2e benefits of the Internet is through implementing regulation ensuring the non-discriminatory exchange of data.

The appeal of the argument lies in the fact that everyone knows that the Internet has been an incredible success ever since its inception. In addition, it is widely known that the Internet's network architecture is unique. Success is often a result of design. The suggestion therefore that one particular design principle is responsible for the Internet's success is intuitively very appealing.

It may be true that networks designed and functioning on an e2e basis do pose significant advantages over non-e2e designed networks. It may also be true that the Internet benefits significantly from network neutrality regulation in terms of innovation and access. The suggestion however, that the proposed net neutrality legislation attempts to revive the benefits associated with the original design features of the Internet is a gross distortion of reality. First, if there were such a connection, the current proposals would be incomplete because they only address one out of two necessary aspects to create the e2e benefits. More importantly however, the Internet has never built on an e2e basis. Its architectural history and early business models suggest a bias towards differentiated services as the following sections explain.

7.3.1 An incomplete solution

A successful e2e-based communication network in terms of openness and end-user innovation however, would require more than a neutral network alone. It would also require end-user devices that allow for modification by end users, devices that would allow them to cater for their specific needs and allow end users to develop novel applications. Whereas the average personal computer does possess this quality, it remains to be seen to what extent the all-purpose personal computer will remain the standard device for accessing the Internet of the future. Increasingly, end users connect to the Internet through devices like iPhones, Xboxes and TiVos.[458] These devices distinguish themselves from the traditional personal computers in their design and in their modifiability by end users. Unlike personal computers they are designed for a specific purpose rather than for general use. These special-purpose devices typically only allow for modification by their vendors and selected partners whereas general-purpose devices typically allow for modification by their end users who write computer programs serving their particular needs. A continuation of this trend towards a widespread use of special-purpose devices would sig-

---

[458] A TiVo is a digital video recorder that can record films using the Internet.

nificantly harm what Zittrain has called the 'generative' quality of the Internet, that is, the Internet's capacity to produce unanticipated change through unfiltered contributions from broad and varied audiences.[459]

Zittrain's exposition however, is rather an overstatement. The use of what he calls 'tethered' appliances is of course marginal compared to the worldwide use of personal 'all-purpose' computers. This is not to say however that the ability for a network architecture built on e2e principles to stimulate openness and innovation depends as much on the dumbness of the system as on the availability and ability for the end users to modify their devices in order to create innovative applications at the end points of the network. Thus even if the network neutrality legislation restored the neutrality of the network to its original e2e model, it would only guarantee one side of the innovative coin, i.e. the dumb, allegedly nondiscriminatory nature of the network. In order to establish the open character of the web and create innovation, it would need to guarantee the use of 'generative' devices. Consequently, from an e2e point of view, if anything, the network neutrality regulation is at most a partial attempt to restore or retain the open and innovative character of the Internet.

Nevertheless, even when assuming that Internet access with non-generative devices is unlikely to stagnate overall innovation if net neutrality is guaranteed, the e2e metaphor in relation to net neutrality regulation cannot be upheld. A second reason why the proposed legislation could never serve as instrument for restoring the actual e2e situation is that the current Internet is rather more complicated than the e2e picture suggests. It is becoming increasingly difficult to distinguish between the dumb network core and the smart applications at the endpoint of the network.[460] Storage and manipulation of information is increasingly conducted location-independent on the web instead of on the computers of the end users and the combined use of end-user devices to distribute processes over multiple locations suggests that the traditional end user/network distinction is not tenable anymore in the current Internet configuration. Consequently, it is not straightforward to view the broadband development as a violation of the e2e situation. In addition, the current technical Internet reality actually requires discrimination between data. Good traffic management in terms of congestion and security, require operators to distinguish between types of information.[461]

In sum, even if the net neutrality regulation would restore the e2e situation on the Internet, it would only establish a partial attempt to restore the situation since it does not address the increased availability and use of tethered appliances. In addition, a restoration of the e2e situation is simply not feasible (politically and technically) because it has become increasingly difficult to distinguish between the ends and the core of the Internet network. In other words, the net neutrality regulation is

---

[459] Zittrain, J.L., 2008, p. 70.

[460] Ibid., for example, popularity of online search algorithms created by Google and other search operators have given way to the creation of social network sites like YouTube and MySpace.

[461] The discriminatory practice in the context of good traffic management is generally acknowledged, as is explicitly confirmed in: FTC (2008).

unable to fix the alleged original e2e nature of the Internet even if it were to foreclose discrimination by network operators.

7.3.2   The biased nature of the Internet

The assumption that the e2e design principle, as the founding principle of Internet
design, somehow hardwired the non-discriminatory exchange of data into the
Internet's very architecture is perhaps the oldest, but certainly the most persistent
misconception informing the net neutrality debate. The network of networks we
now call the Internet has always been technically partisan towards types of information. In addition, as of its early commercial beginnings, the business models
driving the Internet's development have distinguished between different levels of
service on the network. Also a close examination of the first paper describing the
e2e design principle, suggests a less strict interpretation of the relation between the
e2e design principles and the Internet architecture. In sum, as the following explains, the e2e design principle is rather an idealized organizing principle of systems design rather than a foundational principle on which the Internet was built.

The technical bias of the Internet

Although the Internet seems to be the archetypical communications system built
according to e2e design principles, even before Saltzer's paper describing the principle in 1984, the Internet distinguished between different types of traffic and defined informational flags for prioritization of packets travelling over the TCP/IP
networks. The various standards issued by the Internet Engineering Task Force
(IETF)[462] before 1984, suggest that the proposed information-neutral data transmission associated with the e2e design principle has never been hardwired into the
Internet architecture as is often suggested. In fact, a look at the Request for Comments (RFCs)[463] demonstrates that prioritization, the opposite of net neutrality, has
always been an important design characteristic for TCP/IP.[464] RFC 675 (1974), for
example, explains that outgoing packets (packets moving from the respective host)
should be given priority over other packets to prevent congestion on the ingoing
and outgoing pipe.[465] IETF RFC 791 (1981) for example describes a way of distinguishing between high and low priority traffic.[466] In addition, after 1984, the IETF
RFCs show a continued development of standards for distinguishing between types
of traffic.

---

[462] See also Chapter 5 'Interdependence and Technical Standardization' in this inquiry which contains an elaborate exposition of the workings of the IETF and the way in which Internet standards are
implemented.
[463] Ibid., standards developed within the context of the IETF are always posted as requests for
comments.
[464] Hahn, R.W. et al., 2007, p. 601.
[465] IETF RFC 675.
[466] IETF RFC 791, p. 39.

Perhaps one of the more important RFCs in the light of the current Internet developments is RFC 1639 (1994), proposing a solution for the problems arising due to bandwidth constraints that typically cause problems when real-time applications are used transmitting voice and video messages. Acknowledging that real-time applications need additional bandwidth compared for example to text, this RFC includes suggestions for a preferred treatment based on the type of information.[467] Since the technical community posts RFCs as solutions to generally recognized problems, IETF RFC 1639 particularly shows that the Internet has never been neutral. Real-time applications are a considerably disadvantaged type of communication on the Internet due to their need for a better quality of service. Subsequent RFCs confirm the need for distinguishing between different types of information. IETF RFC 2475 for example, also contains architectural proposals for far-reaching differentiated services[468] and the IPv6 addressing standard, designed to cater for the increased number of Internet connections, contains provisions anticipating differentiated services.[469] In the light of these developments, it does not come as a surprise that the Internet Assigned Numbers Authority (IANA), a technical subsidiary of the ICANN,[470] in describing its general protocol values also distinguishes between types of data. Protocols directly interacting with humans should be processed on a low-delay basis, while for example data transfers involving large blocks of data should be treated on a high-throughput basis. In sum, there is no basis for suggesting that the Internet has ever been specifically designed on a neutral basis with respect to the kind of traffic travelling over the networks.

The business model bias of the Internet

From a business perspective, the alleged neutrality of the Internet is also completely misplaced. Hass,[471] for example, shows that, from the Internet's inception as publicly available 'commercial' network, the business model underlying the content and access provisions has allowed for different quality of service agreements and associated price differentiation. The result was a tiered access structure in which top-tier providers building the large (often national) networks and connecting with other networks agreeing to peer with each other and passing traffic on behalf of downstream customers that used the networks to connect to the Internet. Lower-tiered providers, typically catering for smaller areas, made agreements with top-tier providers paying for connectivity and peering. Consequently, the lower-tiered provid-

---

[467] IETF RFC 1633.

[468] IETF RFC 2475.

[469] IETF RFC 2474. More information on the additional complications regarding the next generation Internet addresses can be found in Chapter 5, 'Interdependence and Technical Standardization', in Section 5.5.3 'Standard setting in action: IPv6 and privacy'.

[470] More information on ICANN can be found in Chapter 4 'Interdependence and Global Governance'. Chapter 5 'Interdependence and Technical Standardization' explores the role of standardization in the development of the Internet.

[471] Hass, D.A., 2007.

ers were a step removed from the equal access of the Internet's backbone[472] purchasing bandwidth from top-tiered providers. Soon this model developed into more sophisticated differentiated business models that continue to dominate today's access markets. Since 1998, the differentiation of individual traffic flows and the prioritization of particular applications, for example by using distributed servers on the network, have become important industries for companies like Cisco Systems and ImageStream.[473] In addition, today's consumers and content providers paying for additional bandwidth, have an effective advantage in terms of quality of service because more bandwidth means that data can travel 'side by side' over the Internet and provide faster, hence differentiated data transmission.[474] In sum, also from a business model perspective, the Internet has never been neutral since its inception as a publicly available network despite the alleged qualities that net neutrality proponents impute to the e2e design principle.

The e2e principle revisited

The e2e glorification within the net neutrality debate largely originates in the seminal paper on the topic written by Saltzer et al.[475] In this paper, they explain that designing a system for transferring files from computer A to computer B consists of a variety of steps, namely: (1) reading file X on computer A, (2) creating the packets and making them transport-ready, (3) transporting them over the network nodes, (4) reassembling the packets, and (5) saving file X' on computer B. The crux of the paper is that they explain that most features in the middle of a communications system are redundant if this means that the end user must implement these features a second time on an e2e basis. For example, it is generally inefficient to build error checks into every subsequent step of the process because in order to guarantee a safe delivery of information an end-to-end check at the terminating phase in the process needs to be performed anyway. Hence, any intermediary check is redundant and is likely to slow down the system. This is why Saltzer, Reed and Clark suggest that system designers should preferably build the higher-level functions, requiring a lot of processing, into the servers and host at the end points of the network. However, as Yoo pointed out, Saltzer, Reed and Clark and other technologists, rather take the e2e design principle to be one of several important organizing principles of systems design than as an established, empirically certified and imperative principle of Internet design.[476] The subsequent popularization of the e2e design principle in connection with the Internet's success is mainly due to a unfortunate simplification of the complex reality of the Internet infrastructure. Consequently, the 'revival' of the Internet's benign characteristics based on the mythical

---

[472] See Chapter 3 'Globalization, Interdependence and the Internet' and particular Section 3.2 'The Internet Architecture' for a more elaborate exposition of the Internet.

[473] Hass, D.A., 2007.

[474] See for a more elaborate account: Sidak, J.G., 2007, p. 69ff.

[475] Saltzer, J.H., 1984. See also the exposition in Chapter 3 of this inquiry.

[476] See, ibid., and Yoo, C.S., 2004.

features of the e2e design principle is based on a misconception of both the design principle and the Internet reality.

7.3.3   Conclusion

The forgoing sections showed that the idea that net neutrality is about maintaining the desirable qualities of an architectural design principle is ill founded. The argument from design, that the architectural principles that made the Internet successful are under threat and can only be retained or revitalized by implementing net neutrality regulation, is based on a myth. Even when assuming that the e2e principle was the founding principle of the Internet's architecture, the net neutrality proposals are insufficient for restoring the original e2e situation on the Internet that allegedly was the secret to the Internet's success. Attempts at restoring the 'generative' qualities of the Internet only address the neutrality of the network and not the need for generative devices. In addition, the technical reality on the Internet forecloses a clear distinction between ends and core of the Internet, in effect making the objectives of a net neutral Internet technically unfeasible. Moreover, today's Internet also requires discrimination between types of traffic in order to maintain security and avoid congestion on the servers as part of good network traffic management.

More importantly however, the e2e origin of the Internet, suggesting that the best way to design a communication network with a 'dumb', 'neutral' network core and the 'intelligence' located at the outer ends of the network, is not backed by historical evidence. Both the early technical and the early commercial Internet reality invalidate the thesis that the Internet was founded on the e2e design principle. Instead of being a principle forming the *basis* for the Internet architecture, the e2e design principle is rather a design principle *inspired* by the Internet as a communication network structure. This conclusion is also confirmed by the re-examination of the Saltzer's (1984) paper and the observation that even at the time the Internet did not answer to the idealized e2e format. Both the Internet protocol history and the business models that have made the Internet to its current success suggest a bias towards differentiation, reaching its expression in the tiered access model developed in the nineties forming a precursor to the current state of play.

Consequently, the e2e design principle and its associated benefits are merely idealizations, platonic ideals useful to gain some understanding of the basis features of the Internet architecture but not suitable as an argument for implementing net neutrality regulation based on some kind of technological conservatism. Instead of a romantic longing for an e2e ideal with mythical qualities, the net neutrality discussion is essentially concerned with the question whether and how States should stimulate the development of the Internet. Before taking up this topic, however, it is useful to determine to what extent the current regulatory practices are able to do just this; provide a remedy for the fears of the net neutrality proponents and stimulate the development of the Internet in terms of access, competition and innovation.

7.4   THE CURRENT INTERNET REALITY

The Internet is a fast-changing technical environment. Both the complexity of the technical aspects of the Internet and the complexity of its fast changing business environment create a tendency to interlard Internet debates with metaphors. As the previous section showed, this can be misleading since the metaphors sometimes blur rather than clarify the actual situation on the Internet. The following exposition is also a simplification. Particularly the picture of the Internet as a three-layered model is an unsophisticated representation of reality. Nevertheless, this simplification does not serve as a foundation for developing an argument or model for implementing new legislation. It merely serves to clarify the current technical and business reality to get a better understanding of the issues informing the net neutrality debate, and serves as background information for establishing to what extent today's legal practice is able to tackle the problems that the net neutrality legislation seeks to address. The simplification involved in the following sections only involves a simplification in *degree* of complexity unlike the e2e principle used by the net neutrality proponents, this is not a simplification eliminating the essential features of the actual situation.

7.4.1   The technical and commercial reality

Chapter 3 describes the Internet as a two-layered model. The *communication* layer handles the way in which applications (hence users) communicate with one another. The *interconnectivity* layer arranges the connections between hosts and the transmission of data. For the purposes of this chapter it is useful to subdivide this second layer into (a) a logical or network component consisting of protocols establishing interconnectivity between hosts, and (b) a hardware or physical component comprising of the material cables over which the information is transmitted. The three layers thus distinguished; content layer, network layer and physical layer each have their players and characteristics.

At the content layer, we find two types of players. The first type consists of (end) users operating as prosumers, i.e., they operate both on the supply and demand side of the spectrum.[477] The second type of player consists of professional content providers that compete in the provision of content, services and applications like e-mail, voice and video. Competition at the content level has been one of the major objectives spelled out in the Clinton green and white papers[478] and has played an important role in shaping the Internet environment as we encounter it today. In addition to creating novel business opportunities, the Internet has also changed the business model of traditional information suppliers that are now offering their prod-

---

[477] The neologism 'prosumer' consisting of a contraction of the words *pro*ducer and con*sumer*, illustrates the dual role of the Internet user, which transcends the traditional distinction between consumers on the one hand and producers on the other.

[478] NTIA, 1998a; 1999b.

ucts on line. Moreover, the Internet has become an important tool for marketing purposes for both virtual and non-computer generated products and services.[479] For many players acting at the content level, advertisement is a significant source of income.

At the network level, we encounter a different type of competition. The Internet as a network of connected networks is not a uniform competitive area. It is a tiered business structure. At the top of the chain are the Internet backbone providers owning or leasing the international infrastructures that link different continents or regions. The companies in this category include: AT&T, BT Ignite, Cable and Wireless, France Telecom and WorldCom.[480] The second tier consists of national and regional players, providing fiber and cable infrastructures in smaller regions. At the third tier, we encounter a myriad of ISPs providing the direct connections to the customers. ISPs provide consumers and content providers access to the Internet core by linking the host computer to a local Point of Presence (POP) which in turn establishes the connection with the high speed hubs that form the 'Internet backbone' network either through national, regional providers, or directly, thus establishing a tiered services model. Since the ISP needs to ensure that its customers can access all the other hosts available on the Internet, they pay for bandwidth use to a local backbone provider, which also provides the interconnection with other networks. Agreements establishing this latter connection vary from peering agreements enabling them to use each other's services free of charge, to buying access to other networks. Combinations of the two also exist.[481]

The physical layer is the most basic layer of the Internet. The existence of a network of nodes effectively ensures the ability of the packets to reach the same host by different routes (the secret of the packet switching technique).[482] The physical link itself may vary from copper telephone wires to fiber and (tv) cable connections. There are various means enabling the end user to connect to the network. Currently, the preferred means for connecting to the net are broadband connections, which form the focus of the network neutrality debate.[483] The number of competing backbone (tier one) providers haled to a minimum of price differentiation and at this level it is relatively easy for ISPs to switch Internet backbone service provider.[484]

The net neutrality problem concerns the connection from the Internet backbone to the end user or content provider. This 'last mile', can form a bottleneck for the

---

[479] In this context the debate on ICANN and the DNS in Chapter 4, 'Interdependence and Domain Name System Management' is also relevant.

[480] Nicol, C., 2003, Part 2, Section 4.

[481] Economides, N., 2005, p. 12.

[482] See Chapter 3, Section 3.2 'The Internet Architecture'.

[483] Wu also discusses the net neutrality debate in the light of wireless connections. As he himself points out, this debate between private and regulator's interests is a battle that is to emerge and decided over the next decade. As such, wireless net neutrality is of less immediate concern to congress and to the topic of this inquiry. For more information on wireless net neutrality; Wu, T., 2007.

[484] Economides, N., 2005.

information exchange when network owners owning both the physical last mile to the end users and acting as an ISP connecting end users to the Internet, use their power to discriminate between signals in terms of origin, nature or content. In practice, this could result in favoring the signals from affiliated over non-affiliated content providers. The competitive situation in the 'last mile' service provided by the broadband providers is such that it is less easily accessible to new market entrants. Consequently, now that traditional telecom and television services increasingly use the Internet and act as ISPs, concerns are raised about the mixed interests of these companies offering Internet services that compete with their original line of business; television and telephone services. Although the proposed net neutrality regulation addresses a broader concern, the integration of traditional communications services with the Internet market is illustrative of the kind of concerns that the net neutrality regulation attempts to address. Two, partly interrelated, concerns dominate the debate. First, there is a concern that the current developments hamper the open character of the Internet, i.e., the ability to access Internet content and connect all types of applications. Secondly, there is a concern that the current developments hamper the innovative character of the Internet. Both concerns are different ways of addressing a fear for discrimination on the Internet. Since the bills calling for net neutrality regulation seem to suggest a legislative gap, the following section explores the current legal practice and shows it is well equipped to handle the most harmful types of exclusionary practices on the Internet.

7.4.2   Current legal practice

The bills that have been put before Congress in order to establish net neutrality all contain provisions for broadband providers to refrain from discriminatory practices by barring them from 'blocking, impairing or degrading access to content and applications'.[485] The rationale for implementing net neutrality regulation is twofold:

---

[485] A number of bills have been put before Congress containing net neutrality provisions. Examples of which are: *S2360* The Internet Non Discrimination Act (2006), prohibits a network operator (an entity that owns, controls, or resells any facility that provides communications services to subscribers) from: (1) interfering with any bits, content, application, or service transmitted over the operator's network; (2) discriminating in allocating bandwidth and transmitting content, applications, or services to or from a subscriber; or (3) assessing a charge to any application or service provider not on the operator's network for the delivery of traffic to any subscriber to the operator's network, whilst preserving the network operators to: (1) protect subscribers from adware, viruses, spam, content deemed inappropriate for minors, and other applications or service that harms the Internet experience of subscribers; and (2) support an application or service intended to prevent such adware, viruses, content, etc. *HR 5252* Communications Opportunity and Promotions Enhancement Act (COPE, 2006), initially anti-discrimination provisions were to prohibit network operators to treat equally all the data passing through their cables. Eventually this act was passed on to the Senate without the anti-discrimination clause. *S 2917* The Internet Freedom Preservation Act (2006), amending the Communications Act of 1934 to establish certain Internet neutrality duties for broadband service providers (providers), including not interfering with, or discriminating against, the ability of any person to use broadband service in a lawful manner. It allows providers to engage in activities in furtherance of certain management and

net neutrality provisions allegedly (1) increase the democratic process by guaranteeing access for consumers to all services available on the Internet on a non-discriminatory basis, that is, unimpaired by intermediaries. Furthermore, net neutrality allegedly (2) stimulate competition, investment and innovation on the Internet because it disables intermediaries to impose restrictions on the ways that consumers use the Internet. Net neutrality legislation would prevent network operators providing access to the Internet to have the power to forestall new end-user driven innovation. Whereas both claims are highly contested and dubious to say the least, there are two ways of looking at this from a constitutional point of view, a rights perspective and an economic perspective.

Access rights

Democracy is often associated with information freedoms. Non-discriminatory access to information and applications in the context of the Internet touches the heart of the fundamental values of the modern State. Particularly the democratic values of a free society presuppose a free flow of information establishing a 'marketplace of ideas', in which the best ideas through deliberation and fierce opposition will

---

business-related practices, such as protecting network security and offering consumer protection services such as parental controls. It further prohibits a provider from requiring a subscriber, as a condition on the purchase of broadband service, to purchase any cable service, telecommunications service, or IP-enabled voice service. Eventually the bill did not come to a vote in the Senate. Recently the bill has been reintroduced as S 215 The Internet Freedom Preservation Act (2007) and HR 5353 The Internet Freedom Preservation Act (2008). *HR 5417* Internet Freedom and Nondiscrimination Act of 2006 – Amends the Clayton Act to prohibit any broadband network provider from: (1) failing to provide its services on reasonable and nondiscriminatory terms; (2) refusing to interconnect its facilities with those of another service provider on reasonable and nondiscriminatory terms; (3) blocking, impairing, discriminating against, or interfering with any person's ability to use a broadband network service to access or offer lawful content, applications, or services over the Internet (or imposing an additional charge to avoid such prohibited conduct); (4) prohibiting a user from attaching or using a device on the provider's network that does not physically damage or materially degrade other users' utilization of the network; or (5) failing to clearly and conspicuously disclose to users accurate information concerning service terms. It furthermore requires a provider that prioritizes or offers enhanced quality of service to data of a particular type to prioritize or offer enhanced quality of service to all data of that type without imposing a surcharge or other consideration. The Act allows non-discriminatorily managing the network to promote security, giving priority to emergency communications or preventing a violation of law or comply with a court order. This bill never became law because of failure to pass in Congress within two years time and has been reintroduced as HR 5994 The Internet Freedom and Nondiscrimination Act (2008). *HR 5273* Network Neutrality Act (2006), stating that among other things, it is the policy of the United States to maintain the freedom to use broadband telecommunications networks, including the Internet, without interference from network operators. It outlines specified duties of broadband network providers to ensure broadband network neutrality, including the duty to: (1) enable users to utilize their broadband service to access all lawful content, applications, and services available over broadband networks, including the Internet; and (2) not block, impair, degrade, discriminate against, or interfere with the ability of any person to utilize their broadband service for lawful purposes. Provides exceptions for providers, including implementing reasonable measures to manage its networks and protect network security. The House committee on Telecommunications and the Internet voted it down by 23 to 8.

prevail and guide the way to make decisions in the public interest.[486] Article 19 of the Universal Declaration of Human Rights (UDHR) states in this context that

> 'Everyone has the right to freedom of opinion and expression; this right includes freedom to hold opinions without interference and to seek, receive and impart information and ideas through any media and regardless of frontiers.'

Article 19 UDHR is often read in conjunction with Article 27 UDHR stating that: 'everyone has a right freely to participate in the cultural life of the community, to enjoy the arts and to share in scientific advancement and its benefits.'

Also the United Nations (UN) link the practice of democracy, as a basic value of the modern State, to communication as a basic human need[487] and within the US, the link between democratic deliberation and information freedoms forms an important argument for net neutrality proponents. Some activist organizations like *SavetheInternet(.org)*, which features Lessig and Wu among its most prominent charter members, even hailed the net neutrality concept as 'the first amendment of the Internet'.[488] Seen in this light, the 'open' or 'forced' access requirements imposed on broadband operators by the proposed legislation almost appear a natural extension of US First Amendment rights guaranteeing free speech. On further inspection however, the connection between the first amendment and access rights is rather thin, not to say non-existent.

There have been several attempts to construct the current concerns in the US about non-discriminatory broadband access in terms of First Amendment rights. On the one hand, equal access can be constructed as a speaker's right to access information.[489] On the other hand, it can be defined as a speaker's (or supplier's) right to gain access to an audience.[490] Both views are rather limited in their application to net neutrality provisions. The first construction is merely relevant in terms of availability of information through public channels such as libraries[491] while the second construction primarily concerns the availability of a balanced view in the light of mass media coverage.[492] Moreover, the First Amendment explicitly prohibits *Congress* from making laws that impair the freedom of speech and assembly.[493]

---

[486] Although he used the term 'free trade in ideas' instead of 'marketplace of ideas', the concept is generally attributed to Justice Holmes in his dissenting opinion in *Abrams* v. *U.S,* 250 US 616 (1919). In his opinion Holmes stated that the theory of the Constitution is that 'the ultimate good desired is better reached by free trade in ideas (…) that the best test of truth is the power of the thought to get itself accepted in the competition of the market, and that truth is the only ground upon which their wishes safely can be carried out.'

[487] WSIS, 2003.

[488] See for examples the remarks at <www.savetheinternet.com/>.

[489] Mathiesen, K., 2008.

[490] Napoli, P. and Sybblis, S., 2007.

[491] Mathiesen, K., 2008.

[492] Napoli, P. and Sybblis, S., 2007.

[493] The first amendment to the US Constitution reads: Congress shall make no law respecting an establishment of religion, or prohibiting the free exercise thereof; or abridging the freedom of speech,

Hence, the Amendment's aim is to promote a free flow of information by placing limits on the powers of government as opposed to private actors.[494] May has even suggested that the proposed net neutrality regulations dictating ISPs choices concerning the dissemination of content, is unlikely to survive a Supreme Court examination on First Amendment grounds. His reasons for holding this view is that the net neutrality regulations would impose a legal limitation of the intermediary's right to edit information the way they see fit which also follows from the First amendment.[495]

In sum, it is hard to find a conceptual foundation for net neutrality legislation in terms of non-discriminatory access based on First Amendment rights. Although extending a right to the media could arguably be a promising avenue for developing access rights in both practicable and conceptual terms,[496] the US prefers to take information access as a basis for its Internet communication policy. The rationale for this (qualified) right as we shall see in the next section, is not grounded in rights designed to further the public interest by guaranteeing individual liberties, but by collectivist motives underlying an economic conviction. Ultimately however, neither an economic point of view stimulating choice, nor a rights-based perspective ensuring equal access[497] makes a compelling case for implementing net neutrality regulation. With the absence of a First Amendment right to gain access applicable to the current broadband reality, the remaining part of this section will show that the current economic regulation is more than capable of stimulating competition and innovation whilst simultaneously protecting the consumer and maintaining a 'marketplace of ideas'.

Competition and innovation

The prevailing economic (textbook and policy) practice holds that within the context of the market economy, innovation is achieved primarily through competition. The economic objective of stimulating competition and innovation is Constitutionally grounded in the State's responsibility concerning the regulation of interstate and international commerce[498] and gave rise to the body of antitrust law starting with the Sherman Act (1890). In conjunction with the Federal Trade Commission (1914), it served as a democratically informed corrective mechanism to the undesirable side effects of the free market by promoting competition and protecting the consumer against unfair methods of competition.[499] In addition, to this general body

---

or of the press; or the right of the people peaceably to assemble, and to petition the Government for a redress of grievances.

[494] See also Chapter 2 'The Modern State' on the role of the Constitution in this respect.

[495] May, R.J., 2007.

[496] Napoli, P. and Sybblis, S., 2007.

[497] Example: Goodman, E., 2007.

[498] Art. I, Section 8 US Constitution: The Powers of Congress.

[499] 15 USC § 45(n) The Federal Trade Commission (1914), especially enacted as the federal agency protecting both consumers and competition, cannot deem conduct unfair 'unless the act of practice

of law, the constitutional responsibilities also gave rise to the Federal Communications Commission (FCC) (1934) regulating interstate and international communications.

The Federal Communications Commission

Within the context of the legislative framework addressing the conduct of private corporations in the communications branch, broadband operators can either be regarded as *communication* or *information* services. Communications services traditionally fall under Title II of the Communications Act of 1934[500] whilst information services fall under Title I of the same Act. Communication networks are subject to a stringent 'common carrier' regime while information services are subject to considerably less restrictive requirements.

The historical roots of common carrier legislation can be traced back to the early railroad system. Because the rail network operators had the power to determine which carriers could use the network, the objective of the common carrier legislation was to increase competition by prohibiting the operators of the railway networks to discriminate unreasonably between persons, businesses, localities and traffic.[501] The Communications Act of 1934 did something similar to the telecommunications network by qualifying their private property right to exclude third parties. The effect of this was that network owners offering services to the general public obtained a general duty of non-discrimination among customers, particularly regarding treatment and pricing policy. As a result, common carriers generally operate on a first come, first serve basis, and are not allowed to differentiate in price between different users. In addition, they have an additional obligation to charge 'reasonable' prices for their services.

The Communications Act conferred extensive authority on the FCC to regulate the rates and business practices of communications entities and expanded the common carrier legislation to the telecommunications network. Consequently, since the early ISPs provided Internet access over the telephone network, they profited considerably from the common carrier provisions guiding the conduct of the network operators who had to (1) 'charge just, reasonable, and non-discriminatory rates', (2) ensure interconnection with independent ISPs, and (3) support universal service goals related to stimulating access.[502] This, despite the threat the Internet posed for the telecom sector offering cheap alternative means for communication.

Net neutrality legislation essentially mimics the traditional common carrier regulation in that it imposes non-discriminatory access and rates in the public interest. In early 2005, the FCC showed a willingness to enforce network neutrality prin-

---

causes or is likely to cause substantial injury to consumers which is not reasonably avoidable by consumers themselves and not outweighed by countervailing benefits to consumers of competition'.

[500] Communications Act, 47 USC 151 et seq.

[501] See for a more extended historical overview of the common carrier regime; Noam, E.M., 1994.

[502] Communications Act (1934), 47 USC § 153.

ciples upon Madison River Communications (MRC), a local telephone carrier providing both traditional telephone services and Digital Subscriber Line Services to their customers. Over a period of 30 months, MRC had blocked Vonage's Voice over Internet Protocol (VoIP) services in order to safeguard its own traditional telephone revenues. Pressured by the FCC, Madison MRC reached a settlement and agreed to pay USD 15,000 as a settlement to avoid further investigations after having been accused of blocking ports used for VoIP applications.[503] The settlement resulted in many statements by large corporations never to engage in blocking practices.[504]

In June 2005 however, the Supreme Court took a different path in the (in-)famous *Brand X* decision.[505] This decision seemed to mark a turning point in broadband policy by labeling high-speed Internet connections (broadband) as an *information* service rather than a *telecommunications* service regulated by the common carrier regime. Under the telecommunications Act, common carrier provisions restrict only telecommunications services, information services are not affected. The Brand X decision was justified by the (then) availability of substitute forms of Internet transmission and various ways in which to connect to the Internet as an end user, notably wireline, cable, terrestrial wireless, and satellite. Consequently, the FCC concluded that broadband services should exist in a minimal regulatory environment promoting investment and innovation in a competitive market.[506] In a second ruling, the FCC extended the same regulatory relief to telephone company Internet access services providing their services by wireline broadband or DSL in order to create consistent regulation in the broadband market.[507]

The foregoing shows that the FCC, as an independent US government agency charged with regulating interstate and international communications by radio, television, wire, satellite and cable, considers the Internet broadband market competitive enough not to impose rigid common carrier restrictions on broadband operators.

The antitrust framework

Although the US Supreme Court ruled in 2004 that the antitrust laws do not apply to regulated telecommunications services,[508] the 2005 decisions by the FCC to label broadband operators as information services did subject them to the more general body of antitrust regulation after all. In the light of the net neutrality debate and its historical association with the common carrier legislation, the *essential facilities doctrine* is perhaps the most promising route in avoiding the perils of broadband operators favoring signals running over their networks in terms of origin, nature or

---

[503] FCC, 2005e.

[504] McCullagh, D., 2005.

[505] *National Cable & Telecommunications Assn. v. Brand X Internet Services* (04-277) 545 US 967 (2005), 345 F.3d 1120.

[506] Taylor, C., 1995.

[507] For a more elaborate exposition see: FCC, 2005b.

[508] *Verizon Communications v. Trinco*, 540 US 398 (2004).

content. The doctrine's seminal case was *U.S.* v. *Terminal Railroad Association* (1912)[509] in which the shareholders of the association substantially limited the number of competing terminals that could be erected in the St. Louis area and allegedly determined the prices for transportation through St. Louis arbitrary and discriminatory. The result of this was that the Terminal Railroad Association was held to provide access to previously excluded parties and was compelled to price on non-arbitrary and non-discriminatory grounds. The classic case, particularly in relation to the net neutrality debate, is *U.S.* v. *AT&T* (1982)[510] in which local telephone companies, when taken over by AT&T, excluded AT&T's competitors from access to local connections. In this latter case, the Department of Justice operated the theory that a firm with a lawful monopoly violates Section 2 of the Sherman Act (monopolizing trade) if it 'leverages' that monopoly to impede or foreclose competition in a related market, even in cases where the firm neither monopolizes nor attempts to monopolize that second market. The idea was that when an essential facility monopoly exists in one market, competition in the adjacent markets can only develop when potential entrants can be assured of fair and non-discriminatory access to the 'bottleneck' facility. The essential facilities doctrine formed the basis for AT&Ts restructuring divesting the local exchange business from the adjacent long distance and equipment markets and implementing equal access and non-discrimination duties on the local exchange companies.[511]

Although the US Supreme Court has never applied the doctrine in so many words, the essential facilities doctrine, then, sometimes requires a monopolist to provide access to a 'facility' that the monopolist controls and that is deemed necessary for effective competition.[512] Prominent scholars like Areeda and Hovenkamp[513] hold that essence of the doctrine concerns vertical exclusion in favor of affiliated services. Put in these terms it captures the essence of the net neutrality debate. Broadband operators build and exploit networks. Broadband Internet service providers provide the service of establishing the connection of the end user to the Internet *using* the Internet connection provided by the broadband operator. Due to the vertical integration of broadband operators and broadband Internet service suppliers, there is a theoretical chance according to the net neutrality proponents, that the network operators will abuse their power to exclude content and application providers in order to stimulate the sales of their affiliated partners. The result of this is a potential harm to non-affiliated content and application providers on the one hand, and the end user being deprived of services offered by non-affiliated parties and possible charged too much for the services he does receive due to a lack of competition. Figure 13, shows the vertical integration of access providers and network operators schematically.

---

[509] *United States* v. *Terminal Railroad Association*, 224 US 383 (1912).
[510] *U.S.* v. *AT&T* 552 R. Supp. 131 (DDC 1982), and; *Aff'd sub nom. Maryland* v. *U.S.,* 460 US 1001 (1983).
[511] Rosenblum, M., 1995.
[512] Cotter, T., 2008.
[513] Areeda, P.E. and Hovenkamp A., 2006, § 771a.

LAYERS	PLAYERS
Communication Layer (applications)	Content Providers/ End-users
Connection Layer (network protocols)	Access Providers/ ISPs
Physical Layer (medium)	Network Operators

Figure 13. Vertical integration of broadband operators

Net neutrality proponents agree that in order to prevent the harmful results of the discriminatory practices an *ex ante* prohibition of broadband operators offering differentiated services is paramount. The fact that broadband operators might not have the tools or the actual inclination to offer differentiated services does not seem to influence their opinions[514] and neither are they convinced by the vast body of economic literature describing the advantages of vertical integration.[515] Nevertheless, it is exactly the body of economic literature that has led to a tendency by the US Supreme Court to intervene on an *ex post* basis applying a rule of reason only when actual harm can be demonstrated in the case of vertical mergers.[516] In contrast to what net neutrality proponents advocate, vertical integration is at times beneficial to consumers, often does not impair competition and can actually enhance economic welfare.[517]

In other words, the essential facilities doctrine as applied to communications networks suggests that there is no principled right for private competitors to gain access to markets, not even in the case when the market is dominated by a legal monopoly. Consequently, when players in adjacent markets like the broadband op-

---

[514] For a recent discussion on the matter, see, Lee, T.B., 2008. Although Lee presupposes the existence of the mythical e2e architecture of the Internet, he shows convincingly that the actual power of the network owners and the tools they employ are too limited to go against the end user's wishes to have access to as much content as they can. Doing so would simply be unprofitable because Internet service providers make money by delivering bits, delivering less bits or cutting content and application providers would go against their own interest.

[515] For an overview of this economic literature see, Yoo, C., 2007.

[516] USDoJ (1985). See also *Leegin Creative Leather Prods Inc.* v. *PSKS Inc.*, 75 USLW 4643 (US June 28, 2007) (No. 06-480).

[517] Yoo, C., 2007.

erators and broadband Internet services providers merge, it does not automatically constitute the abuse of a dominant position. This is why the regulatory authorities, including the FTC and the Supreme Court, have upheld a careful *ex ante* examination on the basis of reasonableness. Since dominant market positions are not considered *per se* harmful and because each dominant position on the broadband market would have its own effects, there is nothing to suggest that the current policy would not be able to adequately fight potential damage occurring from broadband operators favoring signals running over their networks in terms of origin, nature or content. The current basis for economic regulation then, are the free market presuppositions of private property and freedom of contract. Within such a framework, a *per se* right to access private facilities is not available in the broadband market and neither considered appropriate by the regulatory authorities.

A changing trend?

Despite the empirical evidence outlined above, some writers have observed a changing trend suggesting an increased inclination to invoke non-discriminatory requirements *ex ante*.[518] In the context of vertical mergers, the Time Warner merger with America Online is the most striking case since it was approved on the condition that they granted at least three ISPs access to their cable system.[519] Although the case was justified in that the group indeed wanted to pursue the strategy of excluding non-affiliated ISPs, it forms an illustration of how problematic predictions are in terms of market strategy and consumer welfare.[520] Soon after the merger, the group had to abandon its business strategy in favor of a more open approach. Rather than a trend or a case for *ex ante* net neutrality requirements, the compulsory access requirements imposed *ex ante* on AOL-Warner makes a case for a more conservative approach in which an *ex post*, case-by-case assessment when actual harm can be proven, would fit better.

The policy statement adopted on August 5, 2005, stating its adherence to four principles of network neutrality is also taken to imply a shift in regulatory policy in acknowledging an end-user right access lawful Internet content and use applications of their choice.[521] The 2006 merger between AT&T and Bellsouth establishing an USD 80 billion corporation controlling more than half the telephone and Internet access lines in the US was noticeable in this respect since the merger included commitments to non-discriminatory access and pricing commitments for three years to come. These provisions however were voluntarily imposed and were neither formally imposed by the FCC nor the FTC. However, in a commentary on

---

[518] See for example, Pitofsky, R., 2002.

[519] FCC, 2001.

[520] Yoo, C., 2007.

[521] FCC (2005c), recognized that consumers were entitled to (1) access the lawful Internet content of their choice, (2) run applications and use services of their choice, subject to the needs of law enforcement, (3) connect their choice of legal devices that do not harm the network, and, (4) competition among network providers, application and service providers and content providers.

the merger, the FCC chairman Martin and commissioner Taylor Tate were keen to point out that the net neutrality provisions were voluntary in nature. They furthermore denied an active FCC policy towards compulsory net neutrality, which they deemed unnecessary and potentially harmful to infrastructure deployment[522] in line with the prevailing antitrust policy outlined above.

In the four years after its policy (2005) statement, the FCC only once deemed it necessary to base a ruling on this statement. In August 2008, the FCC confirmed a commitment to pursuing its four Internet freedoms, but also confirmed its commitment to a case by case, *ex post* approach concerning the effects of discriminatory practices in the broadband market. The case concerned the Internet cable access provider Comcast Corp., which was held to violate the FCC principles when it selectively blocked peer-to-peer connections in an attempt to manage its traffic.[523] The ruling established that outright blocking of content impedes Internet users' ability to use applications and access content of their choice and poses a substantial threat to both the open character and efficient operation of the Internet confirming the FCC's commitment to *ex post* evaluations, stating that:

> '... (N)ot only is the Internet new and dynamic, but Internet access networks are complex and variegated. We thus think it is possible that the network management practices of the various providers of broadband access services are "so specialized and varying in nature as to be impossible to capture within the boundaries of a general rule".'

In addition, the FCC explicitly acknowledged the importance of reasonable network practices that may justify discrimination on networks and also its advice on how to manage congestion without violating the FCC's principles[524] acknowledges that net neutrality is not the norm on the Internet and actually approves to discriminatory techniques. Recently, the FCC has proposed legislation to codify network policies maintaining its policies on reasonable network practices and confirming its four principles of net neutrality.[525]

7.4.3   Conclusion

The purpose of Section 7.4 was to determine to what extent the current regulatory practice is able to provide a remedy for the fears of the net neutrality proponents and hence stimulate the development of the Internet in terms of access, competition and innovation. In addition, it set out to determine to what extent constitutional

---

[522] FCC, 2006b.

[523] FCC, 2008.

[524] Ibid., Para. 49 'Comcast has several available options it could use to manage network traffic without discriminating as it does. Comcast could cap the average users' capacity and then charge the most aggressive users overage fees or it could throttle back the connection speeds of high-capacity users (rather than any user who relies on peer-to-peer technology, no matter how infrequently).'

[525] Singel, R., 2009. For a complete overview of the proposed legislation see: FCC, 2009.

grounds compel the implementation of net neutrality regulation. Two possible routes were identified. The first one, grounded in the possible value of net neutrality in the light of democratic deliberation focused on access rights. The second route, grounded in the possible value of net neutrality regulation in the light of the States constitutional commitment to promote welfare focused on the competition.

One of the major fears regarding the concentration of power in the broadband market was that discriminatory practices would hamper Internet access. It turned out that in absence of an explicit right to equal access, the current regulatory framework nevertheless maintains the open character of the Internet by condemning outright blocking practices in the broadband market and hence effectively granting access and interconnectivity to end users including content providers. Consequently, there is no constitutional basis for requiring explicit net neutrality regulation on democratic grounds. Neither is there an inclination to invoke net neutrality regulation ensuring non-discriminatory access to applications and content *ex ante* within the context of the context of economic regulation overseen by the FCC and FTC. The current regulatory practice is deemed sufficient to ensure competition, stimulate innovation and protect consumers. The average Internet user has a variety of means available to connect to the Internet[526] and currently many alternatives are in the process of being developed.

In sum, neither a rights-based nor an economic perspective hold compelling reasons for implementing net neutrality regulation in order to fight the perils of the possible abuse of power by broadband operators. The current regulations prevent outright blocking practices, even in the absence of a monopoly, and the authorities consider the market on which the broadband operators compete broad enough not to consider them as essential facilities.

7.5   REFRAMING THE DEBATE

Section 7.3 'The Argument from Design' showed that the need for net neutrality regulation can not be justified by the argument that the Internet's success is due to its unique architecture built on the e2e design principle. Section 7.4 'The Current Internet Reality' showed that there are no compelling constitutional grounds deeming net neutrality regulation necessary on democratic grounds (access to the media/ information) or economic grounds (market access and consumer protection). The current regulatory practices sufficiently maintain the Internet's open character to safeguard the deliberative process and guarantees sufficient market access for content/application providers to provide sufficient consumer choice.

Because the *de facto* ban on total blocking safeguards the traditional State responsibilities in terms of competition (welfare), consumer protection (security) and deliberative process (information freedoms/ democracy), the remaining question at

---

[526] See also: Baumol, W.J. et al., 2007.

the heart of the net neutrality debate essentially boils down to a debate whether *ex ante* government intervention is needed to shape the Internet of the future. More specifically the question is whether to prevent broadband operators from diversifying in terms of quality of service and pricing as part of an explicit Internet policy to establish the conditions that stimulate innovation of the network and on the network. In order to come to a balanced conclusion on this question, the scope of the debate needs broadening in two respects. First, the current situation on the Internet requires an assessment of the current legislative proposals in the context of the availability of alternative network use and technologies.[527] In addition, the Internet's global nature requires an evaluation transcending the inward-looking national (US) focus that dominates the current debate.

The previous sections might have raised the impression that the net neutrality debate is essentially about non-discrimination requirements for broadband operators/ISPs. The bills circulating in Congress demanding unfettered Internet access in relation to the broadband situation seem to confirm this thesis. The fact to the matter is that despite the focus of the currently circulating bills and the focus of the accompanying discussion, the debate about quality of service diversification in broadband markets is only part of the story. Ultimately, the question is about shaping the future Internet, about how to optimize conditions for growth, innovation and development of the Internet. Once this is realized, it becomes immediately clear, that the debate's focus on the broadband market is rather narrow, particularly in the light of the many alternatives available for connecting the end user to the Internet. In its decision to render high-speed Internet services as information rather than as telecommunication services, the Supreme Court already mentioned wire line, cable, terrestrial wireless and satellite.[528] Since this press release, perhaps the most important development is the FCC decision to approve access over the national power line grid. This decision is likely to trigger innovation because the ready availability of the networks is bound to trigger experimentation with new uses and new applications.[529] All the options available for end users to connect to the Internet compete with one another for the end user's favor. A narrow focus on broadband applications underestimates the potential of the alternative networks and is likely to hamper the development of the range of possibilities broadband networks have.

Some writers have attempted to broaden the debate as to include alternative connections. Notably Tim Wu has triggered this issue in the academic world by proposing to extend net neutrality regulation to the wireless situation as well.[530] His proposal was immediately followed by replies varying from pointing out a lack of market failure in the wireless market[531] to explaining that recent Supreme Court

---

[527] Yoo, C.S., 2004.
[528] *National Cable & Telecommunications Assn.* v. *Brand X Internet* Services (04-277) 545 US 967 (2005), 345 F.3d 1120.
[529] FCC, 2006a.
[530] Wu, T., 2007.
[531] Wallsten, S., 2007.

decisions rather suggest that imposing net neutrality regulation to the wireless market might substantially harm rather than benefit the prospects for entry and competition in the industry.[532] In addition, objections were raised against the use of the term net neutrality applied to proposed legislation for the wireless Internet providers.[533] However, with the current FCC proposals pushing for a government-owned nationwide freely available wireless Internet,[534] the wireless net neutrality debate could very well turn into short-lived historical debate altogether. The reason is that a nationwide wireless free Internet would give all users equal access to the Internet and its applications albeit at a slower overall speed than offered by broadband connections. The net neutrality bills circulating in Congress however, do not mention the wireless situation, nor do they take other means of connecting end users to the Internet into account. Consequently, the current discussion in Congress is limited to the broadband situation despite Wu's attempt to broaden the discussion.

The focus on the broadband situation is harmful in more than one respect. In addition to ignoring the possibilities for end users to use alternative means for connecting to the Internet, it also ignores the emergence of alternative networks and alternative network use altogether. Of course, the Internet as we currently know it has many advantages and some of them may indeed be due to the technical characteristics underlying the network. Nevertheless, this is not to say that alternative networks and connections to those networks could not be even more successful, particularly when they expressly designed for the express needs of their client base. The alternative use of networks is not just a hypothetical construct. In fact, they are already in operation. Spam and other security considerations increased the demand for private networks offering enhanced security and monitoring opportunities.[535] Peer-to-peer networks for example already use these techniques on a large scale. In addition, 'tunneling'[536] is a regularly used technique in order to prioritize traffic for heavy users and to increase security on the Internet. In addition, the use of tethered appliances, effectively creating 'closed networks' based on proprietary software and applications[537] establishes novel ways of using the Internet based on access

---

[532] Ford, G.S. et al., 2007.

[533] Hahn, R.W. et al., 2007.

[534] Schatz, A., 2008.

[535] One example hereof is Netalter, which offers network services based on an advanced peer-to-peer technology. More information is available on their website <www.netalter.com>.

[536] Tunneling is a way in which data is transferred between two networks securely. All the data that is being transferred are fragmented into smaller packets or frames and then passed through the tunnel. This process is different from a normal data transfer between nodes. Every frame passing through the tunnel will be encrypted with an additional layer of tunneling encryption and encapsulation, which is also used for routing the packets to the right direction. This encapsulation would then be reverted at the destination with decryption of data, which is later sent to the desired destined node. A tunnel is a logical path between the source and the destination endpoints between two networks. Every packet is encapsulated at the source and will be de-capsulated at the destination. This process will keep happening as long as the logical tunnel is persistent between the two endpoints. Source at: <www.tech-faq.com/tunneling.shtml>.

[537] Zittrain, J.L., 2008.

limitations, hence effectively establishing prioritization of Internet traffic and companies like Akamai, Amazon and others, employ a technique called edge caching. The technique is designed to locate frequently used content closer to the people who access it, in order to create faster services.[538] Thus, when security and other reasons have already spurred the development of alternative network use prioritizing information, it is perhaps time to face reality and allow competition between networks and applications to decide which balance between security and openness or functionality and universal access the end user deems optimal for his purposes. In this respect, the net neutrality regulation rather limits consumer choice rather than improves its options. With the current choice in 'last mile' connections, there are ample alternatives to choose, from even when the broadband suppliers make the worst strategic decisions ever. A lack of consumer base will force them to adjust their policies while optimizing the services for their clients.

It is to the ISPs advantage to acknowledge that access to various types of content is an important element in the success of a network. Discrimination in quality of service regarding Internet content will therefore only have a marginal effect on the availability of content. Network effects inherent to the Internet will ensure the development of new alternative techniques parallel to and in conjunction with the existing Internet since each additional network user not only benefits him, it also creates additional value for every other user of the network. Thus, the larger the network becomes, the more valuable it is to every individual users. Consequently, it is in the interest of the providers to create a maximum amount of opportunities in terms of communications and transactions. A wide reach of available content (and applications) establishes exactly this. Estranging groups of users from the use of the network would simply be an irrational business decision. In order to develop a balanced view regarding the role of the State on the development of the Internet, the debate should therefore include the existence of alternative last-mile connections and the development of next-generation networks, a possibility that a majority of writers on the subject have failed to notice.[539]

The most important shortcoming in the current discussion however, is the national focus of the debate.[540] Due to the Internet's global and interdependency-imposing nature, a national focus is simply too limited. The previous chapters have already shown in the interdependent context of the Internet domestic decisions have transnational consequences and vice versa. This means that national regulation inevitably affects foreign parties in an interdependent context. Consequently, it is

---

[538] Isenberg, D., 2008.

[539] The recent FCC (2009) appears to mark a turning point in the debate since this proposal includes alternative wireless access providers. The fierce opposition of stakeholders, notably the smart phone lobby and wireless services providers at the time of this book going to press, is likely to leave this element in the FCC proposal seriously contested for some time to come.

[540] Some writers have even claimed is predominantly an American problem because the broadband markets for example in the EU are differently organized. Due to the alternatives available to broadband however the situation in Europe and other geographical areas is comparable to that of the US.

impossible to make informed decisions regarding national legislation without considering the transnational situation.

7.6   GLOBAL COMMUNICATION POLICY

Thus far, the systematic analysis of the net neutrality debate has somewhat reduced the need for State-interference in the development of the Internet. In the first sections of this chapter, the 'argument from design', linking the call for net neutrality with the Internet's architectural characteristics was discredited in order to demonstrate that the net neutrality debate, despite its rhetoric, is essentially about the question whether government action is needed in order to stimulate innovation *of* the Internet and *on* the Internet. The subsequent section explored the existing regulatory frameworks and concluded that although there were no specific constitutional grounds for invoking net neutrality regulation, a qualified right to access to information could be inferred from current regulatory practices providing *ex post* remedies for outright blocking practices. Because locally, the current regulation proved capable of handling these outright blocking practices, the question concerning the need for net neutrality regulation was reduced to the question to what extent regulation is needed to stimulate innovation by prohibiting discrimination in terms of quality of service. The last section suggested to take the development and availability alternative connections and networks into account in order make a more balanced decision concerning the development of the (national) communications infrastructure. This latter insight reduced the need for net neutrality regulation even further because a focus on broadband connections reveals an ignorance of the dynamic and fast changing technological environment that shapes the development of tomorrows critical information and communication infrastructures.

The most important shortcoming of the current discussion however, as indicated at the end of the previous section, is its national (US) focus.[541] On the one hand, the interdependent nature of the Internet causes national regulation to affect foreign parties directly. On the other hand, unilateral decisions on the Internet are not significant enough to influence the development of the Internet at large.[542] Both sides in the debate, proponents and opponents alike, tend to overestimate the effects of national regulation. The previous chapters show that due to the Internet's interdependent nature, fundamental decisions affecting the network, as for example regarding domain names or regarding standards, require a global implementation in order to be effective. The same holds for legislation designed to influence the development of the global Internet. The most obvious way in which to achieve this

---

[541] Idem.
[542] As the previous chapters also indicated, individual States can not enforce the implementation of their national policies globally. They simply do not have the power and means to do so.

result is by means of global institutions. This possibility however is completely ignored in current net neutrality proposals.

7.6.1   The UN and the IGF

Milton Mueller is one of those writers acknowledging the need for a global implementation of principles if they are to have any effect on the development of the Internet at large. Mueller is particularly concerned with the role of civil society in shaping the Internet of the future. In this context, he pleads for the UN to endorse net neutrality principles, which he considers principles of Internet governance that are a natural and practical interpretation of the UN's general goals. The UN[543] as the largest intergovernmental organization to date is traditionally strongly involved in the provision of global communications. The UN, by means of its International Telecommunications Union (ITU), coordinated the worldwide telephone number allocation at the end of the 19th century. In addition, at the end of the 20th century, the UN was the driving force behind the World Summit on the Information Society (WSIS), a UN summit devoted to the role of information technology in order to achieve the Millennium Development goals improving living standards for people.

The first reason why Mueller sees an important task for the UN in developing and implementing general principles for Internet governance is that the UN regards the Internet as an important vehicle for achieving its overall aims as mentioned in the Preamble to its Charter.[544] In the light of this preamble, net neutrality provisions could be seen as a practical step to achieve these goals. An important focus in the context of the UN summits is to bridge the divide between rich and poor. Because the Internet can serve an important role in a State's economic and political development, bridging the digital divide between *haves* and the *have-nots*[545] forms an important objective within the UN's overall strategy. Net neutrality provisions invoking non-discrimination requirements on the provision of Internet services seem to tie in nicely with the UN's overall goals to promote equality on a worldwide scale and more specifically with the UDHR in which the information freedoms play an important part as a concrete starting point to fight censorship practices worldwide. In addition, the UN links access to the Internet to the improvement of communication between peoples, which, in turn, helps resolve conflicts and attain world peace.

A second reason for Mueller to urge the UN to endorse these principles lies in its apparent conviction about the UN's role on the Internet, which, according to Mueller,

---

[543] See also the development of the Internet in Chapter 3 'Globalization, Interdependence and the Internet' and Chapter 4 'Interdependence and Domain Name System Management'.

[544] The UN Preamble reads that the UN is to save succeeding generations from the scourge of war to establish conditions under which justice and respect for the obligations arising from treaties and other sources of international law can be maintained, and to promote social progress and better standards of life in larger freedom.

[545] The digital divide runs though other types of Internet Communications Technologies as well, WSIS, 2008.

should be a driving force in the development of the Internet, not only in terms of the digital divide, but also in terms of other decisions of a global nature. Net neutrality as a principle for Internet governance is one such area according to Mueller.

Within the context of the UN, the WSIS in Tunis (2005) expressed the need for developing a global public Internet policy in which the development of globally applicable principles on public policy issues associated with the coordination and management of critical Internet resources forms a distinguished element.[546] The Tunis agenda also created the Internet Governance Forum (IGF),[547] a UN-based think tank aimed at establishing a new forum for multi-stakeholder policy dialogue to address Internet-related public policy issues roughly resembling the multi-stakeholder set-up of the ICANN[548] and the IETF.[549] The IGF was designed as a broad platform for dialogue among stakeholders to address Internet governance issues that are crosscutting and multidimensional. In effect, it set out to form a coordinating umbrella organization for existing and emerging Internet-related public policy issues.[550] Its academic subsection, the Global Internet Governance Academic Network (GigaNet),[551] is where Mueller, as one of its founding members and chair of the program committee, presented his ideas on net neutrality as a global principle for Internet governance.[552]

The IGF was effectively the UN's answer to the EU and Brazilian proposals to make the ICANN accountable to the UN. In line with the overall objectives of the UN, Mueller redefines net neutrality as to include universal access and freedom of expression. Moreover, he goes on to connect these concepts with free trade in goods and services and argues that consequently network neutrality should be seen as a concept against the blocking of communication and content by private actors and governments.[553] Of course, there is an important connection between information freedoms on the one hand and the ideals of a free market and democracy, the two hallmarks of the modern State, on the other hand. In fact, a similar line or argumentation was endorsed in Chapter 6 'Interdependence and Search Operator Censorship', tracing the effects of censorship practices to the free flow of information underlying the aforementioned pillars of the free world.[554] It is however, a grave

---

[546] WSIS, 2005b.

[547] IGF website at <www.intgovforum.org/cms/>.

[548] Compare Chapter 4 'Interdependence and Domain Name System Management'.

[549] Compare Chapter 5 'Interdependence and Technical Standardization'.

[550] WSIS, 2005a, § 40.

[551] GigaNet, website available at <http://giganet.igloogroups.org> has four principal objectives: (1) supporting the establishment of a global cohort of scholars specializing on Internet governance issues; (2) promoting the development of Internet governance as a recognized, interdisciplinary field of study; (3) advancing theoretical and applied research on Internet governance, broadly defined: and (4) facilitating informed dialogue on policy issues and related matters between scholars and Internet governance stakeholders (governments, international organizations, the private sector, and civil society).

[552] Ibid.

[553] Mueller, M., 2007.

[554] See, Chapter 6 'Interdependence and Search Operator Censorship'.

misunderstanding to say that censorship and exclusionary practices, keeping out competitors, are at stake in the current Congressional debate. As the previous sections have shown, blocking practices hardly occur in the US and in the rare event they do occur, they are readily dealt with by current regulatory practices. In fact, the net neutrality advocated by Mueller serves a different primary goal than the US debate is addressing. While both Mueller and the US net neutrality advocates are concerned with the development of the next generation Internet in terms of innovation, there is a difference in focus. Where Mueller's prime concern seems to be aiming at countries trying to impair the availability of information and applications on the Internet, the prime concern in the US debates is the vertical integration of markets and the effects of tiered quality of services and pricing.

Another oddity in Mueller's argumentation is his proposal to apply net neutrality as a principle of Internet governance to the Internet's technical coordinating functions as performed by ICANN. This line of reasoning also rooted the IGF's inception since it was formed in reaction to the allegations that ICANN was too US oriented and in need of legitimate international accountability mechanisms. The IGF would form the UN's platform for discussion in order to commit UN countries to accept and implement general principles that would influence the development of the Internet. By creating global consensus, a strong country-based lobbying organization would be able to counter the private initiatives dominating the Internet. Indeed, due to the interdependence-imposing architecture of the Internet, either a central coordinating organization like ICANN or a well-organized unified majority of States could effectively implement governance principles worldwide. From a governance point of view, ICANN is effective in its functionally determined goals but according to many, it lacks legitimacy[555] and ICANN itself acknowledges the limitations of its mandate.[556] In contrast, the UN is generally regarded as legitimate and has a wide public support for its decisions. However, the UN's problem is that it is highly ineffective in creating consensus strong enough to yield to effective decision making. Consequently, the challenge of the IGF and its associated GigaNet[557] is to find a way to combine ICANN's decisiveness and the UN's public support to find workable principles for Internet governance based on the UN Charter and the UNDHR.[558] Thus in the context of the IGF's inception and its relation with ICANN it is understandable that Mueller also links net neutrality principles with the coordinating role functions of the Internet.

---

[555] Chapter 4 'Interdependence and Domain Name System Management', shows that the legitimacy problem is due to a wrong conception on the nature of the organization. ICANN is held in check by alternative mechanisms more resembling a market rather than the traditional constitutional mechanisms that limit decision making in the public interest.

[556] See ICANN's decision regarding the .xxx domain in; ICANN, 2007. While acknowledging its limited technical mandate is shows that ICANN's awareness of its lack of management and oversight role regarding content leads ICANN to forego responsibilities in these areas.

[557] GigaNet is the Global Internet Governance Academic Network, an academic network associated with the IGF.

[558] Esterhuysen, A., 2008, p. 39. Esterhuysen speaks of 'two cultures' in this respect, an informal Internet culture on the one hand and a formal UN culture on the other hand.

Despite all good intentions to create an effective umbrella organization for Internet governance and despite the modeling after organizations like ICANN and the IETF, the IGF remained just as ineffective as the UN. It has proven to be very hard both in the context of the IGF[559] and the UN in general[560] to create consensus on workable principles and set a coherent agenda for Internet policy. Moreover, in addition to failing to reach the effectiveness of organizations like the ICANN and the IETF, the IGF also has not been able to create enough public support to take on the role as coordinating organization for Internet governance. In effect, to date the IGF is a failure since it lacks the virtues of both worlds; it lacks the effectiveness of technical Internet organizations while it also lacks the general public support that is characteristic of the UN. In sum, the IGF has a long way to go if it is to establish its role in Internet governance. Consequently, the proposal to endorse net neutrality regulation on a global basis by means of the UN is not likely to have on influence the development of the Internet within the foreseeable future, not even if all UN members would agree on endorsing net neutrality as a global Internet governance principle.

7.6.2   The WTO and the OECD

In addition to the UN and the IGF, Mueller also mentions the WTO as a potential candidate for endorsing net neutrality principles. However, despite its 153 member States, the WTO merely serves as a vehicle for liberalizing trade between nations. The only document that touches upon Internet-related issues is the Ministerial Declaration on Trade in Information Technology Products (ITA) and this document specifically states that it is only a tariff-cutting mechanism not allowing additional conditions to be imposed on the products at stake. In addition, the WTO suffers the same handicap as the UN in reaching consensus. A telling illustration hereof is that all proposals suggesting additional product coverage made after the ITA's inception in 1996 stranded due to a lack of consensus between the parties involved. Consequently, the WTO is neither going to have an impact on the development of the Internet infrastructure in terms of net neutrality in the foreseeable future either.

A last theoretical candidate for imposing Internet governance principles into its conditions would be the Organization for Economic Coordination and Development (OECD). The reason is that, particularly in the light of Internet and communication technology, it seeks ways to stimulate innovation in order to contribute to economic growth. The OECD however only consist of thirty member States committed to democracy and the market economy and consequently, its potential effect on the global development of the Internet is not large enough. Nevertheless, the OECD's views on the matter, outlined in its (2007) policy paper on Internet traffic prioritization[561] show a preference for market-based solutions, possible ex-post rem-

---

[559] Malcolm, J., 2008.
[560] WTO, 1996. For a comment see, Mueller, M., 2005b.
[561] OECD, 2008.

edies regarding anti-competitive behavior and call for transparency regarding the behavior of network operators. In addition, they acknowledge that existing as well as emerging technologies might require enhanced quality of service.

7.6.3 Conclusion

Neither the UN, the IGF, the WTO nor the OECD are able to effectively make and impose decisions affecting the global development of the Internet within the foreseeable future. The institutional frameworks either lack the mandate, ability to create consensus or the support to actually implement decisions. Nevertheless, Mueller is right in that certain principles and policies need to be imposed globally in order to affect developments on a global scale. The protocols developed by the IETF and the ICANN-managed DNS are exemplary in this regard since without it, the Internet as a universal interconnected global communications infrastructure would simply break down. The same would hold for net neutrality provisions if you consider these crucial to the development of the Internet. However, lacking effective global means for implementing net neutrality globally, individual States, notably the US, need to incorporate an analysis of the effects of national net neutrality regulation in a wider, international or global context.

7.7   NATIONAL COMMUNICATIONS POLICY

States are traditionally rather effective tools for making and enforcing decisions in the public benefit. Their representative decision-making mechanisms generally only require a majority for making decisions (unlike intergovernmental organizations) and the availability of an effective executive branch including a police force allows for an effective implementation of laws making States excellent candidates for making and implementing decisions in the public interest. Lacking the institutional means for a global implementation of Internet policies,[562] the unilateral imposition of particular principles aimed at influencing the development of the Internet, however, is equally ineffective in an interdependent world, because similar to other global phenomena, policy decisions affecting the core of the Internet and its development can only reach their full potential when implemented globally. This poses challenges for individual States because although national decisions affect foreign actors and vice versa, they are not powerful enough to influence the developments of and on the Internet at large directly. Nevertheless, this is exactly what net neutrality proponent's desire, an Internet policy designed to shape the future Internet through competition and access. Because domestic decisions affect foreign actors and foreign conduct in turn affect national policies,[563] individual States are forced

---

[562] See Section 7.6 'Global Communication Policy'.
[563] This thesis is also confirmed by the three previous chapters.

to assess their national policies in a transnational context. In the net neutrality case, the proposed legislation needs to be assessed in the light of the technical developments and the global positioning of the US. At stake is the US' leading position in e-commerce and Internet technology.

7.7.1   Maintaining a competitive advantage

Whereas there are many ways in which to assess the reasons for rejecting or adopting net neutrality regulation, the interdependent nature of the Internet requires an assessment of the effects of national regulation in a global rather than a distinctive national perspective. Because prevailing economic theory holds that regulation generally tends to hamper rather than stimulate innovation and most western economies are relatively open, the US should carefully evaluate the pros and cons of invoking new regulation in terms of competitive advantage. Currently, the rationale for the net neutrality bills are either based on the e2e myth or on a fear for market power due to vertical integration (of service providers and network operators). Moreover, as the previous sections have shown, the need for enhanced quality of service is essential for time-sensitive applications. Offering enhanced quality of service to guarantee live-video conferencing can significantly cut costs on logistics and coordination for internationally operating corporations. In the entertainment industry, particularly in the field of on-line gaming, the supply of enhanced quality of servers to end users and content suppliers alike, could offer opportunities to the sector they currently do not enjoy and which could trigger the developments of real-time on-line environments for educational purposes (public goal). Conjectures on the future developments aside, the current technological state of play shows a need for enhanced quality of service. Only experimentation will show if tiered business models will stimulate innovation.

The foregoing has direct consequences for the current US situation in an international context. The current services offered on the Internet allow packets to arrive on a 'best effort' basis at which the individual packets do not necessary travel at the same speed over the networks and hence do not arrive in the same order as they were sent. For the average data transmission, this does not pose problems, real-time applications however, benefit considerably from a service that guarantees priority of the traffic used in their applications because the sequence in which data is to arrive in the receiving application matters and enhanced quality of service can guarantee a sequential arrival of packets. Hence, real-time applications and their users would profit significantly from a situation in which network operators and ISPs would allow a diversification in quality of service regarding their (real-time) Internet traffic. Given the current network situation, net neutrality regulation would foreclose the development of a potentially wide US market for on-line conferencing and on-line gaming. This in turn, could have direct consequences for American commerce. Not only would American investors be less inclined to invest in the (potentially large) online gaming market, international trade in general might be impeded by lacking video conferencing possibilities, an ideal cost-saving technique for establishing and exploring international business opportunities. Nevertheless, although net neutrality regulation might also have unforeseen benefits, within an interdependent context, national regulation inevitably affects the current US status as a leader both in Internet technology and in the entertainment industry.

7.7.2   A democratic deficit

As the previous section pointed out, national decisions by the US intended to stimulate innovation on the Internet inevitably affect its position in terms of competitive advantage. They also affect its position and ability to pursue international business opportunities as the real-time examples in gaming and on-line conferencing show. This effect of course, is reciprocal. Potential foreign developments in these areas will miss a vast consumer potential and spending power in the US market. This holds for the network industry in general, but also for the development of applications requiring enhanced quality of service. The interdependence established thusly is not without consequences. Not only does it require an assessment of national regulation in terms of its extraterritorial effects, it also poses questions of a democratic nature at the heart of our constitutional democracy. If the rationale underlying our democratic sense of justice is informed by the conviction that affected parties should be able to participate in the decision-making process affecting the public interest, it would imply that within an interdependent context, the current materialization of our democratic convictions is inadequate and insufficient. In fact, interdependency as created by the Internet and by the globalization process in general creates a democratic accountability problem concerning affected foreign actors.

The origin of the democratic deficit is connected with two phenomena that are a direct result of the transnational interdependence imposed by the Internet. First, it creates a loss of autonomy because it imposes a shift in the costs/benefits analysis of national decision making from a purely national affair to a wider perspective including transnational considerations. Secondly, it creates a loss of sovereignty[564] in the sense that national states become increasingly dependent on transnational regulatory arrangements, whether imposed by intergovernmental organizations or by private institutions like ICANN[565] and the IETF.[566] The consequence of this is that the concept of democracy cannot be defended as a concept confined to what Held has called a 'closed political community' or nation-State.[567] Contesting the notion of the relevant community raises a number of questions connected with democratic decision making varying from the appropriateness of the current electoral processes to the question on how to design adequate mechanisms to incorporate transnational interests in decision-making procedures. One important line of inquiry is the role that civil society could play here, particularly since the Internet has

---

[564] See also Chapter 6 'Interdependence and Search Operator Censorship'.
[565] See on this topic, Chapter 4 'Interdependence and Domain Name System Management'.
[566] See on this topic, Chapter 5 'Interdependence and Technical Standardization'.
[567] Held, D., 1997.

opened up new and potentially effective ways in which to set up civil society groups. The problem with these society groups as advocates of transnational interests however, is that whereas they may hold States in check regarding national choices that have transnational effects, they do not solve the problem in terms of representation. They can merely represent ideals and create awareness but the representative element of the foreign affected parties is not grounded in democratic representation, the key element in democratic theory.[568] In sum, the interdependent situation appears to create a significant threat to the system of democratic accountability that lies at the heart of our constitutional democracy.

7.7.3   Conclusion

The reciprocal relation between transnational actors on the Internet undermines the State's effectiveness. Although traditionally advantaged over transnational organizations in terms of consensus building and enforcement, the Internet poses problems for national States since it requires a global implementation of policies in order to be effective and individual States simply lack the power to exact worldwide conformity to their Internet policies unilaterally.[569] In addition, because national decisions affect foreign actors and vice versa it limits the State in advancing its communications policies nationally because it forces them to evaluate national policies in a transnational context. The same phenomenon also affects the democratic foundations of public decision making because national regulations directly affect foreign actors that are not represented in the domestic procedures.

7.8   ACCOUNTABILITY AND INTERDEPENDENCE

Thus far, the systematic analysis of the net neutrality debate has reduced the impact and hence the need for State-action in the development of the Internet. The first sections of this chapter invalidated the 'argument from design' and showed that the technical argument based on the network's e2e structure does not provide a compelling basis for invoking net neutrality regulation. Section 7.4 showed subsequently that constitutionally neither a rights-based nor an economic approach offers compelling reasons for invoking net neutrality regulation limiting the question concerning the need for net neutrality regulation to whether government action is needed to stimulate competition (at content and network level) and democratic deliberation (guaranteeing access). Because the current regulations secures the open character of the Internet domestically, hence safeguarding the deliberative process in society, the question further reduced to whether *ex ante* government action is needed to stimulate innovation by prohibiting discrimination in terms of quality of service.

---

[568] Anderson, K. and Rieff, D., 2004.
[569] This conclusion is also confirmed in Chapter 4 'Interdependence and Domain Name System Management' and Chapter 5 'Interdependence and Technical Standardization'.

Subsequently, it was argued that a balanced view needs to incorporate the current Internet reality, that is, the development of alternative network-use and end-user connections and its interdependent context.

The following sections set the net neutrality debate in an interdependent context and showed that decisions affecting the core of the Internet, whether concerned with domain names, standards or the development of the infrastructure, require a global implementation in order to be effective. The inability of transnational institutions to achieve this, combined with the Internet's characteristic feature, require individual States to evaluate their policies in a transnational setting. The extraterritorial effects of national policy setting in turn pose problems concerning the democratic character of public decision making. At stake is the very legitimacy of national policies affecting millions of Internet users that are not incorporated in the decision-making processes designed to further the public interest. This affects the State-citizen relation at a rather fundamental level because it poses a shift away from the nation-State ideal of democratic decision making based on representation.

7.8.1 Regulatory competition

The question concerning the legitimacy of national decision making in an interdependent context, however fundamental for the way we understand and implement the concept of democracy in the 21st century, does not necessarily pose significant problems from a practical point of view. In addition to causing problems, the Internet occasionally offers solutions to today's problems. The Internet architecture imposing a reciprocal relationship between actors has one very powerful additional feature. The very medium facilitates an exchange of data on a global scale that is unprecedented in scale and speed.

Although different regions may vary in the ways in which one can use the Internet or connect particular Internet devices as a result of innovation policies, the impossibility of using the Internet in novel ways or using particular applications does not imply that users in those regions are not aware of novel development and innovative products. The marketplace of ideas created by the Internet enables a wide dispersion of 'best solutions' to many problems including those concerning innovation. Although, economic theory and current regulatory conviction in the US hold that regulation not specifically designed to enhance competition (antitrust law), is likely to hamper innovation and progress. Opinions on this matter however differ, as does the interpretation of laws as the net neutrality proposals show.

Ultimately, the proof of the pudding is in the eating. Since the current Internet reality lacks appropriate global mechanisms to enforce developmental policies effectively and forecloses one nation to tilt the developments of the Internet unilaterally, there is no choice to the matter than to have States and regions compete with one another for the most innovative regulatory environment. The Internet plays an important role in this regard since it facilitates the exchange of novel ideas and innovation, in effect establishing a marketplace of ideas. In addition to exchanging ideas concerning innovation, also the underlying legal environments are subject to evaluation and discussion. In other words, the Internet facilitates a competitive environment in terms of regulation, because the results of policy decisions designed to create innovation and to develop the future Internet are easily spread throughout the globe cheaply and swiftly. This democratization of information, or put differently this 'empowerment of the individual' is an important tool for individuals and governments alike to determine how they want to contribute to the development of the Internet. In fact, the model of regulatory competition combines the effectiveness of national decision making and enforcement, with the effective allocating of resources characterizing markets. As such, it is an improvement on the democratic decision making, because it adds an objective evaluation mechanism to the model. A market model allowing for choice between competing regulatory regimes resolves the aforementioned democratic deficit that is a result of the interdependent nature of the Internet. The strength of the model is that competing regulatory regimes can rationally decide which type of regulation is most successful.

Alternative approaches between regions or countries will stimulate competition between networks on a temporary basis only to converge into systems and regulatory regimes more suitable for the needs at that particular moment in time. Within the relatively open economies of the Western world, and especially in the interconnected context of today's Internet, successful innovations will drive a convergence of approaches. In this sense, separate developments of networks and network use on a regional basis are likely to stimulate the further development of the Internet. Of course, the network effects of the Internet infrastructure in combination with the international economic interests at stake, leave the interconnectivity and communication requirements of the Internet in place and prevent the development of completely separated networks.

Regulatory competition between regions in terms of Internet development is not only inevitable given today's state of play, it is likely to create the best environment to create diversity within the unified Internet structure in an interdependent context. The reason is that the Internet facilitates a wide dispersion of innovations even into legislative environments that do not yet cater for those products and services. From a practical point of view then, the democratic accountability of traditional State-based decision making is partly replaced by market accountability between competing legislative regimes. Where traditionally the *international* community of States was readily persuaded by the example of US power, the *global* interdependent community in contrast, only seems perceptive to the power of US example.[570]

7.8.2   Considerations on competition and innovation

Within the context of a market economy, the key to innovation is competition. Competition provides an efficient way of allocating resources because the interplay of supply and demand determines the price of products and the provision of new busi-

---

[570] Clinton, W.J.B., 2008.

nesses and products entering the market. Competition also increases innovation because the availability of individual freedom to allocate resources, whether land, labor of capital, stimulates experimentation with new products and new services. Particularly this latter element is a strong advantage of a market economy over a governmentally planned way of allocating resources; a market economy stimulates individual creativity based on the self-interest of actors. Both economic theory and current regulatory practice hold that obstructing market access forms the prime threat to innovation. This is why access to markets forms an important prerequisite to innovation.

This latter point is particularly interesting when assessing net neutrality regulation. Contrary to what proponents preach, net neutrality regulation limits competition. Fostering the e2e myth, net neutrality proponents tend to stress that the net neutrality proposals guarantee the open character of the Internet stimulating an end-user based development of the network. This thesis is flawed in more than one way. An earlier exposition in this chapter already touched upon the mythical character of the e2e design principle. More important however, with respect to innovation, the type of innovation that, in the theoretical situation of an e2e based network, can be attributed to end users is rather limited. First, because, the type of innovation indicated by the net neutrality proponents concerns the development of user-generated applications while it does not address the developments and the use of networks as such. In addition, innovation in the application market is increasingly dominated by large corporations due to the costs that research and development incur on the developer's budgets, think for example about the on-line gaming market.

Imposing net neutrality restrictions potentially limits the development of the Internet networks by prohibiting broadband operators to diversify in terms of quality of service and pricing. It is useful in this context to recall what is perhaps the most important insight of Nobel Prize winner Hayek,[571] namely that freedom of action is the driving force for economic progress. Whether corporations acting monopolistically or governments imposing legislation restrain the behavior of individual conduct, in both cases the attempts to infringe the freedom to act as individuals is harmful to economic progress. In his words,

> 'The argument for liberty … is an argument against all exclusive privileged monopolistic organizations against the use of coercion to prevent others from trying to do better.'[572]

This argument not only holds for the powers of monopolistic organizations, it also holds for the interplay between legislation on the one hand and economic development on the other hand. Since the strength of economic progress is rooted in the

---

[571] Hayek, F., 1960, Chapter 2 'The Creative Powers of a Free Civilization', pp. 22-38. Notably, modern economic theory and policy confirm his thesis that freedom of action is the driving force for economic progress.

[572] Ibid., p. 37.

power of individual creativity, as long as competition is guaranteed, legislation hampering particular developments is likely to hamper rather than stimulate innovation and progress. Moreover, because the process of formation and modification of human intellect is in continuous flux and depends upon changing values and desires, progress by its very nature is not something that can be planned.[573] Since access problems can be dealt with sufficiently by the current regulatory regimes, and the level of competition in Internet service provision or 'last mile' market is considered sufficient by the FCC as we have seen, the currently proposed net neutrality regulation effectively hampers the development of the broadband networks not only *as* broadband networks, but also relative to other means of access.

The same view is implicit in the FCC's approach and expressly stated in the OECD's report by the Working Party on Telecommunication and Information Services Policies.[574] This latter report explicitly states that the Internet is currently not able to cater for enhanced quality of service needed by many current Internet applications. It furthermore envisions, partly based on security concerns, an increased call for enhanced quality of service. In this light, they promote a market-based solution in which governments could play a role in the protection of their citizens by reducing access barriers for new entrants, for example based on the four principles developed by the FCC.[575] Common ISPs could serve as advocates in this regard by advancing the needs of new entrants by the pooling of demand for Internet access. By guaranteeing competition as a basis for innovation, faster broadband networks and different uses of the network could develop parallel to the existing network. The money generated by early adapters that could develop their services over the 'faster lanes' of the broadband networks could help to build faster networks with enhanced quality of services to cater for the needs of, for example, the existing and new, real-time and video applications. The question is not as such that novel uses of the networks requiring enhanced quality of service will be developed, it is just that they *can* be developed unhampered by unnecessary government infringements as Hayek has pointed out. As such, net neutrality regulation could potentially harm the development of the communication infrastructure both in terms of use and in terms of access. The considerations given in this section are not intended to be conclusive on the question whether or not to impose net neutrality regulation on the US broadband market. It merely explored some considerations that are both in line with current economic theory and the interdependent context sketched in the foregoing sections. Although these considerations show a negative answer to this question, there is some consolidation in these matters confirmed by the findings in this chapter. The first one is that in an interdependent context, States (including the US) simply do not have the power to enforce decisions unilaterally. The second one is that the Internet context creates a system of regulatory competi-

---

[573] Ibid., p. 40.
[574] OECD, 2008.
[575] FCC, 2005b.

tion, in which the proof of the pudding is in the eating and in which market mechanisms rather than governmental foresight is the prime drive behind innovation.

7.9   CONCLUSION

This chapter set out to identify the effects of transnational interdependence on the State-subject relation by examining the US attempts to regulate its information infrastructure. It particularly looked at one aspect of US information policy, the call for net neutrality regulation in its broadband market as part of its Internet development strategy. The current transformation of the telecommunications sector is changing the competitive environment on the Internet, which in turn is likely to affect the innovative capacity of and on the information infrastructure. The vertical integration of corporations providing physical access to (broadband) networks and Internet Service Providers creates incentives to violate a uniform access to content. Since it is expensive to set up networks, network operators contemplate to offer differentiated quality of service at different prices to different groups of customers. Because this practice would necessarily involve selection on Internet traffic based on origin, nature or content, there is an intense debate in Congress to what extent regulation is needed to prevent broadband operators engaged in Internet access provision from imposing the result of their discriminatory practices upon both end users and content providers. In order to prevent this, opponents of this development have proposed bills in order to impose non-discriminatory requirements upon broadband operators, generally referred to as net neutrality requirements as we have seen.

The first phase in the inquiry concerned the relation between the technical design of the Internet and the proposed net neutrality legislation in congress leading to the following conclusions.

(1) Even if the proposed net neutrality legislation would set out to retain the textbook e2e situation on the Internet, it would be insufficient.

Reaping the benefits of an e2e design (user generated innovation) would require two elements: (1) non-discriminatory transmission of traffic and (2) open devices capable of end-user manipulation. The increased use of closed devices (like iPhones and the like) prevents the development of new applications by end users. Without addressing this latter development, the proposed legislation only addresses half of the problem. More importantly however,

(2) There is no connection between the architectural design of the Internet and the current call for net neutrality regulation.

The 'Argument from Design', that the Internet is essentially information neutral due to its very architecture design and that legislation is needed in order to retain the original e2e design of the Internet is ill founded because the Internet is not technologically neutral and was neither specifically designed as such.

The Internet distinguishes between types of content. Particularly, real-time applications are considerably less easy to use since they require enhanced quality of service in order to operate adequately. Consequently, because some content is more suitable for Internet exchange, the Internet is not neutral with respect to types of content. The myth that the Internet architecture was designed on a net neutral basis originates on a misguided interpretation of a paper by Saltzer,[576] explaining a design principle for information network infrastructures rather than an empirically established and historically confirmed observation of Internet design. In addition to Saltzer's explicit acknowledgement, the technical protocols developed by the IETF also confirm that the e2e design has not been an iron law of Internet design. The protocols explicitly mention that discrimination between types of content is desirable for good traffic management.

(3) The current Internet reality forecloses a 'restoration' of the Internet on an e2e basis.

Tunneling and other techniques enable end users to perform operations on the Internet rather than at the end points of the network, making it increasingly difficult to distinguish between the ends and core of the Internet. This would make a reconstruction of the Internet on technical e2e grounds impossible because it would render a distinction between the core and the ends of the network arbitrary at best.

In sum, the link between net neutrality regulation and the e2e nature of the Internet is based on a myth. At base, the net neutrality legislation is not about preserving technical principles, but about how to stimulate the development of the Internet in terms of open communications (stimulating equal access) and innovation (by stimulating freedom of choice).

The second phase in the inquiry was to examine the current regulatory framework in order to determine the additional value of the net neutrality regulation from a constitutional point of view. The most important conclusion in this regard is the following.

(4) The current US regulatory regime retains the open character of the Internet by foreclosing outright blocking practices in terms of both content and competitors.

From a constitutional point of view, there are two ways in which to justify net neutrality regulation. First, by appeal to access rights, secondly by advancing an economic argument arguing that net neutrality regulation is needed to promote competition (and hence innovation). An evaluation of the literature and jurisprudence shows that neither the FCC, nor the FTC and the Supreme Court, recognize a first

---

[576] Saltzer, J.H. et al., 1984.

amendment right to access the Internet *per se*. The only right that could be constructed form the current legal practice is a qualified right to enter markets. In effect, this consumer protection against the outright blocking practices retains the open character of the Internet.

The analyses in the first and second part of the inquiry reduced the debate on network neutrality to a debate on deciding whether *ex ante* government intervention is desirable to promote innovation and competition by prohibiting quality of service (and hence pricing) diversification using broadband networks. The third part of the inquiry concluded that in order to make a balanced judgment the parameters defining the current net neutrality debate need to be widened in two important respects. (a) The net neutrality debate needs to include the probable use of novel, yet undiscovered technologies for the net generation Internet. (b) In addition, the interdependent nature of the Internet requires an evaluation in a global setting.

(Ad a) When developing policies aimed at stimulating the development of next generation networks, it is not sufficient only to consider today's dominant form of Internet access. The multitude of alternative ways to connect to the Internet provide a wide range of possible innovations that would all be conducive to the development of the Internet itself, the applications that are being developed and hence the use of the Internet by end users. The focus on broadband connections therefore shows a very limited view on the development of the broader Internet.

(Ad b) Global challenges sometimes require a global effort in order to be dealt with effectively. The net neutrality regulation imposed on network owners is a solution to an alleged problem affecting innovation concerning the development of the next generation Internet. As such, a policy to this effect would benefit considerably from a global implementation. An evaluation of the proposed bills along these lines suggests the following.

(5) The Internet's global and interdependence-imposing nature limits the State's effectiveness in pursuing policy decisions.

The current global governance mechanisms and institutions are not equipped to serve as vehicles for the implementation of effective worldwide policies, as a consequence they cannot serve as a platform for pursuing net neutrality policies globally. First, they tend to be incapable of reaching consensus in time, which is specifically in a fast-moving context of the Internet problematic. Secondly, they lack effective enforcement mechanisms to implement their decisions. The absence of effective global mechanisms for pursuing Internet policies worldwide poses considerable consequences for States or regions that do have specific ideas on how to develop the next generation Internet, because policies designed to develop the global communications infrastructure require a global implementation in order to be effective. As a result, unilateral enforcement of Internet policies does not affect the Internet as a whole directly.

(6) National decision making in an interdependent context requires an evaluation in transnational terms.

National policies do not tend to be very effective on a global scale. They do however generate externalities. Within the context of the net neutrality debate, positive externalities are for example the end products, innovations that can be used anywhere on the Internet. The negative externalities in case of the proposed net neutrality bills are, for example, a decrease in foreign business opportunities in the US based on products requiring enhanced quality of service. Consequently, instead of focusing on its domestic market, the net neutrality legislation should be developed in terms of its competitive advantage related to Internet innovation and access. For the US this boils down to an evaluation on how to maintain its technological and commercial leadership on the Internet. Both economic theory and current regulatory practice in the US suggest that additional legislation (to the current regulatory practice) is not particularly necessary to advance competition but is rather likely to hamper innovation and hence the development the Internet. Whereas the net effect of national US regulation is not going to affect the overall development of the Internet, the effect of unnecessary legislation can significantly damage the US position in the Internet market.

The interdependent context also poses additional questions of a more fundamental nature.

(7) The Internet's interdependent context reveals problems for democratic theory.

If our democratic convictions are based on the intuition that affected parties deserve a say in the making of policies that promote the public interest, the discrepancy caused by a shift in autonomy and sovereignty of the State reveals a democratic deficit underlying national decisions having direct extraterritorial effects. Although a well-organized global civil society could theoretically serve as an advocate for foreign parties, civil society groups tend to suffer from an even greater deficit in terms of democratic legitimacy since they tend to represent ideals rather than people. A consequence of which is that the inextricable bond between State and subject is waning. From a practical point of view however, it means that a specific form of market accountability partly replaces the notion of democratic accountability.

(8) Interdependency establishes a shift from democratic to market accountability.

From a practical point of view however, the accountability problem mentioned above, is considerably less threatening when realizing that the Internet has additional qualities supporting the policy-setting process in an interdependent context. The effectiveness of national policy setting combined with the quality of the Internet as a marketplace of ideas, facilitates the global distribution of innovative products, innovative uses of the Internet and best practices in terms of stimulating innovation and competition. This effectively creates a system of regulatory or legislative competition. First, the most innovative companies will settle in the most innovation friendly regions. Secondly, the Internet's capacity to enable a nearly instant dissemination of information regarding innovative Internet uses, products and services, indirectly pressures governments for favorable regulation. The effect is a competitive environment with at stake the ability to innovate. Whereas current economic theory (and US economic policy) holds that legislation tends to hamper innovation if not forming a solution to the adverse affects of power abuse by large corporations, proponents and opponents in the current net neutrality debate disagree on the benefits of the legislation for the development of the Internet. The model of regulatory competition effectively provides for a testing ground for ideas. The US, until recently, was able to dominate global developments by its hegemonic power. Increased interdependence undermines this position and even forces the US to shift their policies from the traditional *example of power* to the soft power politics of the *power of example*.

Chapter 8
CONCLUSIONS

After a short reminder of the setup of the inquiry, a summary of the case study findings is presented based on the investigation of US Internet policies. A subsequent section provides a generalization hereof based on the US position as critical and the Internet as extreme case in point for examining the implications of globalization for democratic constitutional governance. The last section of the chapter includes the implications of these findings and presents some recommendations for further research formulated as general hypotheses about the changing nature of constitutional governance.

8.1   INTRODUCTION

This inquiry set out to investigate the effects of globalization on the modern State as constitutional democracy. Because the Internet (1) takes the defining characteristic of the globalization process, the increase in the level of transnational interdependence between actors and activities, to its logical extreme and (2) can be studied in isolation whilst States maintain their constitutional commitments and responsibilities both on and off line, the Internet served as testing ground for examining the changes that a context of increased transnational interdependence puts on traditional constitutional governance. Hence, within this inquiry, the Internet served as lens for investigating the effects of globalization for today's dominant form of political organization, the constitutional democracy.

Constitutional democracies are characterized by democratic decision making, a system of checks and balances and a commitment to maintain individual rights. Their traditional responsibilities involve the provision of (1) security, protecting from internal and external threats, (2) welfare, generally associated with a well-functioning market economy, and (3) individual liberties consisting of both political/ civil and economic rights. Being both inclined and known to react to challenges, the ubiquitous globalization process is likely to affect the modern State.

The empirical part of the study focused on the US, since, as one of the first constitutional democracies, it has become an archetype for constitutional governance. As a result, the case study components of the inquiry focused on the changing role of the US in the interdependent context of the Internet. At stake was how the commitments and responsibilities stemming from the US Constitution material-

R.W. Rijgersberg, The State of Interdependence
© *2010, T·M·C·ASSER PRESS, The Hague, and the author*

ize on the Internet and what effects this has on the US in its capacity as a promoter of its citizen's interest. The four case studies forming the empirical basis of the inquiry were chosen on the basis of their relevance to the general inquiry in terms of interdependency and relevance to US' constitutional responsibilities and commitments (security, welfare and individual liberties).

In order to guarantee a diverse range of relevant case studies, a case study model was developed distinguishing between fields of State influence (communication and interconnection) and mode of influence (institutional and regulatory). These modes subsequently provided the basis for the four case studies designed to identify the consequences of transnational interdependency for the role of the US in the light of its constitutional commitments and responsibilities. The case study investigating domain name system management (Chapter 4) concerned the institutional influence of the US in the field of Internet communication. The case study investigating Internet standard setting (Chapter 5) pertained to the US institutional responsibilities regarding the provision of interconnectivity. The censorship case study (Chapter 6) explored the extraterritorial promotion of individual values provided a case study on the regulatory consequences of communications policy. The last case study, regarding network neutrality (Chapter 7) examined the regulatory implications of US innovation policy concerning interconnectivity on the Internet.

8.2   US Policies and the Internet

The individual case studies each confirmed the hypothesis that transnational interdependence challenges the prevalent constitutional organization of political life. The institutional inquiries into domain name management and standard setting, showed the emergence of specialized global governance mechanisms exceeding the current abilities of intergovernmental organization. The regulatory inquiries into the Global Online Freedom Act and Net Neutrality regulation in turn, showed that, rather than opening up opportunities for the US to export their values directly, the interdependent context of the Internet actually forecloses an effective, direct transnational promotion of US values and US policies.

8.2.1   Institutional challenges

In order to provide the necessary global coordination, private communities have taken over governmental responsibilities concerning the Internet communications infrastructure. The Internet Corporation for Assigned Names and Numbers (ICANN) manages the Domain Name System's (DNS) naming and addressing function and the Internet Engineering Task Force (IETF) has become the most important standard setting organization on the Internet. Both organizations are private in nature and show similar organizational features.

The Internet Corporation for Assigned Names and Numbers

The prevailing form of political organization is that of the State in which constitutions limit government powers. Whereas the constitutional format generally works well on territorially bounded areas, the absence of a global State-based government and the less than efficient operation of intergovernmental organizations has caused the global governance of the DNS to take on another form than the traditional State-based format. First, ICANN has a distinctively functional instead of territorial organization enabling it to focus on the swift development in the field and amend its policies to the changing environment. Secondly, its unique decentralized organization structure brings the assignment and distribution of the TLDs and sTLDs closer to the consumer.

In important respects, ICANN's activities resemble public policy setting. It serves an important role in organizing society by securing a global system for Internet navigation In addition it performs an important security role because it maintains the smooth operation of the prime information infrastructure, the Internet. Because domain names have become valuable marketing tools, ICANN even performs the classic State task of ensuring private property rights (to trademarks) to which end it has developed a (private) Universal Dispute Resolution Procedure. Because ICANN's responsibilities as a private corporation exceed mere technical coordination in the public interest, it has been criticized for its alleged lack of adequate accountability mechanisms.

The assessment in Chapter 4, however, shows that ICANN's accountability mechanisms are sufficient for performing its task. It shows that ICANN's stakeholder participation model does not necessarily require constitutional accountability mechanisms in order to foreclose power abuse. One of the most important reasons for this is that the democratization of information resulting from the Internet enables not only States, but even private end users to gain access to the technical resources necessary to set up, back-up and create alternative systems to the ICANN-based DNS, and hence allows private corporations to take the lead in forming a check on public policy making. What the DNS case study has shown is that, even at a basic security level, that of ensuring a smooth operation of an essential part of the communication infrastructure, private organizations can take the lead and market mechanisms combined with pressure from the international community are able to keep the private parties in check. The case study also showed that ICANN has gained the level of maturity that has rendered additional these private checks on public policy superfluous.

The Internet Engineering Task Force

Standards facilitate trade. They also form an important tool for State control. Accountancy standards establishing a uniform valuation of assets, for example, directly affect the State's ability to levy taxes. Within the realm of technological standardization, standards can influence the State's ability to monitor its subjects' exchange of information. The variety in national communication policies suggest that States have different ideas about the extent of control they deem necessary in order to perform their basic tasks. The Internet however requires universal standards in order to operate globally. Absent a global government, the necessary universality of standards affects the traditional role of States in the standard setting process.

The case study on global standard setting shows that, similar to ICANN, the Internet as a transnational interdependency-imposing communication infrastructure, stimulates private initiative and functional organization over territorially organized governance. The result is again decentralized decision making based on technical expertise. The second important observation is that the private and decentralized nature of Internet standard setting organizations makes them better equipped than State institutions to guard individual liberties and stimulate innovation. Contrary to Lessig's dream outlined in Chapter 5, this case study showed that the State is unlikely to be the best candidate for promoting freedom in terms of individual liberties and innovation in global communication infrastructures. It shows that private initiative is more than capable of safeguarding fundamental values of a free society.

Whereas the privatization of the DNS was a deliberate US choice informed primarily by commercial considerations, the Internet's most important standard setting organization, the Internet Engineering Task Force (IETF), even showed that the technical expertise of its members enabled them to establish themselves as independent organization. As a self-regulating standard setting organization, the IETF not only performs an important traditional State-function in ordering society and maintaining a well-functioning Internet, it also serves an important role as guardian of individual rights, as particularly the example of the US attempt to apply its Communications Assistance for Law Enforcement Act (CALEA) to Internet communications shows. In this respect, the IETF showed to be a more reliable guardian of individual rights than the US.

8.2.2   Regulatory challenges

The case studies investigating the effects of US attempts to regulate private actors on the Internet show that the conditions of interdependence established by the Internet limit an autonomous and effective regulation of private actors. The analysis of both the US battle against corporate censorship compliance under foreign regimes and the current proposals to stimulate Internet development by imposing non-discrimination requirements on broadband Internet service providers confirm this thesis. The case study on the Global Online Freedom Act (GOFA) addressing the effect of transnational regulation of US content providers operating under foreign censorship regimes (notably Google in China), shows that neither a human rights-based approach, nor an approach based on antitrust considerations is able to effectively address US compliance with foreign censorship requirements by focusing on private actors. The assessment of the net neutrality regulation imposing non-discrimination requirements on broadband operators providing access to the Internet shows that the transnational effects of national regulation are insufficient to directly influence the development of the Internet at large. Both types of regulations pose serious challenges to the State as an instrument to promote the interests of its citizens. Moreover, they challenge the democratic foundations of decision making in the public interest.

The Global Online Freedom Act

The GOFA is a bill specifically designed to prevent US corporations from cooperating with foreign censorship activities abroad. The bill proposes to constrain the activities of US corporations abroad. In addition to imposing limitations on the censorship cooperation of US actors, the GOFA specifically requires private content providers to ensure the unimpaired transmission of US sponsored content such as Voice of America. This bill, designed to promote the US values extraterritorially, actually achieves the opposite when passed. Not only does it fail to promote the US' economic interests due to the structure of the bill, it effectively prevents US content providers from operating in countries like China at all.

A critical assessment of the effects of the GOFA revealed that the core of the problem is the incompatibility of legal frameworks. A human rights-based approach is generally impervious to economic considerations. Vice versa, an economic approach tends to downsize human rights-based arguments and incentives. Whereas in a democratic constitutional setting, the economy and the protection of individual (civil and political) rights are inextricably connected ideologically, economic and human rights-based legal frameworks have developed in isolation and today form completely different realms. Consequently, the rights-based GOFA blinds its proponents to economic arguments despite the US' trade imbalance and the fact that China represents a market potential of 20 percent of the world's population. Moreover, human rights are generally concerned with Stately violations against the rights of individuals. The interesting element in the GOFA is that it aims to regulate the behavior of private actors to further democratic ideals abroad, an attempt that is hampered by the (realist) legal ordering of the world consisting of sovereign States each seeking to promote their national interests. This discrepancy underlies the fragmentation of domestic and international legal frameworks and is also the basis for States to employ a degree of autonomy in determining their domestic affairs.

Paradoxically, GOFA's attempt to force US corporations to promote US values violates the very constitutional foundations it seeks to promote. By limiting content providers in their editing capacity, it violates the information freedoms granted in the First Amendment's freedom of speech clause. In addition, it violates the tradition of American constitutionalism developed in response to mercantilist policies in which State objectives (feed the local gold stock) were actively pursued by using private corporations. To some extent, the GOFA can be seen as a return to mercantilist principles because it uses private corporations for national purposes. The only difference between the traditional mercantilism and the GOFA is that the latter compels private corporations to promote national values rather than filling the national treasury. Ultimately however, the fragmentation of legal frameworks prevents US content providers to operate in the Chinese market.

In addition to showing the counterproductive nature of the GOFA's human rights-based approach, this case study also examined the possible use of economic frameworks in order to establish the goals outlined in the GOFA. It showed that adapting the US antitrust regime, maintaining US corporate presence whilst simultaneously fighting US censorship practices in China, opens up promising theoretical opportunities for fighting censorship. However, for this construction to work, the US should be willing to incorporate free trade principles into its antitrust framework by extending the 'relevant market' clause to all types of exclusionary conduct. This step, the US is not willing to take. Ultimately its antitrust legislation is designed to protect US national interests rather than the ideal of a free market in general.

Net neutrality legislation

The assessment of the net neutrality proposals shows that national legislation is rather ineffective in transforming the Internet at large. It showed that the interdependent context even prevents a powerful country like the US from maintaining unilateral control over its national communications infrastructures. Although this conclusion may seem tautological in some respects, national legislation in an interdependent context has some important consequences for US communications policies. This particular examination of US innovation policy showed that an interdependent context forces the US to incorporate transnational interests into its policy considerations in its national decision-making process if it is to take its Internet policies seriously.

Net neutrality regulation is designed to compel broadband Internet providers to observe non-discrimination (hence neutrality) requirements in the provision of their services. More specifically, it prohibits broadband providers from offering enhanced quality of services on the Internet since it requires them to distinguish between traffic based on origin, nature or content. This legislation can have profound implications since it concerns a deliberate choice on how to shape the Internet of the future.

Disproving of the alleged neutrality of the technical qualities of the Internet, invalidating the much-used claim that net neutrality legislation is required on technical grounds, reduced the debate to a question on how to stimulate the developments on and of the Internet in terms of open communications (stimulating equal access) and innovation (by stimulating freedom of choice). Since this research showed that the current regulatory regime maintains the open character of the Internet on a local level by foreclosing outright blocking practices, only the latter objective remained.

The inquiry further revealed that the current debate suffers from two shortcomings. It fails to include the probable use of novel, yet undiscovered technologies for the next generation Internet and it fails to acknowledge the interdependent nature of the Internet. Because the Internet requires a global implementation of principles and policies if they are to yield the desired result, policies designed to affect the development of the Internet ideally require global implementation. Unfortunately, the existing intergovernmental institutions and frameworks fail to reach the consensus needed for effective decision making. Even, the specially designed (UN-based) Internet Governance Forum, set up as an umbrella organization of stakeholders to provide a platform for Internet development, lacks the effectiveness of stakeholder organizations and has failed to attract the relevant Internet communities. Consequently, States are left to their own devices when developing their Internet innovation strategies.

The prevalent economic theories, also endorsed by the US in their policies, hold that the key to innovation is competition. This, however, can be interpreted in various ways. Without compelling reasons from a constitutional point of view, the question whether or not to impose net neutrality regulation on the US broadband market seems arbitrary to some extent. However, the interdependent context imposed by the Internet does affect US policy making in two ways. First, it reduces the effects of national policies, because it prevents the US from determining the developments of and on the Internet unilaterally. Secondly, it imposes the need for an evaluation of national policies in transnational terms. Instead of focusing on its domestic market, the net neutrality legislation requires an evaluation in terms of competitive advantage.

8.2.3   The State and the Internet

The institutional case studies show the limitations of Stately decision making in an interdependent context. The Domain Name System case study shows a transition from governmental control to private management in the public interest. It also shows an increased role for market accountability over democratic accountability. The Internet's success and technical characteristics had already forced a transition from the early host-text-based system to the decentralized structure of the modern DNS. Its transnational expansion stimulated the US to transfer its responsibilities to a grassroots-driven private organization with the explicit condition of incorporating the interests of all stakeholder groups. Despite much criticism, ICANN has developed into a rather successful, responsible organization uninhibited by territorial membership requirements. ICANN as provider of security, welfare and individual property rights shows that privatization of public undertakings can establish an effective liaison between private and public initiatives. Within ICANN's organization structure, States have a dual status. On the one hand, they are consumers. Because they have an interest as States in the TLDs denoted by a specific country code, they generally maintain oversight on the private administrators and distributors of the sublevel domain names falling under the country code domains. On the other hand, they are represented *as States* in the stakeholder model to ensure that ICANN policies do not interfere with national regulation. Its specialized task enables it to reach consensus based on technocratic considerations and the democratization of information on the Internet provides the tools to keep ICANN in check by enabling individuals to run satellite servers and set up alternative DNS systems. Interestingly enough, initiatives employed along these lines were conducted by private organizations. Publicly available records do not reveal any funding or other governmental initiatives to this end.

Although the role of States within ICANN is limited due their marginal institutional role, the standard setting process conducted by the IETF shows an even more peripheral role for the State within an interdependent context. Essentially working on a similar stakeholder basis as ICANN, the IETF process completely separates the development of Internet standards from the interests of individual States. Whereas ICANN can be seen as an improvement on Stately or governmental governance because it is able to reach consensus on a global scale and has developed principles of governance that guarantee transparent stakeholder-based decision making, the IETF takes non-governmental decision making even further by refraining from incorporating States *as States* in their decision-making procedures. Although States can contribute to global standard development, they are not acknowledged as representatives of large groups of subjects. The standards are solely evaluated on technical merits, that is, if they provide feasible solutions to existing problems. Whereas ICANN has developed their private UDRDPs largely in cooperation with the UN-based World Intellectual Property Organization (WIPO), the Request for Comments (RFC) procedure characterizing the IETF decision-making procedure has emerged from the voluntary process that emerged between a few experts in the early seventies. In fact, the IETF was not formally privatized like ICANN but the technical experts coordinating the standard setting procedure simply presumed independence by setting up a government-independent funding agency that would enable them to operate government-independently. Their response to the FBI attempt to amend the CALEA as to include Internet services and its incorporation of privacy enhancing alternatives to the IPv6 addressing system suggest that the IETF is even better equipped than States to secure fundamental values and individual liberties.

From the regulatory case studies, the censorship case showed that regulating private actors extraterritorially, especially on human rights grounds, is not very effective if designed to promote Western (democratic constitutional) values. Nevertheless, the type of regulation is tempting in an interdependent world because, on the one hand, States want to protect their subjects and corporations from what they consider harmful conduct and, on the other hand, the global character of the Internet invites individuals and corporations to fulfill their interests beyond national borders. States in this respect have interests of their own (like advancing national values), which is why they continue to exercise their traditional role of protector also transnationally. States, in this respect, merely acts as a trend followers, responding to changing circumstances. The consequence of this extraterritorial approach, however, is a shift in the system of checks and balances. Whereas national decisions are primarily formed by democratic deliberation in congress (or parliament), the GOFA demonstrates a power shift towards the executive branch because the executive is to select the countries in which the GOFA applies. This has two consequences.

First, it decreases the deliberative process in Congress. Secondly, it creates legal uncertainty for private actors operating abroad since it makes them increasingly dependent on the whims of the executive.

The analysis of the network neutrality case study, investigating the need for national regulation stimulating innovation, also showed that the interdependent context created by the Internet has significant consequences for the modern State. First, because in an interdependent context national decisions have transnational effects, national decisions require an evaluation in transnational terms, notably in terms of competitive advantage because national policies can have negative effects in a transnational context. Secondly, because national regulation also affects for-eign actors, it poses questions concerning the democratic foundations of our na-tional policies. If democratic theory requires a representation of affected parties, the current constitutional structure does not formally include foreign affected par-ties in national policy making procedures. Instead of amending democratic deci-sion-making processes however, the Internet as a global communication infrastructure offers a solution to the problem it poses. The key to the solution is the Internet's role as a marketplace of ideas. The current institutional setup forecloses an effective global setting and implementation of innovation policies leaving States to develop innovation policies unilaterally. These policies, however, are unlikely to be effective if not implemented globally because some policies may, for example, foreclose the use of certain applications. The Internet as a marketplace of ideas offers the possibility of instantaneous exchange of ideas. This allows the export of ideas about both innovative products and innovative regulatory environments. In sum, the Internet creates a transformation of society, combining autonomous demo-cratic decision making with a legislative competition between States or regions.

8.3   CONSTITUTIONAL GOVERNANCE AND INTERDEPENDENCE

A widespread belief amongst the more 'empirically minded' researchers, is that it roves very difficult to generalize case study results when not designing a case study very carefully for a rather limited purpose, eliminating all the irrelevant variables. This research, however, was not designed to identify general laws guiding the de-velopment of political organization. It lacks the positivist pretension to establish law-like models allowing for specific predictions. In contrast to the positivist ap-proach of designing case studies to refute or confirm particular theories, the pur-pose of this inquiry was exploratory, aimed at gathering preliminary information that will help to define problems and develop suggestions for further research. Within the context of this inquiry, the case studies merely served to contribute to our under-standing of the effects of globalization on the modern State in order to improve the theoretical framework for understanding the (continuously) changing organization of political life.

8.3.1   Distinguishing elements in the inquiry

The case studies on US Internet policies formed the descriptive element in the inquiry and were designed with a view to generalize their findings in order to form hypotheses on the effects of globalization on the modern State as a constitutional democracy. This is why the criteria for these case studies concerned their relevance to both the independency-imposing qualities of the Internet and the traditional constitutional responsibilities of States.

Two additional methodological elements justify a generalization of the results. The first element is the focus on US policies. The US serves a critical role in this inquiry. The US Constitution is particularly relevant because it has become an archetype for modern political organization. In addition, as the world's most powerful State in political, economic and cultural terms, developments affecting the US will also affect other constitutional democracies. The second element is the use of the Internet as extreme element in the inquiry. Because the Internet takes the notion of transnational interdependence, the essence of globalization, to its logical extreme, it magnifies and accentuates the political changes resulting from globalization. As such, the Internet serves as lens for studying the effects of globalization delineating the scope of the research while not affecting the constitutional commitments and responsibilities of the modern State.

The interdependent context imposed by the Internet affects every individual user. Hence, it affects all States in which the Internet is available similarly in the employment of their communications policies. The focus on the effects on US communications policy in the light of its constitutional commitments and responsibilities however, limit the generalization of the results to Western constitutional democracies since their structure and responsibilities largely coincide.

8.3.2   Generalization of the results

The choice of case studies based on their relevance to the interdependent character of the Internet (extreme element) and the constitutional commitments and responsibilities of the US (critical element) make the case studies suitable for hypothesizing about the changes that await the constitutional democracy in the light of the globalization process.

The case investigating the management of the domain name system showed that transnational interdependency imposes a change in the performance of public tasks. An interdependent context pushes the national execution of public tasks, traditionally performed and overseen by States, to be handled on a global scale. The problems this poses for intergovernmental organizations, generates a transition from centralized State-based control to a grassroots type of private coordination on decentralized functional grounds.

The case study investigating the consequences of global standard setting showed an identical transition from State-interests pursued by national governments to a privatized type of governance in the public interest, free from governmental oversight and characterized by bottom-up decision making on technocratic grounds. Both the domain name case and the standardization case imply that sometimes, private organizations can be are better at guaranteeing individual rights than States.

The censorship case study shows that within an interdependent context, the protective responsibilities of the State extend beyond national borders. It furthermore shows that using a human rights framework to regulate the behavior of private actors operation abroad is not very fruitful. The fragmentation of legal frameworks and the nature of the legal world order based on sovereign States prevent an effective extension of the State's protective role and the extraterritorial promotion of national values by regulating private actors. As a result, instead of using private actors, an intergovernmental/bilateral approach is likely to have more effect in the short run. Because the fundamental values of the constitutional democracy (the political system of democracy and the economic system of a free market) are intrinsically connected, the best way of promoting these fundamental values is indirectly, through an intensification of trade relations, not by regulating private actors.

The network neutrality case study explored the consequences for 'classic' national legislation of private actors within an interdependent context. Within an interdependent context, the need for a global implementation of policies is increasing. When lacking adequate intergovernmental institutions to implement national policies on a global scale it is up to individual States to design their policies nationally or regionally. The effect of this however, is a decrease in influence because a transnational interdependent context causes a decline of the State's autonomy. More importantly, this case study showed that an interdependent context requires an evaluation of national policies in an international context. Particularly, an evaluation in terms of competitive advantage is likely to improve the quality of national policy making.

Figure 14 captures the results of the case studies by showing the potential implications for constitutional governance schematically. It particularly reveals the political transformations caused by increased transnational interdependence. The starting point is the original position depicted in the first quadrant in which a State, as an autonomous entity, operates in a community of sovereign States. The globalization process poses challenges along two lines. First, there is the transition from autonomy to dependency characterized by an increased influence of national policies by events that are not domestically coordinated. The second transition from an international to a transnational world suggests a shift from centralized State-based decision making in the public interest to a decentralized system of decision making exceeding geographically defined areas and actors.

The first transition is the shift from autonomy to dependency. Within the existing international world order this transition contains a shift in power from the legislative (quadrant 1) to the executive branch in government (quadrant 2) as the prime force in public decision making. Dependency on extraterritorial actors and processes invites States to try to influence decisions that evade autonomous domestic

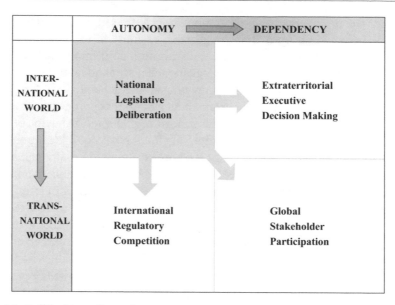

Figure 14. Political transformations

coordination. A traditional way of doing this is by means of intergovernmental liaisons. A relatively new way of trying to influence foreign processes is by using private actors to advance national ideologies abroad. Whereas the former approach has its own disadvantages this latter approach is neither problem free. Characteristic of both approaches is that they show a power shift to the executive branch in government, at the expense of the democratic deliberation in congress and parliament that characterizes domestic decision making.

The second political transformation (resulting from increased transnational interdependence) is suggested by the assessment of the net neutrality regulation and concerns the shift from international world order to a transnational world order. The international world is the world of the currently prevailing legal order built on the Westphalian assumption that the world consists of a collection of self-governing States each seeking to promote their national interests. A transnational world on the other hand, suggests that decisions in the public interest exceed geographical limitations as a matter of course. For States this implies that national decisions have extraterritorial effects just as foreign decisions have their impact on domestic decisions. In its simplest form, leaving the relative autonomy of the State in tact, it shows a transition from democratic deliberation (quadrant 1) to a combination of democratic deliberation and market forces (quadrant 3) as prevailing mechanisms informing public decision making. Because extraterritorial actions have domestic effects, there is a need to evaluate national policies in terms of a nation's competitive advantage. Within the traditional Westphalian conception, the transnational effects of national policies create a democratic deficit if democratic theory requires the incorporation of affected (foreign) parties. Within a transnational framework, however, this problem is overcome by the availability of a global communications network. The Internet creates a 'global marketplace of ideas' by providing a cheap and easy accessible platform for informing individuals, corporations and States about best practices, products and services, instantly and worldwide. The effect of this is a global system of States combining the advantage of autonomous democratic decision making (majority decisions combined with an effective apparatus for enforcement) based on a transnational evaluation of policies with the effective allocation of resources characteristic of the market economy. The availability of information on a global scale is likely to eventually establish conversion towards the best legal culture for creating innovation and competition.

The conversion to a dependency relation with other actors and the transformation of political life from an international to a transnational world order, have additional consequences. Stimulated by global flows of information, goods, services capital and people, both transitions imply an increase in activities in the public interest that would benefit from, or even require, global coordination. The current territory-based intergovernmental frameworks seem to be incapable of effective global governance because they lack the ability to reach consensus. The case studies all confirm that discrepancies in national State-policies paralyze intergovernmental organizations in their consensus-building capacity. Since, in addition, the fragmentation of legal frameworks also hampers the active use of private actors to establish a worldwide distribution of uniform values, the globalization process requires new ways of governing global activities.

The transnational element described above not only implies a boundary-transcending transition in terms of effects; it also implies transcendence in terms of players since interdependence has given rise to non-territorially defined actors operating in the public interest. The institutional case studies are interesting in this respect because they describe actual, real-life non-territory based alternatives to the intergovernmental solutions associated with the international paradigm. They imply a transition from the constitutional State-based promotion of public interests (quadrant 1) to a situation in which transnationally operating private actors increasingly determine public policies (quadrant 4). Both institutional case studies show that transnational interdependency gives rise to private initiatives taking over traditional State responsibilities based on functional rather than territorial grounds The shift to private stakeholder-based type of coordination in the public interest that is technocratic, bottom-up and functional in nature suggests a marginalization of the State as protector of traditional constitutional responsibilities. The inquiries furthermore suggest that a narrow focus of functional governance is an important element in successful functional stakeholder-based governance.

8.3.3   Implications for decision making in the public interest

The political transformations schematically depicted in Figure 14 should not be interpreted dogmatically. They merely represent trends, changes in accents concluded from the case studies examining the effects of globalization through the lens of the Internet in order to obtain a more detailed and clearer picture of the transformations the globalization process has in store for political life viewed from a constitutional perspective. It also serves as a preliminary basis for further investigations into complex and nuanced world of today's political reality. This is not to say that it does not have considerably implications for modern decision making in the public interest.

Instrumentally, this study implies that the State is no longer the sole vehicle for making decisions in the public interest. The shift towards private forms of public policy making suggests that interdependence gives rise to alternative forms of decision making, reducing the relevance of the State as a vehicle for advancing the interests of its citizens. Interdependence forces States to adapt a more facilitating rather than leading role in advancing foreign policy. A practical implication hereof is that the loss in sovereign power requires an evaluation of the transnational effects of the policies, particularly in terms of competitive advantage.

Institutionally, within a constitutional setting, interdependence means a larger role for the executive at the expense of the deliberative legislative process in congress and parliament. In addition, interdependence also increases the need for a global implementation of policies. The lack of intergovernmental consent stimulates functionally defined stakeholder organizations to set global policies in the public interest. Whereas this decreases the role of the State and hence decreases the democratic foundations of policymaking in the public interest, it does pose an interesting alternative to State-based policy making on a global scale. The effect is a shift from constitutional to (hybrid) more market driven decision making mechanisms.

Conceptually, the inquiry pictures a rather complex and nuanced picture. In addition to the aforementioned loss in sovereign State powers and novel decision making mechanisms establish a liberalization of the traditionally inextricably connection between States and their subjects to a degree. The transnationalization of the political reality gives rise to a re-evaluation of the State in terms of constitutional commitments and responsibilities as well as a re-evaluation in terms of political theories. The State as a vehicle for advancing the interests of its subjects is increasingly moving beyond the role it has assumed in the 20th century. The interdependent context tends to decrease the State's ability to maintain its caretaker status. Instead of serving as prime guardian of constitutional values and planner and provider of public goods and services, the State is increasingly adopting a more facilitating role, developing the abilities of its citizens in a transnational context. In this sense, the State becomes akin to a parent, setting the preconditions for successful transnational citizenship, only to serve as safety net, or safe harbor to fall back on when the transnational world fails to live up to expectations.

8.4 IMPLICATIONS FOR FURTHER RESEARCH

This inquiry set out to develop hypotheses for examining the implications of globalization for the modern State in the light of its constitutional commitments (Section 1.2). The implications for further research follow directly from the generalized case study findings. The following list of hypotheses shows the most relevant conclusions.

[HYPOTHESIS 1] The problem of intergovernmental organizations to reach consensus on a global scale is largely due to their territorial foundations.

The results of both the institutional case studies (Chapters 4 and 5), and the examination of the UN's Internet Governance Forum in Chapter 7, suggest that territoriality might be the main reason for the inefficiency of intergovernmental decision making. The essence of the State is its historically determined territorial nature. One important consequence of this is that policies tend to be designed to operate on multiple levels in a complex environment with often conflicting interests. Consequently, States tend to determine their strategies on motives beyond the scope of the immediate problem at hand. The fact that all States share this feature complicates consensus building on territorial grounds in an intergovernmental setting.

[HYPOTHESIS 2] A technocratic functional basis is the future for global policy setting in the public interest.

Both institutional case studies suggest that coordinating global processes on a private, decentralized and functionally limited basis offers an interesting alternative for territory-based intergovernmental governance. An investigation into the possibilities of a technocratic, functional solution to global problems (for example climate change, environmental health and financial crises) could possibly (1) offer a practical solution to the consensus problem mentioned above, (2) provide more insight into the current global decision-making mechanisms, and (3) produce out a roadmap to arrive at a practical solution to the problem itself.

[HYPOTHESIS 3] Constitutional warrants are not strictly necessary for conducting effective and legitimate coordination in the public interest.

As the institutional case studies show, private organizations can take the lead, and market mechanisms combined with intergovernmental and non-governmental pressures can keep private parties sufficiently in check to prevent power abuse of governing organizations without constitutional warrants. Only a combination of States, market players and civil society groups seem to be able to provide the counterweight necessary to foreclose power abuse by governing parties in a globalizing world. The State's traditional provision of security, welfare and individual rights is fading in an interdependent context. The interplay of the three main forces within society deserves more attention in the light of the globalization process, of course, without making the constitutionalization of values within societies obsolete.

[HYPOTHESIS 4] Private stakeholder-based governance may prove a new paradigm for decision making in the public interest in a globalizing world.

The post-WWII world shows a dramatic increase in new players, viz. multinational corporations and non-governmental actors, seeking to influence (global or international) decision making in the public interest. This is why Chapter 3 suggested a permeable model of the modern State, leaving more room to transnationally operating actors to spread their wings.

The Internet, as interdependency-imposing medium, suggests a promising future for private stakeholder-based governance models, particularly for those incorporating a combination of Stately and non-Stately actors. Particularly the ICANN case study showed that functionally organized stakeholder environment can be very successful in integrating a wide variety of interests without resorting to classic democratic accountability mechanisms that are difficult to realize beyond State borders.

[HYPOTHESIS 5] Private, decentralized organizations operating in the public interest can be better equipped than States to encourage innovation.

Private entities generally operate in a (more) competitive environment than States, providing incentives towards more openness/transparency for creating the confidence (trust) necessary for performing their public role. Private decentralized organizations are less inclined to use the same amount of control that States require in the context of fulfilling their constitutional obligations. This is why they are less inclined to impose constraints on private conduct that would prevent innovation. Because the globalization process suggests a privatization of public responsibilities, it serves to investigate more thoroughly the conditions, advantages and disadvantages of the new types of governance emerging in this context.

[HYPOTHESIS 6] Private, decentralized organizations are better equipped than States to guard individual liberties.

The previous section (hypothesis 5) already touched upon the fact that private parties are less inclined and able to control their customers. In this sense, private initiatives taking over traditional State responsibilities can provide better warrant against power abuse from corporations and governments alike, as the institutional case studies suggested. Because private parties lack additional (constitutional) responsibilities, they are less inclined to use their powers the way States tend to do. China's censorship regime (Chapter 6), but also the US interests in standardization and control (Chapter 5) are illustrative in this regard. In addition, the intrinsic connection between political (democratic) values and (market) economic values, render private corporations conducting international trade important actors for promoting the values of a free society.

[HYPOTHESIS 7] The fragmentation of legal frameworks (economic/human rights based and national/international) prevents the development of a global or cosmopolitan world order.

Legal frameworks are designed for different purposes. This is why they do not form a unified body of law that can easily be transposed to a global context. This is also why they render an extraterritorial regulation of private actors designed to promote national values directly unfruitful. The fragmentation of legal frameworks also slows down a conversion into a single global legal framework and hampers a development into a world-State characterized by top down control. Hence, the existing frameworks providing a basis for Stately cooperation also ensure a degree of local autonomy ensuring diversity in legal cultures. Seen from this point of view, the fragmentation of legal frameworks increases the degree of freedom for world-citizens to a degree by preventing the tentacles of the State to gain global in reach. Regardless one's stand on the matter, the connection between cosmopolitanism and legal frameworks deserves more attention in the light of a globalizing world.

[HYPOTHESIS 8] The best way of allocating resources, whether goods, services, capital, people, values or legal systems is through market forces.

Albeit indirectly, the empirical evidence in this inquiry does support this market economic adage. Because State-based organizations have difficulty in obtaining and processing the information necessary to formulate and implement policies, the combined power of individual choice within markets is better equipped to deal with effective allocation of resources as well as transformations of societies. This holds both for the global dissemination of Western (constitutional) values (democracy, market economy and maintenance of individual rights, see Chapter 6) as for legal frameworks guiding innovation processes and market growth (Chapter 7).

[HYPOTHESIS 9] Globalization establishes a shift from constitutional to alternative types of accountability of which market accountability is perhaps the most important and promising alternative.

Both the regulatory competition caused by the shift from an international to a transnational world and the emergence of non-State actors setting public policies imply a declining role for traditional democratic decision making in a globalizing world. More investigation is needed into the limits and applications of alternative types of accountability.

[HYPOTHESIS 10] In an interdependent world, the State's focus shifts from provider of security, welfare and individual rights to facilitator of the preconditions hereof. In addition, it is likely to serve as a last resort, a safety net in providing ultimate remedies.

Global challenges sometimes require global solutions, and because states are increasingly incapable of securing fundamental constitutional responsibilities in an interdependent world, the new role of the State becomes that of a facilitator for individual choice and opportunity, a guardian for individual autonomy creating the preconditions for participation in a transnational world. Viewing the state as a facilitator and ultimate safety net rather than a provider of goods, services and jobs, might help to design effective public policies for a globalizing world.

EPILOGUE

Although the modern State is unlikely to be the end configuration of organized political life, and also a state of interdependence is unlikely to end the successful era of democratic constitutional governance in the public interest, the challenges posed by the globalization process to our much-celebrated archetype of political organization do shake the foundations on which our society is built.

From a philosophical point of view, perhaps the most pressing consequence of the globalization challenge to modern governance is that a state of interdependence inevitably decreases the democratic quality of decision making in the public interest. The privatization of public decision making gives rise to novel, hybrid accountability mechanisms. The ongoing power shift from the legislative to the executive branch of government in an interdependent context undermines the deliberative processes within congress and parliament and the transnational effects of national decisions create a democratic deficit in terms of affected foreign parties, hence limiting the autonomous decision-making capacity of national governments.

Within the traditional conceptual framework of the Westphalian world order, the democratic quality of intergovernmental organizations trying to solve problems globally has long been subject to debate. This examination of the effects of global interdependence for democratic constitutional governance adds additional arguments, and calls for a re-examination of the very philosophical foundations grounding decision making in the public interest from a constitutional perspective. It shows that the globalization process and the accompanying political transformations require a rigorous re-conceptualization of notions such as legitimacy, accountability and the nature of representation. If there is one contribution the empirical evidence presented in this book has made to this debate, it is that it has made the need to answer these questions even more pressing (and more complicated at that).

BIBLIOGRAPHY

Anderson, K. and Rieff, D., 2005
'Global Civil Society: A Skeptical View', in Anheier, H. et al., eds., *Global Civil Society* (London, Sage 2005).

Antitrust Modernization Committee, 2005
Hearings Summary of Exclusionary Conduct Refusals to Deals and Bundling and Loyalty Discounts, 29 September 2005, available at <www.abanet.org/antitrust/at-links/pdf/at-mod/exclusionary_conduct.pdf>.

Antitrust Modernization Committee, 2006
Discussion Memorandum re Exclusionary Conduct, 11 July 2006, available at <http://govinfo.library.unt.edu/amc/pdf/meetings/ExclCond%20DiscMemo060711fin.pdf>.

Areeda, P.E. and Hovenkamp, A., 2006
Antitrust Law: An Analysis of Antitrust Principles and Their Application (New York, Aspen Publishers 2006).

Barboza, D., 2008
'China Surpasses U.S. in Number of Internet Users', in *The New York Times*, 26 July 2008, available at *NYTIMES:* <www.nytimes.com/2008/07/26/business/worldbusiness/26internet.html>.

Barnes, J., 1984
The Complete Works of Aristotle: The Revised Oxford Translation (Princeton, Princeton University Press 1984).

Barnett, R.E., 2001
'The Original Meaning of the Commerce Clause', *University of Chicago Law Review* (winter 2001).

Barnett, R.E., 2004
Restoring the Lost Constitution: The Presumption of Liberty (Princeton, NJ, Princeton University Press 2004).

Battjes, H. and Vermeulen, B., ed., 2007
Constitutionele Klassiekers (Nijmegen, Ars Aequi 2007).

Baumol, W.J., et al., 2007
'Economists' Statement on Net Neutrality Policy', AEI-Brookings Joint Center for Regulatory Studies, 2007, <http://papers.ssrn.com/sol3/papers.cfm?abstract_id=976889>.

Baylis, J. and Smith, S., 2005
The Globalization of World Politics: An Introduction to International Relations (Oxford, Oxford University Press 2005).

Bazyler, M. J., 1986
'Abolishing the Act of State Doctrine', 134(2) *University of Pennsylvania Law Review* (1986).

Benkler, Y., 2000
'From Consumers to Users: Shifting the Deeper Structures of Regulation', 52 *Federal Communications Law Journal* (2000).

Bettinger, T. et al., 2005
   Domain Name Law and Practice: An International Handbook (Oxford, Oxford University Press 2005).
Black, H.C. and Garner, B.A., 1999
   Black's Law Dictionary (St. Paul, MN, West Group 1999).
Braudel, F., 1979
   Perspectives of the World: Civilization and Capitalism: 15th-18th Centuries (Berkely, CA, University of California Press 1979).
Brin S. and Page, L., 1998
   'The Anatomy of a Large-Scale Hypertextual Web Search Engine', 30(1-7) *Computer Networks and ISD Systems* (1998), available at <http://infolab.stanford.edu/pub/papers/google.pdf>.
BBC Staff, 2004
   'China Endorses Private Property', *BBC News*, 15 March 2004, available at <http://news.bbc.co.uk/2/hi/asia-pacific/3509850.stm>.
BBC Staff, 2006
   'China and the Break-Up of the Internet', *BBC News*, 7 March 2006, available at <http://news.bbc.co.uk/2/hi/technology/4779660.stm>.
Brunsson, J., 2000
   'Organization, Markets, and Standardization', in Brunsson, J. et al., ed., *A World of Standards* (New York, Oxford University Press 2000).
Brunsson, J. and Jacobsson, B., 2000
   'The Contemporary Expansion of Standardization', in Brunsson, J. et al., ed., *A World of Standards* (New York, Oxford University Press 2000).
Bygrave, L.A. and Bing, J., 2009
   Internet Governance: Infrastructures and Institutions (Oxford, Oxford University Press 2009).
Department of State, 2008
   'China', 2007 Country Reports on Human Rights Practices, Bureau of Democracy, Human Rights and Labor, 2008, available at <www.state.gov/g/drl/rls/hrrpt/2007/100518.htm>.
Cabinet Office (UK), 2009
   'Cyber Security Strategy of the United Kingdom, safety, security and resilience in cyberspace', 2009, available at <www.cabinetoffice.gov.uk/media/216620/css0906.pdf>.
Cabral, M.B., 2000
   Introduction to Industrial Organization (Cambridge, MIT Press 2000).
Cahier des doleances, 1789
   'Cahier of the Third Estate of Dourdon', 1789, available at <www.historyguide.org/intellect/cahiers.html>.
Calvani, T., 1979
   'What Is the Objective of Antitrust?', in Calvani, T. and Siegfried, J.J., eds., *Economic Analyses and Antitrust Law* (Dordrecht, Wolters Kluwer Law and Business 1979).
Cameron, K., 2005
   The Laws of Identity (Microsoft Corporation 2005).
Cargill, C.F., 1989
   Information Technology Standardization (Alpine Press 1989).
Castells, M., 1996
   The Rise of the Network Society (Cambridge, Blackwell Publishers 1996).

Center for Democracy and Technology, 2007
    The Internet Engineering Task Force (IETF), 'Internet Standards, Technology and Policy
    Project', 2007, available at <www.cdt.org/standards/ietf.shtml>.
Cerf, V., 1995
    IETF and ISOC, 'Histories of the Internet' (Internet Society 1995).
Chalmers, A.F., 1999
    What Is This Thing Called Science? (Indianapolis, IN, Hackett Publishing 1999).
Chemerinsky, E., 2002
    Constitutional Law: Principles and Policies (New York, Aspen Law & Business 2002).
China Daily Staff, 2009
    'China's online shopping jumps 128.5 % in 2008', *Chinadaily online*, 10 February 2009,
    available at <www.chinadaily.com.cn/bizchina/2009-02/10/content_7462219.htm>.
China Technews Staff, 2009
    'Google China Market Share Lower than 30% in Q2 2009', *ChinaTechNews.com,* 29
    July, 2009, available at <www.chinatechnews.com/2009/07/29/10230-google-china-
    market-share-lower-than-30-in-q2-2009>.
Chong, R.B., 2007
    'The 31 Flavors of the Net Neutrality Debate: Beware of the Trojan Horse', ACLP Schol-
    arship Series, 2007, available at <www.nyls.edu/user_files/1/3/4/30/83/Rachelle%20
    Chong%20-%20Net%20Neutrality%20Essay%20-%20December%202007.pdf>.
CIA, 2009
    'Factbook', 2009, available at <www.cia.gov/library/publications/the-world-factbook/
    geos/ch.html>.
Clayton, R. et al., 2006
    'Ignoring the Great Firewall of China', 6th Workshop on Privacy Enhancing Technolo-
    gies, June 2006, Cambridge, available at <www.cl.cam.ac.uk/~rnc1/ignoring.pdf>.
Clinton, W.J.B., 2008
    Expressing his support for Obama at the, Democratic National Convention on 27 August
    2008, available at <http://thegooddemocrat.wordpress.com/2008/08/28/bill-clinton-
    power-of-example-vs-example-of-power/>.
CNNIC, 2007
    'Chinese Search Engine Market Survey Report 2007' (China Internet Network Informa-
    tion Center (CNNIC) 2007).
Congressional Record, 1992
    'Report of the Judiciary Subcommittee on Technology and the Law to Congress of Sep-
    tember 29, 1992, available at <www.fas.org/irp/congress/1992_cr/s920929-crypt.htm>.
Cotter, T., 2008
    'The Essential Facilities Doctrine', in Hylton, K.N., ed., *Antitrust Law and Economics*
    (Edward Elgar Publishing 2008).
Cottier, T. et al., 2005
    Human Rights and International Trade (Oxford, Oxford University Press 2005).
David, P.A., 1985
    'Clio and the Economics of QWERTY', 75 *The American Economic Review* (1985).
De Soto, H., 2000
    *The Mystery of Capital: Why Capitalism Triumphs in the West and Fails Everywhere
    Else* (New York, Basic Books 2000).
De Tocqueville, A., 1856
    L'Ancien Regime et la Revolution, 1856 [English tr. The Old Regime and the French
    Revolution] (New York, Anchor Books 1955).

De Vey Mestdagh C.N.J. and Rijgersberg R.W., 2007
'Rethinking Accountability in Cyberspace: A New Perspective on ICANN', *International Review of Law, Computers & Technology* (2007) pp. 21, 27-38.

De Vries, H.J., 1999
Standardization: A Business Approach to the Role of National Standardization Organizations (Dordrecht, Kluwer Academic Publishers 1999).

De Vries, H.J., 2006
'IT Standards Typology', in Jakobs, K., ed., *Advanced Topics in Information Technology Standards and Standardization Research* (London, Idea Group Publishing 2006).

Dempsey, J.X., 1997
'Communications Privacy in the Digital Age: Revitalizing the Federal Wiretaps to Enhance Privacy', 8(1) *Albany Law Journal of Science and Technology* (1997).

Diffie, W. and Landau, S.E., 2007
Privacy on the Line: The Politics of Wiretapping and Encryption (Cambridge, MIT Press 2007).

Dommering, E.J., 2006
'Regulating Technology: Code is Not Law', in Dommering, E.J., ed., *Coding Regulation: Essays on the Normative Role of Information Technology* (The Hague, TMC Asser Press 2006).

Economides, N., 2005
'The Economics of the Internet Backbone', NYU, Law and Economics Research Paper 04-033, 2005, available at SSRN: <http://ssrn.com/abstract=613581>.

Embassy of the People Republic of China in the U.S.A., 2007
'Non-Party Member Becomes China's New Health Minister', *online news,* 30 June 2005, available at <www.china-embassy.org/eng/gyzg/t335191.htm>.

Erk, J., 2006
'Does Federalism Really Matter?', 39 *Comparative Politics* (2006).

Ermert, M., 2007
'Department of Homeland and Security wants master key for DNS', 30 March, 2007, available at <www.stopnwo.com/docs/department_of_homeland_and_security_wants_master_key_for_dns.pdf>.

Ermert, M., 2008
'ITU Criticized for Its Role in Internet Snooping', *The H,* 27 October 2008, available at <www.h-online.com/newsticker/news/item/International-Telecommunication-Union-criticised-for-its-role-in-internet-snooping-737791.html>.

Esterhuysen, A., 2008
'Reflections on the Internet Governance Forum from 2006-8', in Kleinwachter, D.A., ed., *Internet Governance Forum (IGF) The First Two Years*, UNESCO Publications for the WSIS (2008).

Fletcher, G.P. and Sheppard, S., 2005
American Law in a Global Context: The Basics (Oxford, Oxford University Press 2005).

Ford, G.S. et al., 2007
'Wireless Net Neutrality: From Carterfone to Cable Boxes', *Phoenix Center Policy Bulletin* 17, 2007, available at SSRN: <http://ssrn.com/abstract=985089>.

French, H., 2005
'Chinese Censors and Web Users Match Wits', *New York Times*, March 4 2005, (Late Edition), available at NYTIMES: <www.nytimes.com/2005/03/04/international/asia/04censor.html>.

Friedman, L.M., 2002
  American Law in the Twentieth Century (New Haven, CT, Yale University Press 2002).
Freeh, L.J., 1994
  Statement at the: Digital Telephony and Law Enforcement Access to Advanced Tele-
  communications Technologies and Services: Joint Hearings on H.R. 4922 and S. 2375,
  Subcomm. on Technology and the Law of the Senate Comm. on the Judiciary and the
  Subcomm. on Civil and Constutional Rights of the House Comm. on the Judiciary 103rd
  Congr., at 6.
Frohock, F.M., 1974
  'Notes on the Concept of Politics: Weber, Easton, Strauss', 36 *The Journal of Politics*
  (1974) pp. 379-408.
Froomkin, M., 2000
  'Wrong Turn in Cyberspace: Using ICANN to Route around the APA and the Constitu-
  tion', 50(1) *Duke Law Journal* (2000), available at SSRN: <http://ssrn.com/abstract=
  252523>.
GAC, 2005
  Communique XXIV – Wellington, NZ, 28 March, 2006, available at <www.icann.org/
  en/committees/gac/>.
Gerber, D.J., 2007
  'Competition Law and the WTO: Rethinking the Relationship', 10(3) *Journal of Inter-
  national Economic Law* (2007), available at SSRN: <http://ssrn.com/abstract=613581>.
Germon, C., 1986
  'La normalisation, cle d'un nouvel essor, la documentation francais', Report to the Orga-
  nization for Economic Cooperation and Development (Paris, Organization for Economic
  Cooperation and Development (OECD) 1986).
Giddens, A., 1990
  The Consequences of Modernity (Stanford, CA, Stanford University Press 1990).
Gilpin, R. and Gilpin, J.M., 2001
  Global Political Economy: Understanding the International Economic Order (Princeton,
  NJ, Princeton University Press 2001).
Gilroy, A.A., 2008
  Net Neutrality: Background and Issues, *CRS Report for Congress*, Congressional Re-
  search Service Report RS22444, 24 November 2008, available at <https://secure.wiki
  leaks.org/leak/crs/RS22444.pdf>.
Glaser, B.G. and Strauss, A.L., 1967
  The Discovery of Grounded Theory: Strategies for Qualitative Research (Chicago, IL,
  Aldine Publishing Company 1967).
Goldsmith, J. and Wu, T., 2006
  Who Controls the Internet (Oxford, Oxford University Press 2006).
Goldsteinreport, 2009
  'EU calls for privatized, independent, accountable ICANN with oversight from "G12"',
  Goldsteinreport, 5 May, 2009, available at <http://technewsreview.com.au/article.php?
  article=8041>.
Goodman, E., 2007
  'Media Policy and Free Speech: The First Amendment at War with Itself', 35 *Hofstra
  Law Review* (2007), available at SSRN: <http://papers.ssrn.com/sol3/papers.cfm?abstract_
  id=1009319>.

Google, 2007
    'Censorship as Trade Barrier', *public policy blog*, 22 June 2007, available at <http://googlepublicpolicy.blogspot.com/2007/06/censorship-as-trade-barrier.html>.
Hahn, R.W. and Wallsten, S., 2006
    'The Economics of Net Neutrality', 3(6) *The Economists Voice* (2006), available as EI-Brookings Joint Center Working Paper No. RP06-13 at SSRN: <http://ssrn.com/abstract=943757>.
Hahn, R.W. and Litan E., 2007a
    'The Myth of Network Neutrality and What We Should Do About It', 1 *International Journal of Communication* (2007), available at IJOC: <http://ijoc.org/ojs/index.php/ijoc/article/viewFile/161/87>.
Hahn, R.W. et al., 2007b
    'The Economics of "Wireless" Net Neutrality', AEI-Brookings Joint Center Working Paper No. RP07-10 (2007), available at SSRN: <http://ssrn.com/abstract=983111>.
Hancock, E., 2007
    'CALEA: Does One Size Still Fit All?', in Balkin, J.M. et al., eds., *Cybercrime, Digital Cops in a Networked Environment* (New York, New York University Press 2007).
Harvard Law Review Note, 2001
    'A Most Private Remedy: Foreign Party Suits and the U.S. Antitrust Laws', 114 *Harvard Law Review* (2001).
Hass, D.A., 2008
    'The Never-Was-Neutral Net and Why Informed End Users Can End the Net Neutrality Debates', 22 *Berkeley Technology Law Journal* (2008), available at SSRN: <http://ssrn.com/abstract=957373>.
Hayek, F., 1960
    The Constitution of Liberty (Chicago, IL, University of Chicago Press 1960).
Hayek, F, 1973
    Law, Legislation and Liberty, Vol. 1-3 (Chicago, IL, University of Chicago Press 1973).
Heft, M., 2007
    'Google's Market Share Grows and Grows and Grows', *New York Times Bits Blog,* New York, 28 December 2009, available at <http://bits.blogs.nytimes.com/2007/12/28/googles-market-share-grows-and-grows-and-grows>.
Held, D., 1997
    Democracy and Globalization (Cologne, Max Planck Institute for the Study of Societies 1997).
Held, D., 1999
    Global Transformations: Politics, Economics and Culture (Stanford, CA, Stanford University Press 1999).
Held, D. and McGrew, A.G., 2000
    The Global Transformations Reader: An Introduction to the Globalization Debate (Malden, Polity Press 2000).
Her Majesty's Government (UK), 2006
    'Countering International Terrorism: The United Kingdom's Strategy', 2006, available at <www.mi5.gov.uk/files/pdf/ct_strategy.pdf>.
Her Majesty's Government (UK), 2009
    'Cyber Security Strategy of the United Kingdom, safety, security and resilience in cyber space', Cabinet Office, June 2009, available at <www.cabinetoffice.gov.uk/media/216620/css0906.pdf>.

Hinsley, F.H., 1986
   Sovereignty, 2nd edn. (Cambridge, Cambridge University Press 1986).
Hobbes, T., 1651
   'Leviathan, or, The Matter, Form, and Power of a Common-wealth Ecclesiastical and
   Civil' (1651), available at Project Gutenberg: <www.gutenberg.org/etext/3207>.
Human Rights Watch, 2006
   '"Race to the Bottom" Corporate Complicity in Chinese Internet Censorship', 18(8c)
   HRW Publication (2006).
Hume, D., 1739
   'A Treatise of Human Nature, being an attempt to introduce the experimental Method of
   Reasoning into Moral Subjects' (1739), available at Project Gutenberg: <www.gutenberg.
   org/etext/4705>.
Hunter, D., 2003
   'ICANN and the Concept of Democratic Deficit', 36 *Loyola of Los Angeles Law Review*
   (spring 2003), available at SSRN: <http://ssrn.com/abstract=400000>.
Hutton, W. and Giddens, A., 2000
   Global Capitalism (New York, New Press 2000).
IAHC, 1997
   'Recommendation for Administration and Management gTLDs', International Ad Hoc
   Committee, 1997, available at <www.gtld-mou.org/draft-iahc-recommend-00.html>.
IEEE, 1990
   *IEEE Standard Computer Dictionary: A Compilation of IEEE Standard Computer Glos-
   saries* (New York, Iftikahr 1990).
ISO/IEC, 2004
   ISO/IEC Guide 2: Standardization and Related Activities – General Vocabulary, 8th edn.
   (Geneva, 2004).
IANA, 1998
   'Generic Top-Level Domains', 1998, available at <www.iana.org/gtld/gtld.htm>.
IANA, 2002
   Index by TLD Code (2002), available at <www.iana.org./root-whois/index.html>.
ICANN, 1999a
   Minutes of the Meeting, 27 May 1999, available at <www.icann.org/en/minutes/minutes-
   27may99.htm>.
ICANN, 1999b
   ICANN's Universal Dispute Resolution Procedure, 26 August 1999, available at
   <www.icann.org/en/udrp/udrp.htm>.
ICANN, 2007
   Adopted Resolutions form ICANN Board Meeting, 30 March 2007, available at <www.
   icann.org/en/minutes/resolutions-30mar07.htm>.
ICANN, 2008
   ICANN Accountability & Transparency Frameworks and Principles, 10 January 2008,
   available at ICANN: <www.icann.org/en/transparency/acct-trans-frameworks-principles-
   10jan08.pdf>.
ICANN, 2009a
   ICANN Board Unanimously Approves Voting Board Seat for At-Large Community,
   27 August 2009, available at ALAC: <www.atlarge.icann.org/announcements/announce
   ment-27aug09-en.htm>.

ICANN, 2009b
    Affirmation of Commitments, 30 September 2009, available at <www.icann.org/en/an-nouncements/announcement-30sep09-en.htm>.
ICANN, 2009c
    Bylaws, as amended 30 September 2009, available at <www.icann.org/general/bylaws.htm>.
IETF RFC 675
    Specifications of Internet Transmission Control Program, available at <www.faqs.org/rfcs/rfc675.html>.
IEGF RFC 791
    Internet Protocol, DARPA Internet Program Protocol Specification, available at <www.ietf.org/rfc/rfc791.txt>.
IETF RFC 819
    Domain Naming Convention for Internet User Application, available at <www.faqs.org/rfcs/rfc819.html>.
IETF RFC 882
    Domain Names: Concepts and Facilities, available at <www.faqs.org/rfcs/rfc882.html>.
IETF RFC 883
    Domain Names: Implementation Specification, available at <www.faqs.org/rfcs/rfc883.html>.
IETF RFC 1633
    Integrated Services in the Internet Architecture: An Overview, available at <www.faqs.org/rfcs/rfc1633.html>.
IETF RFC 1958
    Architectural Principles of the Internet, available at <www.faqs.org/rfcs/rfc1958.html>.
IETF RFC 2464
    Transmission of IPv6 Packets over Ethernet Networks, available at <http://tools.ietf.org/html/rfc2464>.
IETF RFC 2026
    The Internet Standards Process – Revision 3, available at <https://tools.ietf.org/html/rfc2026>.
IETF RFC 2474
    Definition of the Differentiated Services Field (DS field) in the IPv4 and IPv6 headers, available at <www.ietf.org/rfc/rfc2474.txt>.
IETF RFC 2475
    An Architecture for Differentiated Services, available at <www.ietf.org/rfc/rfc2475.txt>.
IETF RFC 2804
    IETF Policy on Wiretapping, available at <www.ietf.org/rfc/rfc2804.txt>.
IETF RFC 2850
    Charter of the Internet Architecture Board, available at <www.iab.org/about/charter.html>.
IETF RFC 2925
    A Mission Statement for the IETF, available at <www.ietf.org/rfc/rfc3935.txt>.
IETF RFC 3041
    Privacy Extensions for Stateless Address Autoconfiguration in IPv6, available at <www.ietf.org/rfc/rfc3041.txt>.
IETF RFC 3160
    The Tao of IETF – A Novice's Guide to the Internet Engineering Task Force, available at <www.ietf.org/rfc/rfc3160.txt>.

IETF RFC 3490
    Internationalizing Domain Names in Applications (IDNA), available at <http://tools.ietf. org/html/rfc3490>.
IETF RFC 3833
    Threat Analysis of the Domain Name System (DNS), available at <www.rfc-archive.org/ getrfc.php?rfc=3833>.
Introna, L.D. and Nissenbaum, H., 2000
    'Shaping the Web: Why the Politics of Search Engines Matters', 16(3) *The Information Society* (2000), available at SSRN: <http://ssrn.com/abstract=222009>.
Isenberg, D., 2008
    'Bogus WSJ Story on Net Neutrality', *Circleld*, 15 December 2008, available at <www. circleid.com/posts/20081215_bogus_wsj_story_on_net_neutrality>.
ISOC, 2007
    Statement of Activities and Changes in Net Assets, *Annual Report 2007*, available at <www.isoc.org/isoc/fin/financials2007.pdf>.
Jameson, F. and Miyoshi, M., 1998
    The Cultures of Globalization (Durham, NC, Duke University Press 1998).
Jensen, M., 1970
    The Articles of Confederation; An Interpretation of the Social-Constitutional History of the American Revolution 1774-1781 (Madison, WI, University of Wisconsin Press 1970).
Joelson, M.R., 2006
    An International Antitrust Primer: A Guide to the Operation of United States, European Union, and Other Key Competition Laws in the Global Economy (Alphen aan den Rijn, Kluwer Law International 2006).
Keohane, R.O., 2002
    Power and Governance in a Partially Globalized World (London, Routledge 2002).
Kessler, J.L., 2006
    International Trade and U.S. Antitrust Law (St. Paul, MN, West Group 2006).
Kewney, G., 2005
    'China Blocks Skype, VoIP', *The Register*, 12 September 2005, available at <www.the register.co.uk/2005/09/12/china_blocks_skype/n>.
Klein, H., 2001
    'The Feasibility of Global Democracy, Understanding ICANN's at-Large Election', 4(3) *Journal of Policy, Regulation and Strategy for Telecommunications Information and Media* (2001), available at: <www.internetgovernance.org/pdf/igp-icannreform.pdf>.
Klein, H. and Mueller, M., 2005
    'What to Do about ICANN: A Proposal for Structural Reform', *Internet Governance Project*, 5 April 2005, available at <www.internetgovernance.org/pdf/igp-icannreform. pdf>.
Koenig-Archibugi, M. and Zorn, M., 2006
    New Modes of Governance in the Global System: Exploring Publicness, Delegation and Inclusiveness (Basingstoke and New York, Palgrave Macmillan 2006).
Kortman, C.A.J.M., 2004
    'The French Constitution', in Prakke, L., and Kortman, C.A.J.M., eds., *Constitutional Law of 15 EU Member States* (Deventer, Kluwer 2004).
Kreijen, G., ed., 2002
    State, Sovereignty, and International Governance (Oxford, Oxford University Press 2002).

Kuerbis, B. and Mueller, M., 2007
'Securing the Root: A Proposal for Distributing Signing Authority', Internet Governance Project, 17 May 2007, available at <www.internetgovernance.org/pdf/SecuringThe Root.pdf>.

Landau, S.E., 2006
'National Security on the Line', 4 *Journal of Telecommunications and High Technology Law* (2006) pp. 409-447.

Law, D.S., 2008
'Globalisation and the Future of Constitutional Rights', 102 *Northwestern University Law Review* (2008), available at SSRN: <http://ssrn.com/abstract=975914>.

Lee, T.B., 2008
'The Durable Internet, Preserving Network Neutrality without Regulation', *Policy Analysis* 626 (2008), available at CATO: <www.cato.org/pubs/pas/pa-626.pdf>.

Lemley, M., and Lessig, L., 2000
'The End of End-to-End: Preserving the Architecture of the Internet in the Broadband Era', *UC Berkeley Public Law Research Paper* 37 (2000), available at SSRN: <http://papers.ssrn.com/sol3/papers.cfm?abstract_id=247737>.

Lessig, L., 1999
Code and Other Laws of Cyberspace (New York, Basic Books 1999).

Lessig, L., 2006
Code: Version 2.0 (New York, Basic Books 2006).

Locke, J., 1689
Two Treatises of Government: In the former, the false principles, and foundation of Sir Robert Filmer, and his followers, are detected and overthrown. The latter is an essay concerning the true original, extent, and end of civil government (Awnsham Churchull, 1690), Second Treatise, available at Gutenberg Project: <www.gutenberg.org/etext/7370>.

Lokin, J.H.A. and Zwalve W.J., 2001
Hoofdstukken uit de Europese Codificatiegeschiedenis (Deventer, Kluwer 2001).

Lowe, T. et al., 2006
American Government (New York, W.W. Norton and Company 2006).

Lu, P., 2008
'China Search Engine Survey Report', Beijing, IntelliConsulting Corporation, 16 September 2008, available at <www.iaskchina.cn/en/Report/view/id/13>.

MacKinnon, R., 2006
'China's New Domain Names: Lost in Translation', *RConversation,* 28 February 2006, available at <http://rconversation.blogs.com/rconversation/2006/02/chinas_new_doma. htm>l#comment-14511452>.

Malcolm, J., 2008
Appraising the Success of the Internet Governance Forum, Internet Governance Project, 21 November 2008, available at <www.internetgovernance.org/pdf/MalcolmIGFReview. pdf>.

Mathiason, J., 2009
Internet Governance: The New Frontier of Global Institutions (New York, Routledge 2009).

Mathiason, J. et al., 2004
'Internet Governance: the State of Play', 9 September 2004, Internet Governance Forum, available at <www.internetgovernance.org/pdf/ig-sop-final.pdf>.

Mathiesen, K., 2008
'Access to Information as a Human Right' (2007), available at SSRN: <http://ssrn.com/abstract=1264666>.

May, R.J., 2007
'Net Neutrality Mandates: Neutering the First Amendment in the Digital Age', 3(1) *Journal of Law and Policy for the Information Society* (spring 2007), available at SSRN: <http://ssrn.com/abstract=994470>.

McCullagh, D., 2005
'Telco agrees to stop blocking VoIP calls', *CNET News*, 3 March 2005, available at <www.news.com/Telco-agrees-to-stop-blocking-VoIP-calls/2100-7352_3-5598633.html>.

McMillan, R., 2007
'Feds Pull the Domain Name Plug on State of California', *Infoworld*, 4 October 2007, available at <www.infoworld.com/article/07/10/04/Feds-pull-domain-name-plug-on-California_1.html>.

Merrill, T.W. and Smith, H.E., 2007
Property: Principles and Policies (New York, Foundation Press 2007).

Mifsud Bonnici, J.P., 2007
Self-Regulation in Cyberspace (diss., Groningen, 2007).

Mifsud Bonnici, J.P., 2008
Self-Regulation in Cyberspace (The Hague, TMC Asser Press 2008).

Montesquieu, C.D.S. and Varnet, J.J., 1748
De l'esprit des loix ou du rapport que les loix doivent avoir avec la constitution de chaque gouvernement, les moeurs, le climat, la religion, le commerce, &c., (Geneva, Chez Barillot, & fils 1748), available at Gutenberg Project: <www.gutenberg.org/etext/27573>.

Morris, J. and Davidson, A., 2003
'Policy Impact Assessments: Considering the Public Interest in Internet Standards Development', *Telecommunications Policy Research Conference,* Augustus 2003, Arlington, Center for Democracy and Technology, available at CDT: <www.cdt.org/files/pdfs/pia.pdf>.

Moteff, J. and Parfomak, P., 2004
'Critical Infrastructure and Key Assets: Definition and Identification', report for Congress, 1 October 2004, Library of Congress, available at <www.fas.org/sgp/crs/RL32631.pdf>.

Mueller, M., 2001
'Competing DNS Roots: Creative Destruction of Just Plain Destruction?', ITU Strategy and Policy Unit Lunch Seminar, 23 November 2001, Geneva, available at ITU: <www.itu.int/osg/spu/seminars/mueller/tprc2001.pdf>.

Mueller, M., 2002
Ruling the Root: Internet Governance and the Taming of Cyberspace (Cambridge, MIT Press 2002).

Mueller, M., 2005a
'US Unilateral Control of ICANN Backfires in WSIS', *Politechbot,* available at <www.politechbot.com/2005/10/03/us-unilateral-control>.

Mueller, M., 2005b
'Five More Years! There Was No "Deal" and WSIS Resolved Nothing', *Circleid*, 17 November, 2005, available at <www.circleid.com/posts/no_deal_wsis_resolved_nothing>.

Mueller, M., 2007,
    Net Neutrality as Global Principle for Internet Governance, Internet Governance Project,
    5 November 2007, available at <www.internetgovernance.org/pdf/NetNeutrality
    GlobalPrinciple.pdf>.
Napoli, P. and Sybblis, S., 2007
    'Access to Audiences as a First Amendment Right: Its Relevance and Implications for
    Electronic Media Policy', 12 *Virginia Journal of Law and Technology* (2007), available
    at <www.fordham.edu/images/undergraduate/communications/audienceaccessrev.pdf>.
Nicol, C., 2003
    ICT Policy Handbook, Association for Progressive Communications (2003).
Nielsen/Netratings, 2009
    'Usage and Population Statistics' (2009), available at <www.internetworldstats.com/
    stats.htm>.
Noam, E.M., 1994
    'Beyond Liberalization II: The Impending Doom of Common Carriage', 18(6) *Telecom-
    munications Policy* (1994), available at <www.citi.columbia.edu/elinoam/articles/
    BeyondLiberalizationII-ImpendingDoomofCommonCarriage.pdf>.
Norris, P., 2008
    Driving Democracy, Do Power-Sharing Regimes Work? (Cambridge, Cambridge Uni-
    versity Press 2008).
NRC, 1996
    Cryptography's Role in Securing the Information Society, National Research Council
    (Washington, DC, National Academies Press 1996).
NRC, 2005
    Signposts in Cyberspace: the Domain Name System and Internet Navigation, National
    Research Council (Washington, DC, National Academies Press 2005).
NTIA, 1998a
    'A Proposal to Improve Technical Management of Internet Names and Addresses', dis-
    cussion draft 30 January 1998, available at <www.ntia.doc.gov/ntiahome/domainname/
    dnsdrft.htm>.
NTIA, 1998b
    'Management of Internet Names and Addresses', 6 April 1998, available at <www.ntia.doc.
    gov/ntiahome/domainname/6_5_98dns.htm>.
NTIA, 2005
    'United States Principles on the Internet's Domain Name and Addressing System', 30
    June 2005, available at NTIA: <www.ntia.doc.gov/ntiahome/domainname/USDNS
    principles_06302005.htm>.
O'Connor, J.J. and Robertson, J.F., 2003
    'Jean Baptiste Joseph Delambre', School of Mathematics and Statistics, St. Andrews
    (2003), available at <www-gap.dcs.st-and.ac.uk/~history/Biographies/Delambre.html>.
OECD, 2008
    'Internet Traffic and Prioritization, An Overview', Working Party on Telecommunica-
    tions and Information Services (2008), available at <www.oecd.org//dataoece/43/63/
    38405781.pdf>.
OpenNet Initative, 2005
    'Internet Filtering in China, A Country Report 2004-2005', *Open Net Initiative Country
    Studies* (2005), available at SSRN: <http://papers.ssrn.com/sol3/papers.cfm?abstract_
    id=706681>.

OpenNet Initiative, 2006
'China Tightens Controls on Internet News Content through Additional Regulations', *ONI Bulletin* 012 (July 2006), available at <http://opennet.net/bulletins/012/>.

OpenNet Initiative, 2009
'Research Profile China' (2009), available at <http://opennet.net/research/profiles/china>.

Ordover, J., 1995
'Bingaman's Antitrust Era. The Division's Intensified Enforcement and Internationalization Agenda', 40(2) *Antitrust Bulletin* (summer 1995), available at CATO: <www.cato.org/pubs/regulation/regv20n2/reg20n2c.html>.

Palfrey, J.G., 2004
'The End of the Experiment: How ICANN's Foray into Global Internet Democracy Failed', Harvard Public Law Working Paper No. 93 (2004), available at SSRN: <http://ssrn.com/abstract=487644>.

Palmer, J., 2005
'Turkey Abandons ICANN', *ICANNWatch,* 3 July 2005, available at <www.icannwatch.org/article.pl?sid=05/07/03/2210254&mode=thread>.

PDO Staff, 2006
'China Adds Top-Level Domain Names', *People's Daily Online*, 28 February, 2006, available at <http://english.people.com.cn/200602/28/eng20060228_246712.html>.

Pierson, C., 2004
The Modern State (London, New York, Routledge 2004).

Pitofsky, R., 2002
'Antitrust at the Turn of the Twenty-first Century: The Matter of Remedies', *Georgetown Law Journal* (November 2002).

Post, D., 1999
'Governing Cyberspace "Where is James Madison when we need him?"', *ICANNWatch*, 6 June 1999, available at <www.icannwatch.org/archive/governing_cyberspace.htm>.

Prakke, L. and Kortman, C.A.J.M., eds., 2004
Constitutional Law of 15 EU Member States (Deventer, Kluwer 2004).

Price, E.T., 1995
Dividing the Land: Early American Beginnings of Our Private Property Mosaic (Chicago, IL, University of Chicago Press 1995).

Puffert, D.J., 2005
'Path Dependence in Spatial Networks: The Standardization of Railway Track Gauge', 39(3) *Explorations in Economic History* (2005).

Reding, V., 2005
'Opportunities and Challenges of the Ubiquitous World and Some Words on Internet Governance' (2005), available at <http://ec.europa.eu/commission_barroso/reding/docs/speeches/ubiquitous_world_20051017.pdf>.

Reis, G.
Capitalism (Ottawa, IL, Jameson Books 1996).

Reporters without Borders, 2005
'The 11 Commandments of the Internet in China' (2005), available at RSF: <www.rsf.org/The-11-commandments-of-the.html>.

Rhoads, C., 2006
'Endangered Domain' (interview with Paul Vixie), *Wall Street Journal* (Eastern edn.), New York, 19 January, 2006, available at <http://209.85.229.132/search?q=cache:cmo6d9jfzyUJ:bev.berkeley.edu/ipe/readings/Endangered%2520Domain.doc+Endangered+Domain,+Wall+Street+Journal+paul+vixie&cd=3&hl=en&ct=clnk&gl=uk>.

Ritzer, G., 1998
The McDonaldization Thesis: Explorations and Extensions (London, Sage Publications 1998).

Ritzer, G., 2008
The McDonaldization of Society (Los Angeles, CA, Pine Forge Press 2008).

Rosenblum, M., 1995
'What We Can Learn from the Telecommunications Industry about Possible Ways to Assess Pro and Anticompetitive Behavior in Other Network Industries', Supplemented Statement of Mark Rosenblum Vice President-Law and Public Policy, AT&T Corp. before the Federal Trade Commission (1995), available at FTC: <www.ftc.gov/opp/global/attcom.shtm>.

Saltzer, J.H. et al., 1984
'End-to-End Arguments in System Design', 2 *ACM Transactions on Computer Systems* (1984), available at <http://web.mit.edu/Saltzer/www/publications/endtoend/endtoend.pdf>.

Sassen, S., 2006
Territory, Authority, Rights: From Medieval to Global Assemblages (Princeton, NJ, Princeton University Press 2006).

Schage, E., 2006
'The Internet in China: A Tool for Freedom or Suppression?', Committee on International Relations, U.S. House of Representatives, Washington, DC 20515-0128, 15 February 2006, available at <http://conservativeusa.org/internet_in_china.htm>.

Schatz, A., 2008.
'White House Opposes FCC Free Wireless Internet Plan', *The Wall Street Journal,* 10 December 2008, available at WSJ: <http://online.wsj.com/article/SB122895080737596191.htm>l?mod=googlenews_wsj>.

Screpanti, E. et al., 2005
An Outline of the History of Economic Thought (Oxford, Oxford University Press 2005).

Sen, A.K., 1973
On Economic Inequality (Oxford, Clarendon Press 1973).

Sen, A.K., 1985
Commodities and Capabilities (Amsterdam, North-Holland 1985).

Sen, A.K., 1999
'Democracy as a Universal Value', 10 *Journal of Democracy* (1999).

Sen, A.K., 2009
The Idea of Justice (Cambridge, MA, Harvard University Press 2009).

Shaw, M.N., 2003
International Law (Cambridge, Cambridge University Press 2003).

Sidak, J.G.
'A Consumer-Welfare Approach to Network Neutrality Regulation of the Internet', 2(3) *Journal of Competition Law & Economics* (2006), available at SSRN: <http://ssrn.com/abstract=928582>.

Simons, C.A.J. 1995
'Kiezen tussen Verscheidenheid en Uniformiteit', Inaugural speech accepting Professorship in Standardization Studies at the Erasmus University Rotterdam (Rotterdam, Erasmus University Rotterdam 1995).

Singel, R., 2009
'FCC Approves Net Neutrality Rules, Now the Fight Begins, *Wired,* 22 October, 2009, available at <www.wired.com/epicenter/2009/10/fcc-net-neutrality/>.

Singer, H.J., 2007
'Net Neutrality: A Radical Form of Non-Discrimination', 30(2) *Regulation* (2007), available at SSRN: <http://ssrn.com/abstract=1001480>.

Skinner, Q., 1989
'The State', in Ball, T., Farr, J. and Hanson, R.L., eds., *Political Innovation and Conceptual Change* (Cambridge, Cambridge University Press 1989).

Smith, A., 1776
An Inquiry into the Nature and Causes of the Wealth of Nations, (London, Printed for W. Strahan, and T. Cadell 1776), available at Gutenberg Project: <www.gutenberg.org/etext/ 3300>.

Tanenbaum, A.S., 2003
Computer Networks (Upper Saddle River, NJ, Prentice Hall 2003).

Tassay, G., 2000
'Standardization in Technology-Based Markets', 29(4-5) *Research Policy* (2000), available at <www.nist.gov/director/planning/researchpolicypaper.pdf>.

Taylor, C., 1995
'Invoking Civil Society', in Taylor, C., ed., *Philosophical Arguments* (Cambridge, MA, Harvard University Press 1995).

TDN Staff, 2005
Press release, *Turkish Daily News,* 23 June 2005, summary available at <http://inaic.com/ index.php?p=tukish-daily-news>.

Tomlinson, J., 1999
Globalization and Culture (Chicago, IL, University of Chicago Press 1999).

Transatlantic Consumer Dialogue, 2008
Resolution on Net Neutrality, Doc. No. INFOSOC 36-08 of March 2008, available at TADC: at <www.tacd.org/cgi-bin/db.cgi?page=view&config=admin/docs.cfg&id=331>.

Tribe, L.H., 2000
American Constitutional Law (New York, Foundation Press 2000).

Turner, R.V., 2007
Magna Carta: Through the Ages (Harlow, Longman 2003).

US Census Bureau, 2007
'Top Trading Partners-Total Trade, Exports, Imports' (2007), available at <www.census. gov/foreign-trade/statistics/highlights/top/>.

US Census Bureau, 2008
'Trade with China' (2008), available at <www.census.gov/foreign-trade/balance/ c5700.html#2009>.

USDoS, 2009
'Background Note China', October 2009, available <www.state.gov/r/pa/ei/bgn/18902. htm>.

Van Eijk, N., 2006
'Search Engines: Seek and Ye Shall Find? The Position of Search Engines in Law', *IRIS plus* (Supplement Legal observations of the European Audiovisual Observatory) (2006), available at <www.obs.coe.int/oea_publ/iris/iris_plus/iplus2_2006.pdf.en>.

Vermeulen, B.P., 2007
'Magna Carta (1215-)', in Battjes, H. and Vermeulen, B.P., eds., *Constitutionele Klassiekers* (Nijmegen, Ars Aequi Libri 2007).

Verschuren, P. and Doorewaard, H., 1999
Designing a Research Project (Utrecht, Lemma 1999).

Villeneuve, N., 2005

'Why Exaggerate', blog of 13 July 2005, available at <www.nartv.org/2005/07/13/why-exaggerate/>.

Villeneuve, N., 2006

'The Filtering Matrix: Integrated Mechanisms of Information Control and the Demarcation of Borders in Cyberspace', *First Monday* 11, 2006, available at <http://firstmonday.org/htbin/cgiwrap/bin/ojs/index.php/fm/article/view/1307/1227>.

Villeneuve, N., 2007

'Evasion Tactics, Global Online Censorship is Growing, But so Are the Means to Challenge It and Protect Privacy', 36(4) *Index on Censorship* (2007), available at <www.nartv.org/mirror/evasiontactics-indexoncensorship.pdf>.

Wallsten, S., 2007

'Wireless Net Neutrality?', Progress & Freedom Foundation Progress Snapshot Paper 3.2 (2007), available at SSRN: <http://ssrn.com/abstract=976749>.

Wang, G., 1994

Treading Different Paths: Informatization in Asian Nations (Norwood, NJ, Ablex Publishing Corporation 1994).

Weber, M., 1919

Politik als Beruf (Duncker & Humblodt, Muenchen) (transl. in English as *Politics as a Vocation*, Philadelphia, PA, Fortress Press 1965).

Weber, M., 1978

Economy and Society: An Outline of Interpretive Sociology (Berkeley, CA, University of California Press 1978).

Weinberg, J., 2000

'ICANN and the Problem of Legitimacy', 50(1) *Duke Law Journal* (2000), available at SSRN: <http://ssrn.com/abstract=252524>.

Woolsey, R.J., 2000a

Former CIA Director Woolsey Delibers Remarks at Foreign Press Center, Foreign Press Center, 7 March, 2000, available at <http://cryptome.org/echelon-cia.htm>.

Woolsey, R.J., 2000b

'Why We Spy on Our Allies', *Wall Street Journal,* 17 March, 2000, available at <http://cryptome.org/echelon-cia2.htm>.

WSIS, 2003a

'Plan of Action', WSIS-03/GENEVA/DOC/5-E. 2003, available at, ITU: <www.itu.int/dms_pub/itu-s/md/03/wsis/doc/S03-WSIS-DOC-0005!!PDF-E.pdf>.

WSIS, 2003b

'Building the Information Society; A Global Challenge in the New Millennium', WSIS-03/GENEVA/DOC/4E, 2003, available at ITU, <www.itu.int/dms_pub/itu-s/md/03/wsis/doc/S03-WSIS-DOC-0004!!PDF-E.pdf>.

WSIS, 2005a

'Report on the Working Group on Internet Governance Château de Bossey', 05.41622 (2005), available at WGIG: <www.wgig.org/docs/WGIGREPORT.pdf>.

WSIS, 2005b

'Tunis Agenda for the Information Society', WSIS-05/TUNIS/DOC/6(Rev.1)-E (2005), available at ITU: <www.itu.int/wsis/docs2/tunis/off/6rev1.html>.

WSIS, 2008

'ITU, Report on the World Summit on the Information Society', (2008), available at ITU: <www.itu.int/wsis/stocktaking/docs/2008/WSIS-Stocktaking2008-e.pdf>.

WTO, 1996
Ministerial Declaration on Trade in Information Technology Products, available at WTO: <www.wto.org/english/docs_e/legal_e/itadec_e.htm>.

WTO, 1999
'Trade and Labour Standards: Subject of Intense Debate', briefing note (1999), available at <www.wto.org/english/theWTO_e/minist_e/min99_e/english/about_e/18lab_e.htm>.

Wu, J., 2005
Understanding and Interpreting Chinese Economic Reform (Mason, Thomson/South-Western 2005).

Wu, T., 2007
'Wireless Carterfone', 1 *International Journal of Communication* (2007) p. 398, available at SSRN: <http://ssrn.com/abstract=962027>.

Yoo, C.S., 2004
'Would Mandating Broadband Network Neutrality Help or Hurt Competition? A Comment on the End-to-End Debate', 3 *Journal of Telecommunications and High Technology Law* (2004), available at SSRN: <http://ssrn.com/abstract=495502>.

Yoo, C.S., 2007
'What Can Antitrust Contribute to the Network Neutrality Debate?', 1 *International Journal of Communication* (2007) p. 493, available at SSRN: <http://ssrn.com/abstract=992837>.

Zijderveld, A.C., 1999
The Waning of the Welfare State: The End of Comprehensive State Succor (New Brunswick, NJ, Transaction Publishers 1999).

Zittrain, J.L., 2008
The Future of the Internet – and How to Stop It (New Haven, CT, Yale University Press 2008).

LAWS AND REGULATIONS

INTERNATIONAL INSTRUMENTS

International Covenant for Civil and Political Rights (ICCPR).
United Nations Charter (1948).
Universal Declaration of Human Rights (1948).
OECD Guidelines for Cryptography Policy (1997), Recommendation of the Council concerning Guidelines for Cryptography Policy, 27 March 1997, available at <www.justice.gov/criminal/cybercrime/oerecs.htm>.
Rome Statute of the International Criminal Court, United Nations Doc. A/CONF.183/9, available at <http://untreaty.un.org/cod/icc/statute/romefra.htm>.

EUROPEAN LAW AND REGULATIONS

Council Directive 98/83/EC of 3 November 1998 on the quality of water intended for human consumption, available at <http://eur-lex.europa.eu/LexUriServ/LexUriServ.do?uri=CELEX:31998L0083:EN:NOT>.
Directive concerning the EU Global Online Freedom Act, draft proposal, available at <www.julesmaaten.eu/_uploads/EU%20GOFA.htm>.
European Charter for Local Self-Government (1985, ETS No. 122), available at <http://conventions.coe.int/treaty/en/Treaties/Html/122.htm>.
European Convention on Human Rights (1950), see <www.hri.org/docs/ECHR50.html>.
EC Regulation (EC) No. 661/2009 of the European Parliament and of the Council of 13 July 2009 concerning type-approval requirements for the general safety of motor vehicles, their trailers and systems, components and separate technical units intended therefore, available at <http://eur-lex.europa.eu/LexUriServ/LexUriServ.do?uri=OJ:L:2009:200:0001:01:EN:HTML>.
Treaty Establishing a Constitution for Europe 2004/C310/01, available at <http://eur-lex.europa.eu/JOHtml.do?uri=OJ:C:2004:310:SOM:EN:HTML>.

UNITED STATES LAW AND REGULATIONS

Unanimous Declaration of the Thirteen United States of America (1776), also known as the Declaration of Independence, available at <www.earlyamerica.com/earlyamerica/freedom/doi/text.html>.
Articles of Confederation and Perpetual Union (1776).
Constitution of the United States of America (1787).
A Framework for Global Electronic Commerce (1997), available at <www.technology.gov/digeconomy/framewrk.htm>.
Revised U.S. Encryption Export Control Regulations (2000), RIN: 0694-AC11.

Restatement (Third) of the Foreign Relations Law of the United States (2006), American
Law Institute.

USA Patriot Act (2001), Uniting and Strengthening America by Providing Appropriate Tools
Required to Intercept and Obstruct Terrorism Act, *Public Law Publ. L.* 107-56, available
at <http://frwebgate.access.gpo.gov/cgi-bin/getdoc.cgi?dbname=107_cong_bills&
docid=f:h3162enr.txt.pdf>.

- **Bills**

Digital Telephony Proposal (1992), FBI, available at <http://cyber.eserver.org/clipper/
fbi_phne.txt>.

Cyber Security Act (2009), S.773, available at <www.opencongress.org/bill/111-s773/text>.

Global Online Freedom Act (2009), HR 2271.

- **Code (USC)**

Sherman Act (1890), 15 USC § 1-7.

Clayton Act (1914), 15 USC § 12-27, 29 USC § 52-53.

Federal Trade Commission Act (1914), 15 U.S.C §§ 41-58 (as amended).

Sexual Exploitation of Children, 18 USC § 2251.

Foreign Assistance Act, 22 USC 32.

Arms Export Control Act, 22 USC 2571-2794.

Water Quality Standards and Implementation Plans, 33 USC § 1313.

Communications Assistance for Law Enforcement Act (1994), 47 USC 1001-1010.

Omnibus Crime Control and Safe Streets Act (1968), 42 USC § 3711.

Communications Act (1934), 47 USC 151 et seq.

Federal Motor Vehicle Safety Standards, 49 USC 571.

Foreign Intelligence Surveillance Act, 50 USC §§ 1801-1811, 1821-1829, 1841-1846, and
1861-1862.

Export Administration Act, 50 USC App. 2401-2420.

- **Congressional and Administrative News (USCCAN)**

HR Rep. No. 97-686 (1982), reprinted as 1982 USCCAN 2487.

- **Contracts**

USDoC and ICANN

(1998a) IANA contract 1998, available at <www.ntia.doc.gov/ntiahome/domainname/iana/
ianacontract_081406.pdf>.

(1998b) Memorandum of Understanding between the USDoC and ICANN, available at
<www.ntia.doc.gov/ntiahome/domainname/icann-memorandum.htm>.

(2003) Affirmation of Responsibilities of ICANN Private Sector Management (Joint Project
Agreement), available at <www.icann.org/en/general/JPA-29sep06.pdf>.

USDoC and NSI
(1998) Amendment 11 to Cooperative Agreement Between Network Solutions Inc. and US
  Government, 1998, available at <www.icann.org/en/nsi/coopagmt-amend11-07oct
  98.htm>.

- **Department of Justice**

USDoJ (1984), Non-Horizontal Merger Guidelines, Department of Justice, available at
  <www.usdoj.gov/atr/public/guidelines/2614.pdf>.
USDoJ (1988), Antitrust Enforcement Guidelines for International Operations, November
  1988, reprinted in *4 Trade Reg. Rpt.* (CCH) § 13,109.
USDoJ (1992), Justice Department Will Challenge Foreign Restraints on US Exports under
  Antitrust Laws, Department of Justice Press Release, 3 April 1992, available at
  <www.justice.gov/atr/public/press_releases/1992/211137.htm>.
USDoJ (1995), Antitrust Enforcement Guidelines for International Operations, April 1995,
  available at <www.justice.gov/atr/public/guidelines/internat.htm>.

- **Federal Communications Commission (FCC)**

FCC (2005a), Communications Assistance for Law Enforcement Act and Broadband Ac-
  cess Services, Federal Register.
FCC (2005b), FCC 05-150A1, Report and Order of Notice of Proposed Rulemaking.
FCC (2005c), FCC 05-151, Policy Statement.
FCC (2005d), FCC 05-153, Policy Statement.
FCC (2005e), FCC 05-543, Consent Decree.
FCC (2006a), Press Release: 'FCC Accepts Memorandum Opinion and Order to Broadband
  Over Power Lines to Promote Broadband Service to All Americans', August 2, 2006.
FCC (2006b), WC Docket No. 06-74, Joint Statement of Chairman Kevin J. Martin and
  Commissioner Deborah Taylor Tate, re: AT&T Inc. and Bellsouth Corporation Applica-
  tion for Transfer of Control, December 29, 2006.
FCC (2008), FCC08-183, Memorandum Opinion and Order, August 1, 2008.
FCC (2009), FCC 09-93, Proposal for Legislation, October 22, 2009.

- **Federal Trade Commission (FTC)**

FTC (1980) Policy Statement on Unfairness.
FTC (1983) Policy Statement on Deception.
FTC (2001) Decision and Order, America Online/Time Warner, Docket No. C 3989.

- **Other US Material**

Congressional Hearing (2006), The Internet in China: A Tool for Freedom or Suppression,
  House Committee on Foreign Affairs, 2nd session, Washington, available at
  <www.foreignaffairs.house.gov/archives/109/26075.pdf>.

ENGLISH LAW AND REGULATIONS

Magna Charta (1215), tr. in English from Latin, available at <www.yale.edu/lawweb/avalon/medieval/magframe.htm>.

Magna Charta (1297), tr. in English from Latin, available at <www.archives.gov/exhibits/featured_documents/magna_carta/translation.html>.

Navigation Act (1651), available at <www.constitution.org/eng/conpur_ap.htm>.

An Act Declaring the Rights and Liberties of the Subject and Settling the Succession of the Crown, aka Bill of Rights (1689), available at <http://avalon.law.yale.edu/17th_century/england.asp>.

Tea Act (1773), available at <ttp://ahp.gatech.edu/tea_act_bp_1773.html>.

FRENCH LAW AND REGULATIONS

French Constitution (1958), tr. in English, available at <www.assemblee-nationale.fr/english/8ab.asp>.

Conseil Constitutionnel, July 16, 1971, Decision No. 71-44 DC.

Conseil Constitutionnel, January 15, 1975, Decision No. 74-54 DC.

Declaration of the Rights of Man and of the Citizen (1789), available in English at <www.historyguide.org/intellect/august4.html>.

LOI organique no. 2003-704 du 1er août 2003 relative à l'expérimentation par les collectivités territoriales, available at <www.legifrance.gouv.fr/WAspad/UnTexteDeJorf?numjo=INTX0300039L>.

LOI organique no. 2003-705 du 1er août 2003 relative au référendum local, available at <www.admi.net/jo/20030802/INTX0300060L.html>.

LOI organique no. 2004-758 du 29 juillet 2004 prise en application de l'article 72-2 de la Constitution relative à l'autonomie financière des collectivités territoriale, available at <www.legifrance.gouv.fr/WAspad/UnTexteDeJorf?numjo=INTX0300131L>.

LOI organique no. 2004-809 du 13 août 2004 relative aux libertés et responsabilités locales, available at <www.legifrance.gouv.fr/WAspad/UnTexteDeJorf?numjo= INTX0300078L>.

LOI Gayssot (1990) Tendant a reprimer tout acte raciste, antisemite ou xenophobe.

GERMAN LAW AND REGULATIONS

Basic Law for the Federal Republic of Germany (1946), available at <www.iuscomp.org/gla/statutes/GG.htm>.

German Criminal Code (1998), tr. from Strafgesetzbuch, (StGB), available at <www.gesetze-im-internet.de/englisch_stgb/index.html>.

SCOTTISH LAW AND REGULATIONS

Declaration of Abroath (1320), tr. in English is available at <www.geo.ed.ac.uk/home/scotland/arbroath_english.html>.

LIST OF CASES

Abrams v. *U.S.*, 250 US 616 (1919).
Aff'd sub nom. Maryland v. *U.S.*, 460 US 1001 (1983).
Berger v. *New York*, 388 US 41 (1967).
California Dental Ass'n v. *FTC*, 536 US 756 (1999).
Conservative and Unionist Central Office v. *Burrell (Inspector of Taxes)* [1982] 1 WLR 522.
Continental Ore Co. v. *Union Carbide & Carbon Corp.*, 370 US 690, 706 (1962).
FTC v. *Sperry & Hutchinson Co.*, 405 US 233 (1972).
Gibbons v. *Ogden*, 22 US (9 Weath.) 1, 193-98 (1824).
Hartford Fire Ins. Co. v. *California*, 509 US 764 (1993).
Hoffmann-LaRoche Ltc. v. *Empagran S.A.,* 542 US 155, 161 (2004).
InterAmerican Refining Corp. v. *Texaco Maracaibo Inc.*, 307 F. Supp. 1291 (D. Del 1970).
Katzenbach v. *McClung*, 379 US 294, 298 (1964).
Katz v. *United States*, 389 US 347 (1967).
Leegin Creative Leather Prods Inc v. *PSKS Inc.* 75 USLW 4643 (2007).
Mannington Mills Inc. v. *Congoleum Corp.,* 595 F.2 1287, 202 USPQ 321, 1979-1 Trade Cas. (CHH) P 62547 (3rd Circ. 1979).
McCulloch v. *Maryland*, 17 US 316, 420 (1819).
Meyer v. *Nebraska*, 262 US 390 (1923).
National Cable & Telecommunications Assn. v. *Brand X Internet Services* (04-277) 545 US 967 (2005), 345 F.3d 1120.
Northern Pacific Railway Company v. *United States*, 365 US 1, 6 (1958).
Timberlane Lumber Co. v. *Bank of America,* 549 F.2d 1378 (9th Circ. 1976).
Timberlane Lumber Co. v. *Bank of America,* 749 F.2d 1378 (9th Circ. 1984).
United States v. *AT&T* 552 R. Supp. 131 (DDC 1982).
United States v. *Darby*, 312 US 100, 118-119 (1941).
United States v. *E.I. du Point de Nemours & Co.*, 351 US 377 (1956).
United States v. *Lopez*, 14 US 594, 559-560 (1995).
United States v. *Socony-Vacuum Oil Co.,* 310 US 150 (1940).
United States. v. *Terminal Railroad Association*, 224 US 383 (1912).
United States Watchmakers of Switzerland Info. Ctr. Inc. (SDNY 1965).
Verizon Communications v. *Trinco*, 540 US 398 (2004).
Wickard v. *Filburn Heart of Atlanta Motel* v. *United States*, 397 US 241, 257-258 (1964).

INDEX

INFORMATION TECHNOLOGY & LAW SERIES

1. E-Government and its Implications for Administrative Law – Regulatory Initiatives in France, Germany, Norway and the United States (The Hague: T·M·C·ASSER PRESS, 2002) Editor: J.E.J. Prins / ISBN 978-90-6704-141-6
2. Digital Anonymity and the Law – Tensions and Dimensions (The Hague: T·M·C·ASSER PRESS, 2003) Editors: C. Nicoll, J.E.J. Prins and M.J.M. van Dellen / ISBN 978-90-6704-156-0
3. Protecting the Virtual Commons – Self-Organizing Open Source and Free Software Communities and Innovative Intellectual Property Regimes (The Hague: T·M·C· ASSER PRESS, 2003) Authors: R. van Wendel de Joode, J.A. de Bruijn and M.J.G. van Eeten / ISBN 978-90-6704-159-1
4. IT Support and the Judiciary – Australia, Singapore, Venezuela, Norway, The Netherlands and Italy (The Hague: T·M·C·ASSER PRESS, 2004) Editors: A. Oskamp, A.R. Lodder and M. Apistola / ISBN 978-90-6704-168-3
5. Electronic Signatures – Authentication Technology from a Legal Perspective (The Hague: T·M·C·ASSER PRESS, 2004) Author: M.H.M. Schellekens / ISBN 978-90-6704-174-4
6. Virtual Arguments – On the Design of Argument Assistants for Lawyers and Other Arguers (The Hague: T·M·C·ASSER PRESS, 2004) Author: B. Verheij / ISBN 978-90-6704-190-4
7. Reasonable Expectations of Privacy? – Eleven Country Reports on Camera Surveillance and Workplace Privacy (The Hague: T·M·C·ASSER PRESS, 2005) Editors: S. Nouwt, B.R. de Vries and J.E.J. Prins / ISBN 978-90-6704-198-0
8. Unravelling the Myth Around Open Source Licences – An Analysis from a Dutch and European Law Perspective (The Hague: T·M·C·ASSER PRESS, 2006) Authors: L. Guibault and O. van Daalen / ISBN 978-90-6704-214-7
9. Starting Points for ICT Regulation – Deconstructing Prevalent Policy One-Liners (The Hague: T·M·C·ASSER PRESS, 2006) Editors: B-J. Koops, M. Lips, J.E.J. Prins and M. Schellekens / ISBN 978-90-6704-216-1
10. Regulating Spam – A European Perspective after the Adoption of the E-Privacy Directive (The Hague: T·M·C·ASSER PRESS, 2006) Author: L.F. Asscher / ISBN 978-90-6704-220-8
11. Cybercrime and Jurisdiction – A Global Survey (The Hague: T·M·C·ASSER PRESS, 2006) Editors: B-J. Koops and Susan W. Brenner / ISBN 978-90-6704-221-5
12. Coding Regulation – Essays on the Normative Role of Information Technology (The Hague: T·M·C·ASSER PRESS, 2006) Editors: E.J. Dommering and L.F. Asscher / ISBN 978-90-6704-229-1
13. Customary Law of the Internet – In the Search for a Supranational Cyberspace Law (The Hague: T·M·C·ASSER PRESS, 2007) Author: P.P. Polánski / ISBN 978-90-6704-230-7
14. Fighting the War of File Sharing (The Hague: T·M·C·ASSER PRESS, 2007) Authors: A.H.J. Schmidt, W. Dolfsma and W. Keuvelaar / ISBN 978-90-6704-238-3
15. Constitutional Rights and New Technologies – A Comparative Study (The Hague: T·M·C·ASSER PRESS, 2008) Editors: R.E. Leenes, B.J. Koops and P. De Hert / ISBN 978-90-6704-246-8

16. Self-Regulation in Cyberspace (The Hague: T·M·C·ASSER PRESS, 2008) Author:
     J.P. Mifsud Bonnici / ISBN 978-90-6704-267-3
17. Trustmarks in E-Commerce – The Value of Web Seals and the Liability of their Pro-
     viders (The Hague: T·M·C·ASSER PRESS, 2009) Author: P. Balboni /
     ISBN 978-90-6704-296-3
18. Universities and Copyright Collecting Societies (The Hague: T·M·C·ASSER PRESS, 2009)
     Author: D.K. Mendis / ISBN 978-90-6704-298-7
19. The State of Interdependence – Globalization, Internet and Constitutional Governance
     (The Hague: T·M·C·ASSER PRESS, 2010) Author: R.W. Rijgersberg /
     ISBN 978-90-6704-331-1